No Regrets

Other Books
by Barry Neil Kaufman

Happiness Is a Choice

Son-Rise: The Miracle Continues

PowerDialogues

To Love Is to Be Happy With

Giant Steps

A Miracle to Believe In

A Sacred Dying

FutureSight

OutSmarting Your Karma and Other Preordained Conditions

The Book of Wows and Ughs

Son-Rise

NO REGRETS

Last Chance for a Father and Son

BARRY NEIL KAUFMAN

H J Kramer

New World Library

An H J Kramer Book

published in a joint venture with

New World Library

Editorial office:
P.O. Box 1082
Tiburon, California 94920

Administrative office:
14 Pamaron Way
Novato, California 94949

Edited by Kevin Bentley
Cover design by Mary Ann Casler
Text design and typography by Tona Pearce Myers

Library of Congress Cataloging-in-Publication Data
Kaufman, Barry Neil.
No regrets : last chance for a father and son / by Barry Neil Kaufman.
    p.   cm.
  ISBN 1-932073-02-7 (alk. paper)
  1. Grief. 2. Bereavement—Psychological aspects. 3. Fathers—Death—Psychological aspects. 4. Loss (Psychology) 5. Fathers and sons. 6. Kaufman, Barry Neil. I. Title.
  BF575.G7K385 2003
  155.9'37'092—dc21   2003000178

First Printing, May 2003
ISBN 1-932073-02-7
Printed in Canada on acid-free, partially recycled paper
Distributed to the trade by Publishers Group West

10 9 8 7 6 5 4 3 2 1

First and foremost, this book is dedicated to anyone who ever wanted a more nourishing relationship with a parent and who wanted to express love and caring even when the doors didn't seem open. The challenge of a life-threatening illness gave my dad and me an opportunity to find our way back to each other. We challenged decades of conflict in an attempt to forge a relationship that neither of us had probably thought possible. It was possible. I learned, in a deeper way, to never give up. We don't have to give up on our parents or ourselves. We can learn to fly above our yearning for acknowledgment, approval, or even agreement from our fathers and mothers and possibly catch a golden ring of common ground more fantastic than any we might have imagined.

To Abe:

You did not build a skyscraper with your name on it. You didn't write a best-selling novel, become a movie star, or sing a famous tune. Your name will not appear in the history books. And yet what you did, Pop, will be as enduring and memorable as any work of art. You lived simply, with dignity and integrity, passing this way and leaving some of us richer for having known you and having experienced your love. Were you perfect? Hardly. Did you make mistakes? Sure. But did you learn to fly? Absolutely. Like a bird. You were never the father of my dreams, but in the end, you became the father of my heart. Who will be left to remember what we did, whom we loved, and how we cared? Who will be left to remember? I will, Pop. I will remember.

To Rosie:

You gave everything you could . . . and then some — boldness, daring, and determination to create a safe place for the man you loved even when you were scared. Those very human qualities make you a towering figure in my life.

To Samahria:

Heaven has blessed me with over four awesome decades of your deep, powerful, and abiding love. You are my most important teacher — and my greatest inspiration.

ACKNOWLEDGMENTS

This book begins and ends with Rosalind Kaufman, Rosie, whose example of love and courage "under fire" remains an inspiration. She cried the first time I told her I was considering putting our journey down on paper. She believed my father would have been delighted as well as surprised to have these years of his life and the lessons we all learned memorialized in a book. Each time I wrote a section, I submitted it to Rosie for accuracy, input, or adjustment. We had the best time together — crying at the same sections and enjoying memories of great tenderness and personal transformation. I feel an overwhelming sense of gratitude to Rosie, who not only became my mother in a stellar second marriage with my father that spanned almost thirty years, but also became a best friend in the true sense of that expression as together we walked the path documented in this book.

I have been blessed to have a most amazing partner who

not only plays the most pivotal role in my life but also has been the wellspring of tenderness and support that enabled and encouraged me to jump into the best places within myself and reach out to my father with a steady and loving hand. For me, Samahria Lyte Kaufman defines love-in-action, and her many personal examples of daring, wisdom, and trust in God permeate all the pages of this book.

I have been further blessed by the presence of six children (and now, by their children). At the time of the events detailed in this book, many of my children had become young adults, and because some of them had moved away, not all of them took an active role in this extraordinary adventure. Nevertheless, I feel such gratitude for their presence in my life.

I would like to specifically acknowledge my daughter Bryn Hogan, who not only supported our family and her grandfather with warm and deep caring but supported me very specifically with her unending expressions of love and her very useful mentoring questions. A key director and gifted teacher at The Option Institute, our learning and training center, she took the skills that she uses daily to help families and individuals throughout the world and graciously applied them in helping me. For that, I am most grateful. I want to express a big hurrah to my son Tayo Lukanus Kaufman, who supported his grandparents with his understated power and warmth, running errands and asking continually what he could do to help. Tayo made a huge contribution. A big thank-you to my son, Raun K. Kaufman, who used the same thoughtful and insatiable curiosity that made him a legendary teacher, trainer, and innovator at the Option Institute to prod me to dig deeper in understanding and to explain every aspect of the events detailed in this book. A sweet smile of appreciation to Sage L. Kaufman, who expressed such sweetness and delight to her grandfather — and whose smile and energy he so appreciated.

I owe a significant debt of gratitude to our colleague and dear, dear friend, Zoe Goldstein, who stood beside Samahria and me, embracing my father and mother as family — and then extending herself like an angel sent from heaven. She is the most giving person I have ever known. I feel such deep appreciation for Caiseal Orsini, who gave her intelligent, insightful, and energetic support on this project when she was not working at the Option Institute as dean of Professional Training, passionately helping people or supervising training programs. I am grateful to have her friendship and crucial input. To Margaret Boydston I owe much appreciation. At different times during the development of this book, she reviewed the contents, making many large and small editorial suggestions that helped enhance the clarity of my writing. Many other staff members of the Option Institute, who are also close friends, extended love and caring to my dad and my family during this great adventure. Even the program participants at the Institute greeted my father with notable respect and dignity as he moved across our rural campus with obvious difficulty. Thank you all.

Additionally, I want to cite the warm and caring folks at the Cancer Treatment Center of America in Tulsa, Oklahoma. We had searched near and far for a treatment facility that would care for my father not only with medical expertise but also with warmth, caring, dignity, respect, and love. We had also wanted an organization that would incorporate standard medical options with alternative protocols such as nutrition, meditation, group counseling, yoga, and exercise. The health-care team there delivered excellence in all these areas, making my father's treatment palatable and imparting a sweetness to his care that made his stay there a deeply moving experience. Marge Affleck, the leader of his care team, took in my parents as if they were her own; her support, guidance, and love took our breath away.

Admiration and gratitude to Kevin Bentley, whose keen editorial eye and savvy insights helped spotlight what was most meaningful to express as well as the tangential ingredients that could be deleted. Without a doubt, he helped make this a much better book.

Last, but not least, my extraordinary thanks go to Linda Kramer, who expressed such love and enthusiasm for this book and had such a passion to publish it. She is a woman of great power and strong beliefs, and I feel honored to have had this very special project in her capable and caring hands. To her, and to the folks at H J Kramer and New World Library, I am very grateful. An additional thank-you to Linda and her husband, Hal Kramer, who also enthusiastically supported and published a previous book of mine, *Son-Rise: The Miracle Continues,* our story of entering the world of our son's autism and helping him transform himself into a bright, warm, extroverted, and highly effective young man who has become a gifted teacher, seminar facilitator, and lecturer. Thank you, Linda. Thank you, Hal.

INTRODUCTION

A sequoia can live two thousand years. A squid has a four-year life span. A mayfly — born with the dawn and gone by dusk. Each life is a whole life, complete in itself. The quality of an individual life has nothing to do with its longevity but everything to do with how it is lived. For me, the greatest tragedy in dying would be to have been known and loved for who I am *not* rather than to be assessed, judged, embraced, or even discarded for who I *am*. Saying what's on our minds and in our hearts throughout our lives — being authentic — is ultimately easier than dying with our omissions and lies.

We all stand before God naked, yet we hide from each other. As we faced his death together, my father, with whom I'd had a difficult relationship, finally allowed himself to be naked in my presence as I had learned to be with him. He learned to share his innermost thoughts and feelings. He let go of his judgments as I let go of my need for his approval, and our letting go allowed us, in the end, to discover each other anew and create nurturing legends about each other. Two glorious years reversed decades of misunderstandings and emotional distance. The catalyst: approaching death.

Death was not our enemy but our friend, offering us an incomparable opportunity. It knocked on our door, reminding us that life celebrates itself through constant change and that the illusion of permanency is just that — an illusion. People live. People die. And death is not only the grand equalizer (it visits us all, rich or poor, young or old) but also the great whisper from the universe that urges us to swim with the current and "let go, let go, let go." When we stop clinging to our children, our relationships, our jobs, even our reputations, we make more personal space in which to be flexible, generous, and fulfilled. The more we welcome death as part of life, the more we free ourselves to live.

In his eighty-fourth year, my father began a twenty-four month journey into himself. I have written this account in the hopes that his adventure might serve as a road map for all of us with aging, chronically sick, or dying parents. Among the many challenges we will face in life, caring for elderly mothers and fathers (and "letting go") as well as parenting our children (and "letting go") will be among the greatest.

Like a committed athlete, I have spent a massive portion of my adult life in a rigorous personal training program. My focus has not been on tossing hoops with expertise, flipping gracefully on a balance beam, or running quarter-mile races with lightning speed. Instead, I have made my playing field the inner stadium of thoughts and emotions, developing each day, week, and year more muscle to help me become accepting and empowered in my embrace of myself, others, and the situations I encounter. Whether in the field, leading workshops or presenting motivational talks; in the trenches at the Option Institute, mentoring individuals, couples, or families facing adversity; or in my living room, confronting challenges within my own family, my life has been an exquisite classroom within which to practice, practice, and practice opening my mind and heart to the challenges and miracles around me.

When my wife and I had a child diagnosed as irreversibly autistic, functionally retarded, and neurologically impaired, we realized that we had worked diligently, as if toward an unknown goal, to transform ourselves before his arrival, a critical factor that allowed us to meet this challenge successfully.

That's exactly what happened again, two years ago, when I received a telephone call for help from my father. As I listened to him share startling information about his body being riddled with cancer, I knew, in that very instant, that I had trained all my life for this unfolding opportunity. This would be my Olympics, where I would ask myself to deliver all that I had learned for the love of this man. And all that I had learned would serve as a foundation, enabling the healing of a forty-year discordant parent-child relationship and a gentle passage through death's door.

I believe my loved ones and I— Pop's wife, Rosie, my wife, Samahria, and our children — found a way to make my dad's living and dying not only bearable, but also a deeply spiritual, transformative, and sweet adventure, one that deepened our connections to him and to each other. The fundamental attitudes and codes of conduct that enabled us to safeguard his dignity and gave him endless opportunities to connect to those he loved, allowing him a "good life" and a "good death," were straightforward and simple. My hope is that just as the lessons we learned in helping our son Raun to blossom have rippled outward to change the lives of so many other autistic children and their parents, so may the following insights from our experience help others who are dealing with a dying parent.

ONE

My left hand cradled your head against the pillow. The fingers of my other hand created a soft cocoon around your arm, which lay limply on the blanket. I had been sitting cross-legged on the bed next to you for hours in that exact position. The room had become a cathedral where the lines between life and death blurred. I did not know whether you could still hear me, but I kept talking anyway.

"You're doing great, Pop. It's Bears. Rosie is here. She's doing fine. She loves you. Dad, you have the best wife. And in her eyes and our eyes, you're the best guy. We're here with you as you take this journey. It's okay now to let go. It's okay now to have your visit with God. Pop, we love you."

These words echoed in the quiet of the room. As I listened to my own voice, I felt love emanating from every cell in my body. I adored you. And I can hardly believe that I adored you. We had come such a long way together.

When did we first lose each other? Was it when I was fifteen and went, against your wishes, to visit my friends in Manhattan? Was it when I grew my hair long and sympathized with the antiwar and civil rights movements of the sixties, foolishly identifying you and Mom as the complacent and conservative middle class? Was it even earlier, when I hated you for letting me languish at military school for six additional months after I had begged you to let me come home? It took years, Pop, for me to finally understand and acknowledge that you had always done the best you could. Only as an adult did I realize how my unyielding rebelliousness must have confused you and challenged all the principles you lived by. Maybe it wasn't one particular event that strangled our relationship. Maybe it was an endless series of clashes, as I tramped awkwardly through my teens, searching unsuccessfully to make sense of myself and a world that appeared so unreasonable and unjust. I made you the symbol and the target of all my discontent.

Now, having fathered my own six children, I can easily recognize that I must have seemed like a child from hell for you. But I finally changed, Pop, as I know you did. It took us almost forty years to find our way back to each other. Forty years! A mayfly, born at dawn and gone by dusk, lives a whole life across the span of one glorious day. We had passed by each other for more than fourteen thousand of those glorious days without touching each other's hearts. We said our hellos, had our phone conversations, and sat together for many meals: you at your end of the table, I at mine, all without really connecting.

Your recollection of those years must have differed dramatically from mine. That's how it works, Pop. We each live in our own worlds, peering out from the non-neutral lens of our eyes. Ultimately, I had made peace with the belief that you would never really know me — that you didn't want to really know me. Then, what a surprise and an opportunity you gave to both of us over these past two very special years. How honored I felt and continue to feel! That you allowed me to hold your hand while you traveled this final road has been such an unexpected blessing.

In years past, you poked fun at the heart and soul of my work and lifestyle, often reacting with impatience and anger when I talked about workshops and seminars. "Too many of those 'why' questions!" you'd bellow, flipping your hand in the air as if to swat a fly.

It's okay, Pop — this was a bit of karmic retribution for my having given you such a hard time when you, the straight-talking man whose youth straddled the Great Depression, who had found your own sense of dignity and pride through providing housing and food for your family, had to put up with me, a self-absorbed and ungrateful teenager, poking fun at the safe haven you worked so diligently to maintain for all of us.

"I'm here, Pop. Right beside you. I will not leave you. You can count on me, on all of us. We all want the best for you. Rosie is doing fine. Bryn came to visit a few hours ago. You were sleeping, Pop, but she talked to you anyway — just like I'm talking to you now. She told you how you're her special grandpa; she so enjoys your gruff, understated affection toward her. She loves you and Rosie so much. But, Dad, I know you know that. We're all having the best time loving you. Are you in any pain? Just give me a sign if you are — squeeze my hand, nod your head. We want to make you as comfortable as possible."

I watched for a signal — any gesture, a fluttering from your closed eyelids. Hours had passed since you drifted back into yourself. I couldn't help but admire the dignity you showed. And then you nodded, ever so slightly, indicating pain. Kenny, who had returned with Denise and Jessica from the motel, noted your movement in the same moment I did. He and I glanced at each other and then looked down at the morphine pump that supplied you with pain medication every thirty minutes. For too long, Kenny and I had been brothers only in name, but right now the distance separating us evaporated as we moved in concert, focused on helping you.

Although the hospice nurse had advised us that you could have extra medication whenever you needed it, Rosie lobbied against it. For her, more morphine meant that comfort took precedence over healing, signaling that your death approached. Rosie wanted more time. The three decades you'd spent together suddenly seemed like an instant; she wanted more years, more months, and now more days and more hours with you. She grasped at any additional time she could get. Just having you there, Pop, asleep in bed, comforted her. For Rosie, that morphine machine represented the end of an amazing thirty-year love relationship. Each time I noticed you wincing with pain, I wanted to respect her yearning, but I wanted to help you as well.

I checked to see what Rosie was doing. She stared out the window, gazing at the valley and mountains beyond — a vista that had been a source of such pleasure for you over these past four weeks. I dipped my head as a covert signal to Kenny, who coughed loudly to mask the whining sound the pump made when I slid the manual control under the quilt and pressed the button. Rosie turned toward us, peered curiously into our faces, and then returned to her own reflections, continuing to stare out the window. Maybe on some level she knew what we had done.

Rosie had kept a constant vigil at the foot of your bed, like a warrior knight fighting the good fight on your behalf. I knew how much Rosie — your wife, lover, companion, best friend, and, more recently, health care advocate as well as caring nurse — had touched and inspired you with her love. I have always felt similarly about my relationship with Samahria (pronounced suh-MA-ree-ya), whose camaraderie and caring have blessed me all these years. Although I struggled against the walls of silence and judgment that prevailed in our family as I grew up, I always appreciated and wanted to emulate the way you treated Mom and then Rosie, treasuring them. You came off as a tough guy, a superman — but not with the women in your life. With them, you were so gentle and loving...so fiercely protective and loyal.

I remember a case in point; I must have been about twelve years old. You had just finished dinner with Mom as I entered the kitchen doorway, unobserved. What I witnessed then stunned me, for you never really expressed affection physically, at least not toward me. You enforced a dress code in our home, requiring us to be fully dressed at all times, no walking around in undergarments. We never discussed human anatomy or talked openly about love or sex. And there you were, Pop, by the kitchen counter, standing behind Mom with an uncharacteristically mischievous smile on your face. You slipped your arms very gently around her, and then, to my surprise, you cupped her breasts in your hands and jiggled them. Then you both laughed. I didn't quite know what to do with what I had observed. I felt so lighthearted in that moment, watching you two play together. You appeared so much more approachable, more human. I liked you more at that moment than any other time previously. I liked your smile and your laugh. (I had hardly ever heard you laugh.) You and I, Pop, have talked so much about life, love, God, and death since you became sick, but I hadn't remembered this incident until right now. So, although I've expressed my gratitude to you many times over these past months and weeks, I never before thanked you for this one memory. Thank you, Dad.

The extra morphine began to have an impact. The muscles in your face relaxed. Every time I told you that you could let go, leave your body, and have your visit with God, Rosie eyed me defiantly. I could see her love, her confusion, and her panic. But she and I kept talking, Pop. Samahria had been taking walks with her every morning. Both she and Rosie claimed that they used the time to "solve the world's problems." I knew Samahria used the time to help her get ready for you to leave her. Remember last week, when you gave Rosie some bills to process, how you started to cry, telling her that she will have to learn to take care of herself and live alone without you? She tried to stop you from speaking, but we all heard your message. Somehow, I think you were staying with us a bit longer until you knew Rosie would be ready. She's been coming around, Pop. Really, she has.

The sun faded from the sky, bathing the room with a golden light. Although you had not been able to sit up for days, the huge Victorian windows that were set in stone over one hundred years ago brought the countryside close to your bed. I wanted you to have the best room in the house, Pop — so I gave you this one.

. "Everyone's gone for the moment, Pop. Kenny took a walk with Denise. Jessica's on the phone, calling home. Samahria and Rosie went downstairs a few minutes ago to prepare some food for everyone. Those two have developed such a warm friendship since you both came to live here. All kinds of magic is happening right around you — and because of you.

"Your grandchildren are coming to see you. Tayo came home from football practice a few minutes ago, ready to eat everything in sight. I can't believe the enormity of his shoulders. At seventeen, he's a bull — but, deep down, very sweet and gentle. A lot like you, Pop — not a big talker and not quick to reveal his inner thoughts. Samahria and I keep encouraging him to share more. Sage will be coming home this weekend, after her last class at school tomorrow. She might drive from Boston with Raun; he wants to see you as well.

"I love having all the children home or at least as many as can be here. Funny, how they have all become young adults, yet they will always be my children. Do you see me that way, too, Pop? Even if I were a hundred years old, I would still be your child. And I would still call you 'Pop' or 'Dad.' I like those names. It's a bit of history. Our history is pretty muddled at times. But we're all finding our way in this family. And me, I'm still actively parenting my children as I care for you.

"We're taking turns, you and I. You held me when I came into the world; now I hold you as you leave it. Why does this feel so natural? It's just part of living. I can feel your grip on my hand tighten, Pop. I'm going to hold onto you tighter. Are you in pain?"

"No," you whisper.

"Are you comfortable?"

You nod your head affirmatively.

"Do you want to talk?"

You shake your head no.

"Do you hear me when I talk?"

You nod your head again.

"Do you like when I talk to you?"

Again you nod.

"I love you, Pop. Thank you for letting me help you. I feel so honored to be able to serve you in this way. I so enjoy getting to know you and have you get to know me. You have really opened your heart to me with such sweetness."

You increased your grip on my hand once again. One side of your mouth curled upward into a faint smile. My tears started to flow — not tears of sadness but of gratitude. I could see what an enormous effort it took for you to communicate. Your ability to engage bodily kept diminishing. I didn't want to disturb you even though I wanted you to feel our presence and our abiding love for you. I had done everything in my power over the past four weeks to help you have a good death — the best death.

For thirty years I have worked with individuals, couples, families, and groups, and during this time I have witnessed so many people living in anguish because of one difficult or traumatic event that haunts them from the past. With the encouragement of friends and therapists, many of these people have repeatedly revisited a particular painful experience and thereby relived their discomfort over and over again, sometimes decades after the actual event.

During a brainstorming meeting with the senior teaching staff at our learning center, I proposed a course entitled "A Single Act of Love" that would offer a contrasting possibility. In this program we would teach people how to take one powerful love-filled event in their lives, amplify it, and make it a wellspring of inspiration and good feelings for the rest of their lives. Indeed, if we magnified all the details, made them big enough in our thoughts and in our hearts, any single experience of love could overwhelm, and possibly obliterate, the space we normally allot for reliving distressing experiences from the past. The teaching staff appeared excited by this concept, but in truth, scarcely anyone registered for the workshop. It was a hard sell for people buried in memories, but I still treasured the idea.

Pop, I believe you and I have brought this idea to life. These two years together, and especially these recent weeks, have taken up all the space in my mind that I used to give to the abyss of heart separation that once characterized our relationship. I feel as though I have successfully backfilled a forty-year chasm with love.

Last Monday, you sat on the front porch with me, holding my hand and gazing at the meadows and mountains spread out before us. Way off to the right, some Option Institute program participants sat together, obviously engrossed in a passionate discussion. Off to the left, down at the bottom of the hill, several deer darted through the woods. You smiled as you watched them. But the most dazzling part of this scene was what we were doing as we sat in those chairs. There you were, almost eighty-six years old, holding hands with me, your fifty-four-year-old son, in a gesture as sweet and timeless as the Earth itself. You were my parent and yet, in some way, my child. One day my children will parent me in turn. On this day, you and I held hands as dear and cherished friends.

"Bears," you said, accenting the word with a theatrical flourish as you still struggled to make the nickname, which Samahria had given me thirty years ago, more commonplace on your lips. "What more could any man want than to be surrounded by so much love?" You tightened your grip on my hand. We looked into each other's eyes.

"I love you, Pop."

You smiled one of those soft smiles, rare in prior years but expressed so much more frequently during these past weeks. "I love you, too," you said.

A single experience of love, Dad — yet warm enough and powerful enough to fill any void and inspire appreciation for a lifetime. This will be my new vision, Pop, one I will remember forever. Everything that happened before in our relationship will be rendered insignificant by the magnificence of these unfolding hours. This is what I have been trying to teach myself, as well as others, most of my adult life: what happens in life is not nearly as significant as what we make up, or believe, about what happens. We are not in charge of many of the events or activities that occur around us, but we do fully control how we choose to see and experience those events and activities, as well as how we respond to them. Loss, or fulfillment? Moving away, or moving toward?

It's the game of "make-believe," Pop — making up beliefs. When you grimaced at me or shook your head with annoyance, which you did often when I was an adolescent, I made up the belief that you really didn't like me. When you yelled at me or hit me, I made up the belief that you probably didn't love me either; or if you did, that I had to get out of the way of your love. I never told you about these notions I made up inside, my "make-beliefs," nor did I ever ask you for verification of my assumptions. You and I passed each other like strangers speaking different languages, not only during my formative years but also throughout the decades that followed.

I could make up a legend about how we wasted all those years. Or I could see that time as spent perfectly — each of us finding our way, gaining new insights into ourselves and the world around us, so that we could come together in those moments, moments containing the power and content of centuries' worth of communion. I could choose to feel empty, focusing on the loss of all those years we butted heads, or I could choose to feel full with the wonder of our recent adventure together. I like the second version or "make-believe" about our relationship much more than the first, Pop.

We make up beliefs about people all the time — about their thoughts, feelings, motivations, intentions — often based on speculation, as if we could read minds. Then we pass judgment on each other or the events around us, but we use our own standards or value systems to do so, basing our judgments on our own particular make-beliefs. Thus, one person's patriot becomes another person's terrorist. When I lived with you as your son, I never realized that I constantly made up beliefs about you and about us. I just assumed everything I thought was valid, factual. I felt no need to question such conclusions, and so I boxed myself in, taking the road to discontent and fear. You didn't do that to me. I did that to myself, and rather self-righteously, too.

See, Pop, when I take full ownership for the craziness in my head, then I'm not a victim. I like believing I have a choice; I like believing I always had a choice. When the doctors diagnosed Raun as autistic and retarded, they pointed to that special little guy and called our son a tragedy. I can still hear the echo of their words across the landscape of more than twenty-five ensuing years. But Samahria and I followed what we had been teaching and made up a completely different and optimistic perspective regarding our son. We chose (yes, we *chose*) to see him as a special human being presenting us with the opportunity of our lives. It was more "make-believe," but make-believe designed for hope and possibility.

You loved the success we had with your grandson, Pop, although at the time you didn't want to hear about the attitude and belief-making that allowed us to accomplish all we did. And initially, I wanted desperately for you to understand our work. We saved Raun from the supposed inevitability of an institution, and you cheered when he graduated with high honors from high school and college. But you brushed aside all the "philosophy," as you called it, and I resigned myself finally to letting go of my "need" for you to know me. I imagined that when you died, you would have connected with your other children but would still hold me at a distance. I made peace with that possibility by making up numerous lessons for myself: What mattered was that I be happy even when you didn't acknowledge or understand me, that I let go of any judgments I had of you, even when you seemed to be judging me.

As I reflect on these thoughts, I realize that you must have had had a completely different experience from the one I used to believe you were having. Perhaps you had decided to be awesomely tolerant in the face of my endless questions about your state of mind and emotions, about the quality of your marriage and about your views of family and parent-child relationships. Thirty years ago, my still-exploding love affair with questions and dialogue had become all encompassing for me. I had taught myself to be a mentor by using a Socratic style of inquiry that I had learned and then used to change my own life. But, in those days, my mentoring outside of formal sessions or seminars probably felt more like tormenting, for you and everyone else. I was asking you to share, to be self-reflective, and to dig deep within yourself when you were giving me clear messages to back off, labeling my inquiries intrusive and impolite. I wanted to save you not from yourself but from my make-beliefs about you. I wanted to create opportunities for sharing with you, but I must have seemed like a misguided missionary intent on converting you to a worldview you didn't want to buy. Though we shared the same genes, you and I hailed from such different ideational planets.

The situation became only more frustrating. As a result of my constant questioning, you became hypersensitive to any question I asked. I telephoned you once in the early evening and inquired, "How are you?"

"Don't start with your damn questions!" you shouted.

I felt a bit lost and didn't know how to talk to you. I decided that the next time I called you, I would start detailing the weather conditions in the northeast (always an interest of yours) and then try to be as noncontroversial as possible. It didn't work. You said something about being annoyed at a neighbor. I went brain-dead for a few seconds and popped a question to you about your annoyance. You pounced on me. I laughed, and you exploded. Oil and water, Pop.

Now I imagine that your make-believe about our difficult

interactions made you the good guy, "in the right," just as my make-believe cast me as the good guy, out on a limb trying to build a bridge between himself and his father. We tell ourselves the stories we want to hear and make ourselves either the heroes or the victims. Henry Wadsworth Longfellow wrote, "If we could read the secret history of our enemies we should find in each man's life sorrow and suffering enough to disarm all hostility."

Pop, what have we come to know recently that we didn't seem to know back then? The answer is clear now: Love. Love for each other. You and I were reasonably good people trying to do a good thing. Each of us had the best of intentions, but we didn't know how to love each other. I now believe that everything happened perfectly, Pop. All those events served as our rites of passage, bringing us together so I could hold your hand as I did that afternoon on the porch. No regrets, Pop. No wrong moves. Only you and I, making up stories and legends about ourselves and our lives.

TWO

The mammoth white ship glided across the water easily, negotiating its way through floating icebergs as it neared the great walls of ice that thundered into Glacier Bay, Alaska, at irregular intervals. Samahria and I held hands as we leaned against the railing, awestruck by the brooding sky, which seemed to hover only a few hundred feet above the surface of the ocean. Then suddenly, as if making a dramatic entrance on cue, a blast of early afternoon sunshine broke through the clouds and cast an intense beam of light across the face of a nearby glacier. Within minutes, a giant clap of thunder rippled across the boat's deck and a twelve-story wall of ice collapsed theatrically into the water, sending misty geysers shooting into the air and creating an advancing wave that rocked the huge ship. As I gazed at this ancient force of nature expressing itself continually with or without my permission or observation, I felt humbled in the face of events born in a distant past and reaching forward toward an unknown, beckoning future. You and I, Pop, Samahria and Rosie, my siblings, and all my children and their children — we get to participate for a fleeting instant, and then, like the falling walls of ice, we too melt into and disappear beneath the ever-flowing waters of time.

The ship, which had left Juneau the night before, would be cruising at sea for three days, and I welcomed the respite from my eager exploration of each Alaskan port we had visited. Normally Samahria and I would have taken a more active vacation — climbing up a mountainside in Switzerland or trekking through a redwood forest in northern California or hiking through virgin meadows in Vermont. But everything had changed.

As recently as four months ago, before those long hours I sat cross-legged on the bed beside you, you were still exercising vigorously despite the progressive and virulent growth of the cancerous lymphatic tumors that had been nesting in your body since the initial diagnosis almost two years ago. Lately, though, I had noticed that you walked much more slowly, rested much more, and appeared extraordinarily tired. Samahria, too, had been active and vigorous until a degenerating spinal injury and other physiological challenges began to overwhelm her vitality. The idea of cruising Alaska's coastline, dotted with snow-capped mountains and immense relics of the Ice Age, had attracted us for years, so we set out. Nevertheless, we both knew the trip was a compromise, arising from the need to accommodate her weakened body and growing inability to take even short walks.

I held Samahria close as we stood on the deck. Pop, I knew that your time with me, with all of us, was drawing ever more rapidly to a close. I wondered whether I would lose her as well.

I thought about Bryn and her congenital heart condition, which at times in the last five years has threatened her life. Each time I say good-bye to her, I am acutely aware that it could easily be the last. I love my daughter so deeply; she has become such a champion of our work, a gifted teacher and therapist and such a supportive presence in our lives. But, Pop, I have come to know that if I cling to her, fearing some future loss, I will be distracted by my distress and miss the enjoyment of loving her today. That's it, Pop — today — that's all any of us have. And today I have my daughter Bryn, my precious wife Samahria, and you, sweet man, very much alive in my life.

How many times I had thought of you in the week since we left Massachusetts for Alaska. The vision of Rosie and you smiling and waving to us in the rearview mirror of our van as we left your cottage in New York after our last visit still danced playfully in my mind. Did you believe me when I told you that I thought you looked elegant without any hair? Well, Pop, I meant it. You are one stunning creature — yes, sir. You have never denied your cancer. We have stood together for two years looking it right in the face. When your complexion turned a greenish yellow cast, I suggested you might be ready to play a character on *Star Trek*. Sure, my spin on events might have seemed too playful and optimistic at times. Yet we always acknowledged and took steps to deal with your changing physiology and the treatments you believed would be helpful and tolerable. No denials — just acceptance of the "comings" and "goings" in life and support for your desire to live on — to be a senior usher at the theater on weekends, to play competitive Ping-Pong and whip players twenty-five years your junior, to take walks with Rosie, to eat another slice of chocolate pie, to visit with your grandchildren and great-grandchildren, and yes, to participate freely and with noted excitement in those deep and moving conversations with me that you once so intensely resisted.

Jessica said recently that you always rushed to get off the phone with her. Kenny told me once that you were not very forthcoming with information. David described you as "not a big talker." As I listened to my siblings' complaints, not so different from my own just a few years back, I realized that you had let some walls down with me. I wanted you to take those walls down with your other children as well. Instead, you anointed me your personal press secretary, keeping them at a distance. I never wanted the press secretary job, and I told you so, Pop, but I did want to support you in every way I could. My siblings didn't always enjoy my style of communicating or asking questions, even before I took on this assignment. Too damn outspoken, too direct — foot-in-mouth syndrome. Even though in my circle of friends this style of communication is valued, it made me unpopular with most of my siblings.

As the cloud cover thickened, the temperature dropped precipitously. Samahria and I went back to our cabin to find an envelope marked "urgent" taped to our door. I held my breath, instinctively trying to hold back time, to hold back the walls of ice, to hold on to you, Pop, as you had become so precious to me. I opened the envelope immediately; it contained a telex from Bryn.

Dear Popi:

I am sorry to intrude on your vacation, but I know you would want me to contact you if anything happened to Grandpa. Two days ago, he was taken to the hospital. I visited him just this morning. He's much,

much sicker than when you left. Grandma seems real scared. I think you should come home right away. I think he's dying. Please call me anytime. I have enclosed the hospital phone numbers. I love you and Mom so much. I will do whatever I can to help.

Love, Bryn

My subsequent phone conversation with Bryn startled me. She said you had been in intense pain for hours when she arrived at the hospital. You did not want her to see you in such a desperate situation, so you asked her to remain just outside the door to your room. Later, you allowed her to enter. When Rosie began to feed you, you looked at Bryn and told her you loved her but said you would appreciate her leaving since you did not want her to observe you being so unable to care for yourself. After talking with Bryn, calling Rosie, and consulting with the doctors, I was convinced that your condition had turned grave and your death seemed imminent. I couldn't believe that after being totally available to you for the past two years, now that the situation had become critical I was stuck on a ship that would not touch port again for three days. I consulted the man at the front desk and explained my dilemma. He appeared sympathetic but informed me that there would not be an opportunity for us to leave the ship for days.

"What about a helicopter?" I asked.

"We don't have a helipad. And this part of Alaska is desolate, so there's no place to let you and your wife off. It's impossible; I'm sorry."

"Listen, we have to find a way to reframe this situation. Nothing's impossible. Can I talk to your supervisor?"

"Sure, just a minute." He returned with another gentleman

wearing a naval uniform. Though sympathetic to our plight, he gave a similar answer. I would have to wait until we arrived in Valdez, three days away.

I returned to my cabin, all the while engaging in a continuous silent dialogue with you. I visualized my words traveling thousands of miles to whisper messages of comfort in your ear. Rain had begun to fall. The ocean's surface had become increasingly turbulent. All I could think about was getting to you, Pop. I returned to the front desk and asked to see the same manager again.

"Yes?" he said expectantly.

"I know this might seem unreasonable, but I really want your help in finding a way to get me off this ship. My father is dying and I really have to be there with him. Do you understand?"

"Of course, of course," he chimed in emphatically. "I understand, but there's nothing we can do. My own father died four years ago and I wasn't there, either. I know how you feel."

"I appreciate your kindness, really I do. But if you can't help me find a way off, maybe I'll just have to swim."

"No, no, no," he countered, half smiling and yet cautious as he continued to address me. "This is Alaska. The water is freezing."

"Then help me. Let's be creative! Please." We looked at each other without speaking for several seconds; then I continued. "What about getting a boat from shore to meet the ship? If we can get on land, I know we can find our way back to the east coast."

"But that's not possible right now. I'm very sorry."

As I moved toward the elevators to go back to my room, I kept picturing your face, Pop. Rosie said you were in terrible pain now. I had to get back to you. I whipped around and went back to the front desk.

"Excuse me, again," I said. "I really want to speak to the captain."

"There's nothing more we can do," another clerk informed me.

"I understand, but I want to see the captain anyway."

"Wait here, please." Minutes later another officer appeared.

"Hello, I am the vice captain. We have discussed your situation with the captain and your insistence about leaving the ship. Tomorrow we will be cruising within a few miles of a place on the coastline where there is a small village. We exchange pilots at that point. We can radio for a fishing boat to take you and your wife to shore, and then you will have to make your way from there."

"Thank you. Thank you very much." I leaned over the counter and hugged the man. At first he seemed startled; then he smiled softly.

"We will make the transfer at midday," he informed me. "The concierge will have your luggage picked up and brought down to a lower deck. Our crew will assist you in getting off the ship and into the fishing boat."

Suddenly, I had the image of this huge twelve-deck vessel almost one thousand feet in length meeting a tiny boat on the high seas.

"How do we get from this boat to the other?"

"Don't worry," he said confidently. "The crew will help you."

"My wife's a bit squeamish about these particular types of adventures — standing at the edge of cliffs or tall buildings. We're going, no matter what, but how will we get into that little fishing boat?"

"By ladder."

"Oh!" I grinned thoughtfully. "I don't mean to sound too naïve, but will the ladder be metal...or...or rope?"

"Metal, of course. It will not be difficult."

I thanked him profusely, extending my gratitude to the captain and everyone else involved. He bowed graciously.

Stay alive, Pop, I kept telling you. I'm coming. I will help you. Stay alive. Wait for me if you can, I said to you, jogging down the corridor toward my room. Then I stopped dead in my tracks. I didn't want you to wait for me if it meant more pain. I didn't want you to stay alive if you felt ready to let go. So I changed my running commentary: It's okay, Pop. I'm coming but you don't have to wait for me. Do what's best for you! I'm asking God to help you, Pop. I'm asking God to help me, too.

Samahria couldn't believe that I'd managed to convince the crew to assist us after all those refusals.

"We'll be leaving in the morning. I think we should pack."

"Bears, you know how much I love your father. He's like a father to me, too. I would do anything for him; you know that. But the weather is awful. One of the stewards said we're entering a rainstorm that will last all day tomorrow. How exactly do we get from this monster ship into a small boat in choppy seas?" She caught my smile. "Don't laugh. Answer me."

"How about trusting that we'll get off fine? These people know what they're doing. Whatever we have to do tomorrow, we'll do. Okay?"

"I've got this weird feeling about getting off the boat."

Samahria's fear of heights concerned me. I was sure that if she knew about our method of disembarkation, she would not sleep that night at all. But to my surprise and delight, she did not pursue the issue further.

"I am going to focus on praying for your dad tonight," she said as she crawled into bed next to me. "Should I be praying for us as well?" When I shrugged my shoulders innocently, she shook her head with appropriate caution. "Based on that response, I'll pray for us as well. You know how I always say that I've got God on my side? Well, I've just got to tell God what my side is — and that's peace for Dad. And an easy 'off-the-boat' for you and me. How does that sound?"

"I'm with you!" I whispered as we held hands and closed our eyes.

The next day, the crew took us and our luggage down to a cargo deck about two stories above the water. One of the deck hands slid a huge cargo door aside. The wind and the pouring rain filled the area where we waited. I searched in the mist for the fishing boat. Then, in the distance, we caught a glimpse of what looked like a toy boat by comparison with our huge ship. I could feel Samahria clutching my arm.

"Honey, it's okay," I said, trying to reassure her. "We're going to be okay."

The fishing craft, no more than eighteen feet long, circled around to the cargo opening and then its crew secured it with ropes and metal hooks to the side of our vessel. The ship's crew burst into action, lowering our luggage with ropes. And then, to my surprise, they opened a hatch beneath the cargo door, revealing a flimsy rope ladder riveted at one end to the door's metal casing. They tossed the other end over the side of the ship. This was no neat metal ladder with a reasonable railing to hold on to. No, as in a movie, it was a simple, unadorned rope ladder, now flapping in the wind.

"Oh, God!" Samahria exclaimed as she backed away from the cargo door. "No way. I am not going."

"Honey, we can do this. You can do this. There's no time to discuss it. We have to go, now."

"Please hurry," a crew member urged us.

"In a minute," I said to him. Pop, I turned back to Samahria. I knew I had to invoke your name. I could feel her hands trembling. "It's the only way to get to Pop before he dies. Honey, trust me. You can do this. I'll go first and make sure you get down safely. Okay?" She pulled back from me. "C'mon, you can do this. I know you can. Maybe God is inviting you to be a daredevil today."

Samahria took a single step toward me, then stopped to peer through the rainy mist down to the choppy waves below — *far* below. She took a deep breath, shook her head in resignation, and followed me like a prisoner marching to her execution. For her, it was like jumping out of a skyscraper. My heart reached out to her, Pop, but my head stayed focused on helping her do what seemed unthinkable. I knew we had to move quickly. I barely remember grabbing the rope and backing quickly down the ladder, with Samahria saying, "Oh, my God! Oh, God!" as she watched me descend. Truly, I felt like Spiderman climbing down the side of a high-rise apartment, only my target wasn't a sturdy sidewalk but a little platform, bobbing in the water. Seconds later, I jumped into the boat, which rocked unevenly in the ocean waves.

When I looked up, I saw the crew showing Samahria how to turn around and grab the ladder.

"Don't look down," they called out. "Just follow our directions."

Pop, she looked so frightened, but what a trooper! You would have been so proud of her. She took the first step down. "You're doing great!" I yelled. "Your foot's secure. Yes, that's it;

step down." The rungs of the rope ladder were so thin that only the toes of her tiny feet could secure her. The rain drenched us both, splashing into my eyes as I kept talking to her. The crew added their comments, encouraging her to take the next step and then the next. "Not too much more to go and you're here," I shouted.

Suddenly, Samahria stopped climbing and looked down. Her legs trembled.

"No!" another crewmember shouted. "Don't look down! Look up and we'll guide you."

Samahria acknowledged their directive immediately, regained her balance on the rope and continued her descent. As she came within reach, I touched her leg so she could feel my support. "Only a few more steps to go," I reassured her. Just as she was about to put her foot on the outside ridge of the boat, a wave crested, sending the boat into a dip between swells. It dropped down at least six feet, leaving Samahria's foot dangling precariously in midair.

"Hang on! Don't let go!" I screamed as did some of the crew members. When the boat popped back up toward her, I shouted for her to let go and grabbed her as she dropped into the boat.

Within seconds, one of the fishermen disengaged the small craft from the ocean liner. As their boat cut through the choppy waves, he guided us along a very narrow walkway beside the small cabin. The metal surface of the deck was slick from the rain, and no railing provided protection against a fall overboard. We had to lean against the side of the cabin as we walked, gliding our wet hands along the flat wall. As we finally took our seats next to the boat's pilot, he smiled his welcome, informing us rather casually that, although the seas were rough, they were not as heavy as he might have imagined, given the small craft warnings issued that morning.

Samahria rolled her eyes (as all three of my daughters do — the boys don't seem to have that talent), sighed her relief, then laughed. Suddenly, her face turned deadly serious as her eyes opened wide. "It just hit me! What's it going to be like getting off when this boat touches land?"

"Hey, given your crafty exit on the high seas, I am sure it will be a snap," I responded, holding her hands tightly and looking into her eyes. Her hair, soaked by the rain, curled wetly against her face. We had been together for thirty-six years, yet in this moment, she was my bride. Beautiful. Feisty. Daring. Again and again, as we had done in dealing with Raun's autism, in creating the Option Institute, in helping Bryn deal with her heart, we had jumped together into uncharted territory, each time because we had such a compelling purpose. This time, Pop, you provided that compelling purpose.

Less than an hour later, we landed on shore in a village with a population of less than three hundred people, located a plane to fly us to Juneau, and spent the next thirty hours finding our way back to you.

THREE

On the plane from Alaska I couldn't sleep. I visualized an image of you and held it intently in my mind's eye, trying to keep you alive until I could be there to help you through those last few hours. And yet, I did not want you to stay alive for me or to prolong your pain for even an additional second if you felt ready to let go. You had lost so much weight, and it even seemed that you had lost inches in height. You were smaller than ever. Frail.

When I was young, Pop, you were such an imposing figure in my life. Tall. Energetic. Athletic. Powerful. I guess all fathers appear to be mythical giants to their offspring. My own children used to report having similar impressions of me. Bryn said that when she traveled with Samahria and me, not only did the inside of the car appear huge but also the stature of her parents...especially me. I recall thinking it made sense that my children would view me as mammoth, since I loom over six feet, two inches tall. And yet I knew Bryn and her siblings also held me within the context of their image of father: "He makes everything right." "He saves the day." "He saves us." These are tough expectations to fulfill. I guess I had similar expectations of you, Pop.

While I was growing up, for me you seemed like Superman, only without the tights and cape. I remember when you were in your mid-forties, and doctors told you that you had stress-induced heart palpitations that could lead to a heart attack. One evening, you stood in front of the mirror and told yourself you had to change; you had to stop driving yourself crazy. And that was it! The palpitations stopped. You made a decision, period. Well, for me, Pop, it never came that easy. I had to explore, investigate; I had to dig deep, then deeper. Only after systematically studying my own psychodynamics could I finally change. Now I teach a method of personal transformation that allows me as well as others to quicken the process of change and to make it permanent.

One incident that I remember vividly happened just after my fourteenth birthday. You invited me to accompany you to work for the day. I had recently entered those mind-boggling, obnoxious teenage years, which on this occasion meant I gave you a hard time by pretending I didn't want to go. I resisted you initially but acquiesced finally while camouflaging my secret excitement about seeing you in your element. I knew the story of your life more from my grandmother than from you. Now I wanted to see you in action.

You were born in Russia and smuggled as an infant by your mother across the mountains of eastern Europe, arriving finally in the United States to join your father, and becoming eventually a graduate of the Depression and a shining example of the

American dream. You didn't complain, Pop, even when you lost your sight in one eye during an accident at the lumberyard where you had labored after school to earn money for your immigrant family. You worked hard, in the old-fashioned way, to carve out a respectable niche among your peers.

You worked during the day sweeping floors at a large textile-manufacturing corporation and attended college courses at night. Your industriousness soon landed you a higher position in that organization. Seven years later, when you graduated with a degree in education and history, you decided to stay with the textile company rather than teach. Twenty years later, you were a senior vice president. All these facts had become part of your legend.

Grandma viewed you as the fair-haired son. Your brother Max never had a chance to see his star shine so bright in her eyes. She loved him, but she trusted and admired you. I could tell, Pop, by the way she spoke about you and especially by the way she described your achievements: a suburban home, a four-door Packard sedan, vacations in the country, a loving marriage, and three healthy children. You represented stability and security.

Until that trip to your office in New York City, I had experienced you essentially as my personal disciplinarian — a real jerk! How many times you marched me angrily into the dining room after you came home from the office in order to deliver my well-earned punishment. The list of my problematic behaviors seemed endless: using vulgarity in the house, speaking unkindly to my mother, hitting my brother, coming home past curfew, refusing to do my chores. Mom would diligently list all my daily transgressions, and you, poor guy, would have to deliver my just rewards after scolding me at length. Often, I'd stop listening to your words as you yelled at me, thinking only about the beating to come and your red face. I never realized then how you enacted the best version you knew of parenting, American style, in the 1950s. I viewed you as just a mean bully. I'd have to drop my pants, bend over a chair, usually in front of my siblings (ugh!), and then wait as you ceremoniously withdrew your belt from your pants. I'd close my eyes as you began to whack me, holding back my tears so you wouldn't know how much it hurt.

At the same time, I would want to defy you even more to show you that you couldn't control me. I would imagine blurting out some curse word or saying something else outrageous in order to break your dominance. In the end, I would hold back and hate you instead of owning my own actions or the repercussions of those actions. And as soon as I had the chance, I would break another curfew or grow my hair down to my shoulders in order to assert my power. You, in turn, would parade me back into that dining room and administer my penance. Ironically and apologetically, you would often make the most confounding and confusing statements. First, you said with the greatest sincerity, "This hurts me more than it hurts you." How could that be? I wondered. I am the one with the red ass. Second, you affirmed, "I do this because I love you." I remember thinking that when I grew up I certainly did not want too many people loving me, since being loved involved so much pain.

The parents we counsel now at the Institute confide in us about the anger they sometimes feel toward their children and the way they end up telling them exactly what you told me forty years ago; they say they get angry with their children because they love them. Actually, Pop, they get angry because they are disappointed, because their expectations are not being met, because their children are dishonest and rebellious or, perhaps, too honest and too independent.

We love our children sincerely and deeply; nevertheless, we might scream at our sons and daughters not because we love them but because we, ourselves, are upset, angry, or frustrated. Being loving is a completely different activity than expressing our discomfort. In actuality, our unhappiness distracts us from expressing the tenderness and warmth of love that we feel.

What you might have said more accurately to me back when I made myself a difficult and challenging youngster was that, when you were angry with me and disappointed with my difficult behavior, you expressed disappointment and anger, not love. But you did your best, just like I'm trying to do my best right now. When I say I love you, Pop, it means I accept you, want the very best for you, and am willing to take action, to be useful, to help you get the best. Before I created such an understanding of love for myself, I didn't know how to embrace you, me, or anyone with such focus and caring. Hopefully, I am better equipped now. Love is no longer mysterious or intangible to me but an attitude and sensation that I can choose to feel and express. I choose to love you, Pop, to serve you. Years ago that would have sounded sanctimonious or silly to me; today, I feel grateful to make such a choice. The more love I give you, Dad, the more love I have to give you.

Somebody who knew of those whippings once told me that I was abused as a child. No way. I did not come from an abusive family. I came from a distinctly American family with a father and mother who did what they believed was best. And you know what, Pop? Even though a current psychological fad encourages us to see ourselves as martyrs of dysfunctional families, victimized by what people said or didn't say, what they did or didn't do in our childhood, I hold you in the highest regard — not for all that you did, certainly, but for what I came to understand about the intentions behind what you did.

So there I was, Pop, traveling with Grandma's dream boy into New York City. You introduced me proudly to your co-workers, showed me how raw cotton became cloth to be made into shirts, sheets, and blouses, then invited me to sit beside you in your office while you handled endless meetings and phone interactions. The business world seemed vast and unfathomable, yet you moved authoritatively through it. Although impressed by your knowledge and skill, I withheld from you all of the compliments you truly deserved. After all, I told myself, you were still the guy who whacked me.

The most startling and impressive event of that day occurred on "the Street": Seventh Avenue, the heart of Manhattan to anyone in the textile business, or as you and your colleagues called it, the "rag trade." While walking down that avenue toward a coffee shop to have lunch, just south of Forty-seventh Street, we encountered a very distinguished gentleman wearing a plaid double-breasted suit and a felt hat with a wide brim. When he saw you, he stopped and smiled broadly, greeting you like a celebrity. Before you spoke, you did something with each other that took my breath away. You kissed each other on the cheek. I had never seen you do anything like that except with Mom, and certainly not with another man. Time stopped for a moment as I watched the two of you, like characters in a movie expressing some ancient European tradition. I loved that sweet exchange between the two of you.

Once you introduced me, the man immediately turned his attention to me like an old friend. "Ah, Abe's son! How marvelous! Do you know, young man, what kind of father you have? This man is good for his word, and that's saying something on this street. Just a handshake with Abe. That's all it takes. And you can bet your life on that handshake. That's no small matter, young man. Integrity. That's your father. Mr. Integrity." He squeezed your cheek affectionately, saying, "I love this man."

I don't know if you noticed me standing there with my mouth wide open. What an endorsement! I tried desperately to view you through his eyes. I knew this stranger loved and appreciated you more than I did. You were my dad, and from my teenager's vantage point, you were becoming progressively more and more a pain in the butt. But to this man, you were golden, a real prince. I wanted to be your business associate, not your son. For years afterward, every time we argued, I would dredge up the image of that encounter on Seventh Avenue as a way to remind myself of qualities about you that I had not yet seen or that you had not yet shown me in our normal daily interaction. I wanted you to be the prince in my life instead of a disciplinarian. And yet, that fellow's words and the kisses on the cheek you exchanged humanized you in my mind and in my heart and put a crack in the wall we had built between us.

As I sat on the plane, wide awake, I couldn't help but wonder, How could your life have been transformed from that powerful strut down a Manhattan street and the respectful reception by your associate to the impotency of illness and aging and the prison of a hospital bed? Time had always been your friend, Pop, longevity and health your apparent birthright. The verse seemed written for you: "And goodness will follow you all the days of your life." Had something gone wrong? Had God abandoned you? Could I find ways to be more helpful?

33

FOUR

The plane touched down at LaGuardia Airport in New York City just before eight o'clock in the morning. Samahria and I had passed through four time zones, and we had not slept in almost two days. Given Samahria's weakened condition, this trip had taken its toll on her physically. But I felt acutely alert as I searched the baggage area for Raun, who had driven from Massachusetts to meet us so that we could drive directly to the hospital. Suddenly, his sweet face appeared above the crowd and we were off.

In the car, driving north out of the city toward the hospital, we talked to Raun about you, Pop.

"Honey," Samahria said, "Grandpa will probably look a lot different than when you saw him a week ago."

"I know. I thought about that." Raun said. "It might be weird, but I'll be all right."

"Raun," I added, "Grandpa could die soon. Based on what

Grandma told me on the phone, this could be it. Today. Tomorrow. I know you have a lot of unresolved issues about death; most people do — and I know you really care about Grandpa."

"If it was you or Mom, I don't think I could handle it, not right now. It's not that I don't love Grandpa, but he's not a part of my life like you guys are. I just don't want him to be in pain."

"Neither do we, honey, but that's probably exactly what we'll see when we get to the hospital," Samahria added. "Grandpa might still be in a lot of pain."

Raun stared out the window without responding. He was twenty-three years old — about the same age I was, Pop, when I tried to understand Mom's pain and death. Unfortunately, at that time, none of us had had a forum for talking about death. We did "grin and bear it," then lied to each other, to ourselves, and to Mom, telling her she looked healthier than ever when, in fact, her face had become distorted because of the radiation treatments and her abdomen swelled because of the tumors growing in her liver. We followed your lead, Pop, as we toasted Mom on her final birthday, when you assured her and everyone at the table we would also celebrate her next birthday the following year. I remember choking on the wine; I didn't believe you and I guessed that Mom didn't believe you, either. But we all played the game, Pop, just as you had prescribed, creating a wall of silence mixed with forced smiles and a large dose of misinformation.

You did the best you could. I know how you wanted to support her, love her, and take away her fears. But I think, Pop, we left her isolated, dying alone while still physically alive in the midst of her family and amidst the surface chatter we had all used to mask our real thoughts and feelings. You and I have learned, grown, and changed so much since then. If I could redo Mom's send-off, I would. She's gone, Pop, but you're here and Rosie's here. We're doing your send-off very differently; hopefully, we'll do it better.

"Why can't we just close our eyes and die when it's our time, like some yogi in the Himalayas?" Raun asked. "Why can't it be that easy?"

These were exactly my thoughts, Pop, as I considered your current difficulties. Certainly, your staying alive these past two years has been an unforgettable adventure, requiring real effort and daring on your part. Why couldn't the final moments be easy?

"Raun," I responded, "I have the same question you do. Why can't it be a simple act of will — to be done when we want to be done? Some people, for example, go to sleep at night and never wake up again in the morning."

"That would be my preference, totally." Raun offered.

"Sure, I understand," I nodded, smiling. "Some folks have heart attacks; they die in hours, minutes, seconds. Others have strokes; they die immediately or live on for years with disabilities. Still others have progressively incapacitating and painful illnesses, like multiple sclerosis or cancer. Raun, this might not sound like much of a consolation, but Grandpa has learned so much since being diagnosed with cancer. He shares more. He's opened his heart. And he shows so much more love." Raun smiled, acknowledging your transformation, Pop. "This might sound like a crazy observation," I continued, "but if Grandpa had died in his sleep two years ago, none of this would have occurred. Years earlier, I would have wished him a quiet, peaceful death. But now, I'm not so sure anymore. Grandpa has reaped so many benefits from confronting his mortality with ample time and space to consider his life, his relationships, and his loves. Would you think it insensitive if I also said that these two years have been a gift for me personally?"

"No. I know how much you love him," Raun answered. "We talk and say what we think all the time, but Grandpa's not used to that."

"You're right. Until recently, it was never his cup of tea. My father came from a different generation. He adopted very different values: Stand tough. Be stoic. Keep your inner life private and do not show emotions. His upbringing, and mine, were very different from yours; after all, we've encouraged all you kids to speak up and say what's on your mind and in your heart. This experience of cancer has inspired him to experience very tender parts within himself, to build bridges that didn't exist before. I'd like to believe that our different ways of dying are not cruel occurrences but rather meaningful opportunities to complete our personal journey in this life in the particular way that best suits each of us."

"Yeah, I understand. Makes sense," Raun mused. "But, even so, why not complete our journeys without so much damn aggravation?"

Samahria turned around in her seat and touched Raun's hand gently. "Sometimes we need to hear a loud knocking on the door in order to confront our issues and make our changes," she said. "For most people, cancer would certainly qualify as a loud knock on the door. When you and I — all of us — don't listen to ourselves and our bodies, the messages usually escalate. That happened to me. I ignored feeling ill for years. I believed my work — helping people at the Institute — was much more important than taking care of myself. Until, of course, the pain became so intense and my ability to move so restricted that I couldn't ignore the knock on the door any longer. And my lessons, Raun, are by no means over."

I wondered how you might feel about this conversation, Pop. You'd probably smile tolerantly, especially as Raun talked, since you seem to enjoy him so much. In the end, you'd label the entire discussion "philosophical." These are the kinds of discussions we didn't have as a family when Mom became sick. As a result, death overwhelmed us all, including you.

I remember leaving Mom's bedside in the hospital after her mastectomy in order to go to the bathroom. As I stood in front of the mirror washing my hands, I heard a man in one of the stalls sobbing intensely; in fact, he seemed to choke on his own emotions. The depth of pain expressed by that man sent chills through my body. I didn't know what to do. I thought about trying to comfort him, but he had locked the door to the stall, apparently wanting privacy. I considered getting a hospital attendant or priest, but, here again, I didn't want to intrude on his space with misguided Good Samaritan impulses.

You had taught me well, Pop: Stay away from the private zones in people's lives. Ironically, my entire profession now puts me squarely in the middle of those tender and, at times, turbulent private zones in thousands of people's lives. But back then, just twenty-one years old, I couldn't make sense of my mom's life-threatening condition or the despair and anguish expressed by the man in the toilet stall. As I turned to exit the restroom, I lingered uncomfortably, listening to the gut-wrenching sounds that continued unabated. I could see the top of the man's head visible above the gray partition. Obviously, he stood alone, leaning against the metal cubicle that had become both his refuge and his prison. Finally, I decided to leave him, to avoid intruding on his privacy and his grief. But as I walked to the door, I stopped yet again, disturbed by my own unwillingness to become involved. I looked back toward the toilet stalls.

Something about the top of this man's head seemed suddenly and oddly familiar. I tiptoed toward the cubicles to get a closer look. Pop, you were the man sobbing in the stall.

I backed away stunned, experiencing my own emotional meltdown. I had never seen you cry or display any pain whatsoever. I wanted to reach out to you — to help you, to hold you, but I couldn't. You had taught me to stand alone, as you stood alone in the bathroom stall. Be strong. Be a man! I didn't know how to make sense out of your emotions. Silly as it might sound, I hadn't known you had emotions, at least not the kind that erupted from your throat that day.

I never judged your pain or your grief. I left the bathroom without acknowledging you, an action I believed you would have wanted me to take. At the same time, I berated myself for being a compliant fool. You had made your privacy so precious, and unfortunately, your unavailability left me adrift, on the outside, alone with my waking nightmares. I felt physically sick and nauseated when I returned to Mom's room. I smiled as if nothing had happened, but everything inside seemed poised to explode. Then, some time later, you returned to Mom's bedside, smiling at her, me, and the others in the room. I smiled back at you, Pop, never betraying — no, not for an instant — that I knew where you had been and what you had been doing. When Mom asked you why you had been gone so long, you told her you had been down in the cafeteria.

Maybe it was in that moment, Pop, that I first began to hate the lies. They separated us from each other. They left you without any comfort or caring from others in the face of your grief. They left me confused and angry with myself and with you. They left Mom dangling in a sea of formula smiles. Nevertheless, I played the family game for at least a few more years, certainly until after Mom had died. And later, Pop, when I broke that mandate to lie politely, either by design or by omission, and became outspoken about my thoughts and feelings toward everyone in the family, I crossed an invisible line, becoming the pariah when I only meant to open my heart and inner world to everyone.

Once at the hospital, Samahria, Raun, and I took an elevator, then walked quickly through the hallways in search of your room. Just at that moment, Rosie came out of a staff bathroom, saw us, and began to cry. Samahria and I hugged her; together with Raun we walked toward your room. We could hear you moaning from the hallway, Pop. I said a silent prayer for you as I approached. Once at the doorway, Rosie suggested that I go in first, to see you alone because you might be embarrassed to be seen by others in this condition. I recalled what you had said to Raun only weeks before: "Don't remember me as I am now; remember me as I used to be."

Clearly, you had lost weight. Additionally, the muscles on the side of your face flexed against the waves of distress and pain. Carefully pushing aside the tubing from the intravenous hookup, I sat down next to you and took your hand gently into mine. As soon as you became aware of my presence, you started to cry and turned away from me.

"Bears," you said, " you got here at a bad time. I'm not doing well. I've had enough. I want to be gone. I'm sorry, Bears, but I can't take it anymore."

I sat beside you and wrapped both my hands around yours. "You don't have to be sorry about anything, Pop. You've been amazing. You've been an inspiration. It's okay to feel finished."

"I just want to die," you said, choking on your words as if a man like you couldn't give himself permission to speak so frankly.

Then you pulled one of your hands from mine, banged the bed and tried to push the blanket down off your body. "Get if off. It hurts. Please, get it off!" Immediately, I jumped up, stripping away the cover and the top sheet as quickly as I could. Apparently, just the pressure of its weight against your skin caused intense pain. "Go. You shouldn't see me like this. Don't let Rosie come in."

"Pop, I'm staying. You might not look your best right now, but you're my father and I want to help you." I could hear a second sound track in my mind abandoning the thoughtful conversation with Raun in the car about dying slowly. I now prayed that you would be able to die quickly, as you wished.

You looked over at me and the tears flowed from your eyes. You squeezed my hands tightly, shaking them irritably. "I've had enough. It's too much." You disengaged your hands and slammed them against the bed; the effort drained your remaining strength and left you panting. "It's over. I just want to be gone."

"I hear you, Pop. Listen, maybe I can help you right now with the pain and with what you want for yourself. Okay?" You nodded. "We'll do a visualization together. Okay?" You nodded again.

"We're going to take a few deep breaths together. Try to focus on my voice and follow my suggestions. Here we go. Draw your breath in. Great! Hold it. Good. Now let it go. Draw another breath in. Hold it. Wonderful. Now let it out. Draw yet another breath in. Hold this one a little longer. Good. Okay, now let it out." As you focused on your breathing, the tension in your face diminished, although, from time to time, the muscles in your jaw and arms twitched, releasing energy.

I continued to speak softly to you: "Allow your breathing to follow its natural rhythm, but as you do, monitor each breath.

Each time you take in a breath, be aware of the air moving through your nostrils and mouth, the rising of your chest cavity, the expansion of your abdominal area. Be aware of the sound of each breath being invited into your lungs and then released. Each time you exhale, use it as a way to let go — to let go of any holding in your neck or chest or back or abdominal area, to let go of any holding in your face, your hands, your feet, to let go of any thoughts or worries that might be occupying your mind. Just let it all go each time you exhale." The fistlike grip of your hands softened. You stretched out your fingers and laid them very gently on the blanket. The rhythm of your breathing slowed noticeably. "Stay with your breathing. It will help take you home, to a quiet, peaceful place inside. There's no place to go, nothing else to do, right now, but to be with your breathing. No yesterdays. No tomorrows. Just this moment... and then the next...and the next. Each moment unfolds into the next one.

"Visualize your body floating downward into a vast internal landscape as big as the heavens above. Visualize this landscape filled with a soothing white-yellow light, like a warm summer sun. The light envelops your body. Now imagine relaxing your head, your torso, and your limbs so completely that your cells actually separate a bit from one another, allowing a spaciousness between them so that the warm, soothing light can now move through your body, providing a gentle massage inside — reaching into even the remotest crevices. Allow the energy of the light to help you to be comfortable and to be as free of pain as possible. Let the light melt away the pain." The mild twitching in your face and arms ebbed.

After a few minutes of silence had passed, I spoke again. "Raise the index finger on your left hand if your pain is gone."

No movement. "Raise the index finger on your right hand if you have less pain." Your index finger shot right up. "Raise the same finger again if you have substantially less pain." Again, your finger pointed upward. Awesome, Pop, just awesome. Over the next forty-five minutes, I guided you through a complex meditation/visualization. At different points during this process, I encouraged you to let go of your breathing if you wanted, to let go of your heartbeat if you wanted, to let go of your brain waves if you wanted. If you yearned to die, I wanted to assist you, Pop, but it would have to be your own will, not mine, that would direct you to let go.

At different times, I stared at your chest because your breathing had become barely perceptible. Then, as I invited you to close your entire system down — your breathing, your heartbeat, and your brain activities simultaneously — and to let go into the hands of God, you stopped breathing. I, too, held my breath. The silence in the room became deafening. I started counting the seconds. Ten seconds. Twenty seconds. Thirty. Then, suddenly, you swallowed. I leaned over and whispered in your ear.

"Pop, are you still alive?"

"Yes," you muttered, your parched lips forming a faint smile.

"If you wanted to die, how come you're still alive?"

"That's a very good question," you said with a big grin.

"How are you feeling now?" I asked, smiling with you.

"Better. Much better." Keeping your eyes closed, you put your left hand back in mine. You spoke very, very slowly. Each word you enunciated seemed to require a tremendous amount of energy to vocalize. "I am really glad you're here."

"I'm glad I'm here, too, Pop."

"Being sick like this." You shook your head. "I'm giving everybody a hard time."

"No. At least, not me. I want to be here for you. It's my honor, Pop. Really, my honor." You opened your eyelids and turned your head toward me; then you gazed deeply into my eyes in a way so different from the fleeting glances you'd give me years ago. I felt so much gratitude. My eyes filled with tears. Yours did, too. "Hey, Pop," I whispered, "We're still having our big adventure."

You nodded almost imperceptibly, then drifted off to sleep for a few minutes. When you awoke, you appeared somewhat more energetic.

"I have a question for you, okay?" I asked.

"Okay."

"Before I did the meditation, you said you wanted to be released from the pain and from this life. Yes?" You responded by nodding. "So how come you're still in your body?"

"I don't know," you answered.

"Do you know it's okay with me if you leave, if you set your spirit free from your body?" You nodded again. "Do you know it's okay with Samahria?" Another nod. "And do you know Kenny, Jessica, Alan, and David — they'll all be okay?" Yet another dip of your head. "And what about Rosie, Pop? Do you know she'll be okay as well?"

At first, you gave no response to this last question. Then, you shook your head from side to side adamantly.

"Pop, what does that mean?" You refused to answer initially and just stared at the ceiling. But I knew what your gesture meant. Rosie was not ready to let you go . . . and you knew she wasn't ready. Finally, you acknowledged that awareness.

For the next two hours, Samahria and I walked through the corridors of the hospital with Rosie, explaining to her how helpful it might be for you to know that she was okay and how helpful it would be if she, too, told you she would be okay if you set yourself free from your body and from the pain whenever you wanted.

"I can't do that!" Rosie insisted, annoyed by my suggestion.

"Why not?" I asked gently.

"I just can't. I'm not ready. I'm just not ready!" She began to cry. "Maybe he could still get better. We've had almost two years. Why not two more? Or five more?"

"Rosie, we had a great run with Pop. Two sensational years. Great years for all of us. But he doesn't have the energy to push any more. His body has weakened, the cancer's growing; the pain's increased."

"He just doesn't feel good now, that's all," she insisted. "He's had difficulties before and come out fine. Why should this be any different?" Rosie peered into my eyes as if searching for an answer to a riddle and then abruptly turned away. "Don't say it! Don't you dare say it."

I put my arm around her. I wanted her to feel my support. "Rosie, what don't you want me to say?"

"That it's over. Don't say it's over. I'm not ready for it to be over."

Samahria took her hand and said, "Do you want him to continue to live if he's suffering?"

Tears cascaded down Rosie's cheeks as she held Samahria's hand more tightly and leaned against me more heavily. If I could have magically created what she so desperately wanted, I would have done it. But your words echoed in my ears. You wanted to die. I loved you both. I asked myself, Who do I serve?

You and Rosie had also expressed differing desires at the outset of this journey almost two years ago. At the age of eighty-four years, having lived what you described as a full life,

blessed to have had two amazing and durable love relationships, you wanted to make a graceful exit, without a fuss or a
fight. I recall Rosie's mouth hanging ajar as she listened to you
talk about dying, and dying soon, so matter-of-factly. She
wanted ten more years — well, at least five — and lobbied for
a change of heart. That little sparkle danced in your eyes as you
listened to her; I knew she had hooked you. You adjusted then
and came her way. Now, Pop, I think Rosie will eventually have
to come your way.

"No one knows when it's over, except maybe Dad and God,"
I said to Rosie. "We can only stand by to help him and love him.
Do what you feel is right in your heart. You don't have to say
anything to him, and you don't have to believe his life is over.
You know me, Rosie; I'll tell you exactly what I think, just as I've
done with you and Dad throughout this whole affair. These are
my beliefs, my viewpoints, my guesses, and I believe it would be
helpful for Pop to know that he can die... especially to hear
that from you. Maybe he wants your permission. There I go,
Rosie, with one of my guesses."

Samahria left us to check on you, Pop, and to see how Raun
was doing.

I looked at Rosie and considered a possible additional fear
that had not been addressed. "Rosie, if you give him your permission to die (not that he needs it), that doesn't necessarily
mean he will die in the next minute. Of course, that's certainly
a possibility. We're at the crossroads."

"We don't have to be. He can get through this one like the
others."

"You know I've championed his ability to defy the odds,
whatever the prognosis. I've done that right from the beginning. He's a unique guy. He has real spirit, real heart. And his

ability to bounce back has been amazing. But he's saying something different now, and I want us to hear him."

"Don't you believe he can still come back from this?" she asked me pleadingly.

"If he feels he wants to, if he feels he has the strength, then sure! But, Rosie, that's not what I'm hearing." I closed my eyes for a moment. Could I approach this discussion from a different direction? I wanted to be helpful and supportive to her, Pop, in every way I could. "What do you think, Rosie? What do you hear him saying he wants?"

Rosie glared at me, Pop, with eyes that knew but stalwartly refused to acknowledge her own awareness. She disengaged from the conversation and walked determinedly back to your room. Samahria and Raun had been talking with you, and you appeared so much more comfortable than when we first arrived. From time to time, the nurses came to prod and poke you, activities that you endured with little tolerance. More than once, you remarked that you hated being in the hospital. More than once, Rosie reminded you that this facility provided you with help you could not get at home. You appeared unconvinced.

FIVE

As I sat by your side in the hospital, I thought about the passage of time and about that exceptional phone call I received from you two years earlier. I don't know if I realized then what an incredible gift you deposited at my doorstep in that call. Although we had built some bridges between us over the previous decade, I still felt separate from you. I continued to believe that you had lived and would die without ever knowing me... without even wanting to know me. You viewed the lifestyle I lived and the principles I had adopted as contrary to what you held dear. However, the unexpected, tradition-breaking call that Sunday morning altered irrevocably our father-and-son relationship.

When the telephone rang and I heard you speaking from your home in Florida, I anticipated one of your ritual chats, which would unfold as follows:

"Hello."…"How are you?"…"How are the children?" (Here you'd mention a few of their names.) "How's the weather?"…I would ask you and Rosie about your lives. Your answers would be short, usually "yes" or "no" or "fine." "Okay, okay," you would then say, "this long-distance call is expensive. It's costing too much money. That's enough; good bye." I would offer to call back on my "nickel," but you would refuse, explaining that you had all the other children to call and then had plans to go to the gym or play tennis or compete in a bridge tournament. That was why I suggested that you stop calling me on Sunday and allow me to call you during the week. When I caught you without advance notice in the evenings, especially if I had placed the call, you talked much more freely and appeared significantly more relaxed, even though you interrupted our conversation often to remind me that this call would cost me a fortune. Each time, I told you that I worked very hard and enjoyed spending my money on telephone calls to you. Sometimes, you'd laugh at such comments, then become even chattier.

During those extended phone conversations, you would also be somewhat more forthcoming about your feelings, about your relationship with Rosie, about your concerns regarding finances or relationships with your other children. Still, you asked little about me except to inquire, "How's the action?" referring to the number of people registered in the group programs we taught. If I said, "Good," as I usually did, that meant financial health and stability to you. To me, it meant helping more people. We took the same news and referenced it in completely different ways.

However, when I wanted to tell you about a seminar I had designed or share a story about a client or a program participant's transformation, you often used that as a cue to express impatience and terminate our interaction, whether we were on the phone or talking in person. When I confronted you about this, you would say you didn't have much interest in listening to stories about people's problems and how they changed. You complimented me on helping people, but you weren't interested in the specifics, even though the specific way we work cured your grandson and helped so many other families and children as well.

Usually, our discussions short-circuited when I talked about any of the perspectives underlying our work — for example, our belief that happiness is a choice and love is a choice.

"Don't start with that crap," you'd say.

"What crap?" I'd ask.

"Maybe for the people who read your books and attend your programs happiness is a choice, and people create whatever attitudes they darn well please. But for the rest of us, some things just are. Some people get angry. Some people are more laid back. Some people tend to be aggressive; others are timid. It's just part of our nature."

"That's exactly what I used to think, Pop, until I discovered that I could change what appeared to be in my nature or supposedly in my genes. I could teach myself to think differently, feel differently, and behave differently."

"Look, Bears, enough. The programs are filled. The kids are doing well. Enough."

"You don't have to yell, Pop."

"I'll yell if I want to!" you shouted.

"Sure, that's fine. But if we have a different interpretation of human nature, why do you get so upset with me?"

"Stop asking so many questions. You always have another question. Don't psychologize me!"

"I'm not. I am trying to understand how you feel and what you're thinking so we can communicate better."

"We communicate well enough. I'll talk to you next week. Good bye."

It was difficult for me to live down the excessive missionary enthusiasm I had when I first threw myself into this process thirty years ago. Back then, I wanted to save the world from unhappiness, hate, and violence by helping folks change the self-defeating beliefs that fueled these circumstances — whether they wanted to change their beliefs or not. I still love the evolving Socratic dialogue process we utilize in mentoring sessions and in our work with program participants and helping professionals. The gift of a question is still sacred to me. But years ago, instead of mentoring, instead of asking gentle questions of those who are already seeking to change, my youthful passion sometimes led me to torment unsuspecting friends and acquaintances by tossing rather blunt, unwelcome questions into their laps like explosive grenades.

These days I have mellowed profoundly, and I engage in dialogues only with people who are actively seeking to rethink their fundamental beliefs and learn how to be happier and more loving. Nevertheless, I still see questions as a valid means of enhancing communication and believe that if we truly seek to understand, the questions we ask of each other can help open doorways between us. In truth, I still feel rather socially inept when exchanging pleasantries in conversation. I tend rather to dive deeply into the other person's world and invite them to jump fully into mine.

I jump in heart and soul, Pop — exactly the style of

conversation you avoided like the plague with me. Consequently, most of our interactions, especially those on the telephone, became sleigh rides along the surface. Every time I tried to take us deeper, you resisted and reacted. When I told you that you expressed anger toward me fairly often and that I wondered if you spoke to my siblings that way, you protested the observation and the question, saying you treated all your children the same way.

Rosie disagreed with you. "Abe," she said emphatically during one particular discussion, "you're much harder on Bears. You never yell at Jessica; she's 'the daughter.' You never raise your voice to Kenny, and I know that's because you're afraid to hurt him. And you speak really nicely to Alan and David." She paused to let you absorb her words, then continued. "How many times, after you spoke to Bears, did you tell me you had been too rough on him and wanted to call him back? Only, Abe, you never did call him back any of those times."

"I don't have to call him back. Bears is stronger than they are," you said matter-of-factly, as if that explained your behavior.

"Oh!" I said. "You see me as strong, and so you give me guff?"

"He's right, Abie, that's what you do," Rosie concluded. "But Bears," she said turning her attention to me, "you may not believe this, but he always talks about you in glowing terms to our friends. He lets everyone know his son writes books. He talks about the Institute, where you help people 'from all around the world,' he always adds. And don't think he forgets to tell them that they made a television movie about you, Samahria, and Raun. He doesn't tell you, but he sure tells everyone else. Oh, and you don't get to see him when someone writes an article in a Florida newspaper about your work or in one of those big magazines. He's the first to show everyone!"

"Well, Rosie, I'm blown away, really!" I said, touched, amazed, and at the same time, confused. "Wouldn't it be sweet, Pop, if you talked about me like that to my face as well?" I suggested.

"I tell you," you snapped.

"No, you absolutely do not," I said. "When it comes to talking about my work, you usually yell at me, just like today. Or poke fun at what I say."

"He's right, Abe," Rosie added.

Given this kind of history, your telephone conversation with me that special Sunday morning changed the format for our interactions. You asked all the standard questions, but I could hear a strange lilt, almost a hesitancy, in your voice.

"Is everything okay?" I interrupted. "Your voice — it sounds, well, different. Pop, are you okay?" I braced myself for one of your terse objections to my question, but instead, you surprised me. Rather than responding with annoyance or outrage, you said simply and rather unconvincingly, "I'm okay."

"No, he's not okay," Rosie said, from the other extension.

No one spoke for a few seconds.

"Do you want to tell me what's happening?" I asked.

"Yes," you said in a quiet tone. "Actually, we had planned to tell you."

"Great. I'm ready. What's happening?"

"Well, I have prostate cancer. And they think it's spread because I have swollen lymph nodes in my stomach area and in my groin."

I leaned back slowly into my chair. Your words burst into my world, as the words "autism" and "retardation" first burst into my world regarding our son Raun. I had spent my life changing, training myself to be happier, more loving, more centered, and more self-trusting so that I could greet effectively the unknown challenges beckoning to me from the future. Raun presented one of those challenges. There had been others. So it was that I recognized your pronouncement immediately as giving me the unparalleled opportunity to live to the fullest everything I had been teaching for a quarter of a century. I wanted to give you the best of me. More clearly than ever before, I knew I wanted to love you, Pop, and if you permitted, to serve you.

After several more moments of silence, I formulated a clear intention: to be the most useful, supportive creature that you have ever had in your life. And so, with great sincerity and a spirited voice, I said, "Well, congratulations, Pop! Sounds like you are beginning a whole new adventure in your life."

You laughed and said to Rosie, "See, that's why we called him. Listen to his attitude."

You explained that this diagnosis had been made three months earlier but that you hadn't told anyone. "I don't want to be treated like I'm sick and dying," you said emphatically. "Right now, I'm feeling fine. I go to the gym every day as usual. I want my life to stay as it is."

"Sounds reasonable," I responded. "I want to ask you about any treatment procedures you're having, but first...why did you decide to tell us now?"

"There is no 'us.' I'm telling *you*," you responded. "We don't want the other kids to know. They'll just get upset and worry, and I don't want that. I don't want everyone flying down and treating me like something terrible is happening. I don't want the phone ringing all day with everyone asking me what hurts and what doesn't hurt, how do I look, am I losing weight, and on and on. God willing, I'll keep on living just fine. I want everything to stay the same."

"Then how come you called me? Why are you letting me know?"

"Because I knew you could handle it," you said.

"And we could use some help," Rosie added.

"You got it!" I said.

"Your father's having some additional problems, and we don't know what to do — what treatments he should have. Everyone says something different. The urologist says one thing, the oncologist another."

"Give me the rest of the day to change my schedule for the next week, make sure all my classes are covered. I am sure Samahria can rearrange her session with the families. We will be on a plane tomorrow morning. Okay?"

"You have so many responsibilities. Maybe coming down to Florida right now is too much," you volunteered.

"Not too much. I'll see you both tomorrow. Remember, you're beginning a new adventure."

"Yes," you said, laughing again. "I am certainly having a new adventure."

I had you give me nitty-gritty details about your diagnosis, the results of the MRI and CAT scans, as well as the results of biopsies and blood profiles. You told me that the oncologist suspected that the prostate cancer had not spread but that you had two cancers simultaneously, the second being an aggressive form of large cell lymphoma. I knew that I could be useful by doing as much research as possible to provide you with the most up-to-date information. I finally had a way to show you, in terms you might appreciate, that I really cared and sincerely wanted to help you in any way I could.

That same day, utilizing all the medical reports you had, I called on a network of professionals and colleagues to help provide us with the latest information regarding the prognosis for people with these types of cancer, as well as cutting-edge treatment protocols, conventional as well as alternative. Using the Internet, we scanned public files at the National Institutes of Health and downloaded pertinent medical research at Duke, Johns Hopkins, and other universities. When we arrived at your home the next day, the bounty of our research came along with us, including numerous FedEx packages delivered that morning, filled with brochures and research papers from California, New Mexico, Maryland, and Washington, D.C., as well as from the Bahamas, Switzerland, and Germany.

Both of you seemed so pleased to see us. You had arranged for me to accompany you to consultations with both the urologist and the oncologist. We also made arrangements to meet with a nutritionist who specialized in nutritional approaches to cancer treatment. I had made phone appointments with two nationally renowned researchers who would assist us in locating both alternative cancer treatment centers and conventional treatment centers known for treating prostate cancer and/or large cell lymphoma. You smiled appreciatively. In those first minutes together, I could feel that something had changed between us.

"Before we start looking at all this material, why don't we talk first and get clear about your intentions for yourself so Rosie, Samahria, and I know how to proceed with your treatment plan? Okay?" I asked. Everyone nodded. "What kinds of thoughts and feelings do you have about your medical condition and about your life?"

"You know," you said, "I'm no spring chicken. I'm eighty-four years old. No one lives forever. I've been more fortunate than most. If I have a couple more years, great. I can't complain."

"What do you mean 'a couple more years?'" Rosie protested.

"How do you feel about what he just said?" I asked her.

"Lousy! How else should I feel? What do you mean, Abe, by a couple more years? What about ten more years, fifteen more years? Plenty of people live until they're one hundred. They wish them happy birthday on television. Why not you?"

"Okay, okay, Rosie," you countered, tapping her arm affectionately. "Let's just stay on point. I feel good, even with this problem. No reason I can't keep going on just like I've been."

"What about the pain in your back, Dad?" Samahria asked.

"We've got to do something about his back," Rosie interjected. "It's been getting worse."

You had been taking a hormone inhibitor to slow the prostate cancer but refused to consider any other treatment procedures. "What do you think, Pop?" I questioned. "Time to do something more?" You nodded your head affirmatively. "Great," I said softly. "In the next day or two, in addition to all our appointments, we have to educate ourselves. We have a lot of material to review. Pop, Rosie wants to do natural therapies..."

"Yes," she interrupted, "but I'm not sure. Maybe we have to do everything we can — the alternative therapies as well as, um, the normal medical treatments."

"Like what?" I inquired.

"We're afraid to give him chemotherapy because of his age — you know how sick people get, using those terrible drugs. But I'm afraid not to give him chemotherapy, too," she added.

"How about," I suggested, "we agree that we don't have to make any decisions until we have a lot more information. Maybe, at that point, what to do will be much more apparent. And then you guys decide. And I'm also thinking that reviewing all this literature will show us that you can't necessarily do all different kinds of therapies at once. Often, one type of medication or procedure will be compromised or rendered ineffective if administered together with a competing protocol. So you might have to choose between one or several methods rather than trying to do everything simultaneously."

The appointment with the urologist that afternoon proved inconclusive. He suggested several treatments, including additional hormone blocks, a possible surgical procedure, and a limited form of chemotherapy under the direction of a consulting oncologist. Despite several biopsies, the radiologists felt the tissue samples did not yield conclusive evidence of large cell lymphoma. Thus, an additional biopsy from a mass near your kidney or from a growth beside the vertebrae in your lower back would be helpful. To complicate matters, the lymph cell tumors had pressed against your urethra, rendering one kidney inoperative. Chemotherapy could further endanger either your one functioning kidney or your heart, which had a mild arrhythmia. As the picture developed, I became more and more amazed at how well you functioned, Pop, with all this disease activity going on throughout your body.

When I shared that observation with you, you laughed yet again. "Pretty tough old buck, huh?" you said proudly.

"My compliments, Pop." We shook hands.

After dinner, Samahria, Rosie, and I sat together in the kitchen and began reading through all the materials. You paced in the living room, walking barefoot across the smooth white tiles, occasionally stopping to stretch near one of the two love seats facing each other in front of the decorative Chinese screen attached to the wall. You had been thin since your mid-fifties, when you dropped some extra weight and became an exercise devotee. Now you appeared even a touch more lean, yet still overflowing with a youthful physical vitality. When I invited you to join us, you refused, saying your back hurt and you didn't want to sit. An hour later, you entered the kitchen, appearing distressed.

"Dad, are you okay?" Samahria asked you.

"I'm fine," you said. "But maybe all this fuss isn't necessary. I've lived a long life. What if I just go along, as I have been, and when it's my time, it's my time?"

"What are you saying, Abe? Just give up?" Rosie exclaimed.

"No," you insisted, "it's not giving up. Just, well, letting things take their natural course. And, when I'm gone, I'm gone."

Suddenly, I realized the game plan might not be the one I had anticipated. I thought I had come to Florida, Pop, to help you live. Maybe instead I had come to help you die.

"Whatever you want, Pop," I said emphatically.

"One major question, right now, is what to do about that increasing pain in your lower back," Samahria added.

"Well, that's not my major question right now," Rosie protested as she shook her head. "Abe, I want us to have more years. Do you hear me? At least five or ten. What's wrong with that?"

"I don't want to be a fuss or a burden to everyone. It's not such a calamity to . . . to be at the end of your life."

"You mean to die?" I asked you.

"Okay — to die," you responded.

Rosie winced at the word "die." I also noticed that she could not use words like "cancer" or "tumors" in any of our discussions. Instead, she identified your difficulties using nonspecific terms such as "illness" or "'pressure near your lower back." On a few occasions, she talked about your swollen lymph nodes as if you had an infection rather than a constellation of tumors growing in your abdominal cavity.

"How did you feel, Rosie, when Pop said it would be okay for him to die?" I asked.

"I don't like him talking that way," she muttered.

Most of us have a need to control events and outcomes so we can feel safe and be happy. As the discussion proceeded, I realized that in order to be most helpful to you and Rosie, I had to be unattached to whatever you and Rosie decided about your life and death. I wanted to love you without interfering with your decisions about how to take care of yourself. So for the next several hours, both Samahria and I dialogued alternately with you, Pop, and with Rosie, as we might have done with any couple attending a program or arranging for joint sessions at the Institute.

We explored a host of issues and asked a lot of questions, which, surprisingly, you both answered willingly. How did you feel, Pop, about Rosie's desire that you live longer and make a real effort to accomplish that feat? How did she feel about your desire to avoid being a "fuss," as you declared, and to expire gracefully and perhaps quickly? In the end, you both remained quite solid in your positions. So later in the evening, after everyone had retired to bed, I returned to reading the materials we had received, just in case you changed your mind. At about eleven-thirty, you walked into the kitchen.

"Go to sleep!" you ordered, directing me with your thumb to stand and leave the room. "It's been a long day for you. Time to go to sleep."

"I'm fine, Pop. I have a few more research papers to read and then I'll tuck myself into bed. Just a note — there's really some interesting new work being done in the autoimmune area that has had notable impact on some cancers, especially on large cell lymphomas."

"Okay," you said rather casually, "give me some of that damn literature to read."

I sat back in the chair, clasped my hands behind my head, and smiled, "Well, well, well! Sounds like you've decided to live."

"If Rosie wants me around for another five years or more," you snapped, "the least I could do is make an effort."

"Sounds great, Pop. I'm sure she'll be delighted."

SIX

Our visit to the oncologist the next day presented us with an additional viewpoint that both supported and contradicted the urologist's perspective. This physician wanted you to begin massive, not limited, chemotherapy immediately, arguing, unlike the urologist and radiologist, that the previous biopsies *had* conclusively shown large cell lymphoma. Based on the tissue samples already in hand and on all the CAT scans and MRI results, he felt sure that you, indeed, had two cancers and that aggressive treatment of the large cell lymphoma should be undertaken immediately, since the prostate cancer appeared contained. However, he did agree with the urologist that it would be prudent and useful to perform another biopsy to determine the level of malignancy. He expressed no concern about your age, although we had read literature indicating that one ingredient of the recommended chemotherapy "cocktail" could traumatize the heart of someone advanced in age and that the protocol he suggested tended to have an adverse impact on kidney and liver function. He dismissed the statistics that challenged the validity of his recommendation, asserting that "all cancer therapies involve risk, of course." His "of course" sounded a bit scolding. Although he appeared sincere and quite competent, his resistance to full discussions and his unwillingness to educate us, especially you, with digestible information or useful insights left us baffled, and we were uncertain what course of action to take.

On the way back to your house, Rosie seemed particularly agitated.

"I didn't feel good about him," she said strongly. "What about you, Abe?"

"There's a lot for us to consider," you said thoughtfully, not quite answering her question as you glanced out the car window.

"We have to do something about the swollen nodes that the doctor talked about," she asserted, "and about this illness."

"And we have to do something about your pain, Dad," Samahria added.

"I agree with everyone," I said. "But why aren't we calling the swollen nodes 'tumors,' which they are, and this illness 'cancer,' which it is? Even the doctors avoided those words."

"I don't like those words," Rosie said.

"Why?" I asked.

"Because of what, um, they mean," she responded haltingly. "You know as well as I do that when people hear that word, it's . . . it's like hearing a death sentence."

"And that belief, tied to that word, becomes part of the shuttle that takes us to that final exit door. What we believe has real power in our lives, Rosie! How about we let that word mean something else for us, like a powerful invitation to question how we have been living our lives and a real challenge from our bodies to make some significant changes? Somehow, by not using the 'real' words when we talk about 'nodes' and 'illness,' we keep phantoms lurking in the shadows as if we're all part of some sort of a sinister masquerade. We're not dealing with swollen nodes; we're dealing with a series of growing tumors that can interfere with the function of organs and can press against nerves and cause pain. But they can also shrink in size and go away." I looked at my father's thoughtful expression though the rearview mirror.

"What are you thinking, Pop?"

"Go on. I'm listening."

"Okay. I want to say this so it sounds sensible, not scary. Pop, you don't have a cold or the flu; you have cancer, which means some cells are now growing at a rate different from that of normal cells and they have to be guided to return or change back to normal patterns. Your body's internal dynamics have changed. We don't have to view that as the end of the world; we can view it as useful information to help you decide what action to take. I have a suggestion that I hope doesn't sound too flip or silly. What about beginning by making friends with these words? At the Institute, we do a little exercise with words that we're afraid of or words that have become taboo. We sing them. I know it sounds silly, but let me try. I'll start, then you can join in if you'd like. Okay?"

Using the tune of "Row, Row, Row Your Boat," I started singing, "Cancer, cancer, cancer, cancer, all the way down the stream; cancer, cancer, cancer, cancer, life is but a dream." Through the mirror, I could see you and Rosie looking at each other quite astonished. Then you began to smile. Rosie smiled back at you as she began to sing. Samahria joined us immediately. When you started singing, then our quartet became complete. We switched words, alternately using "tumor" and "malignant." Within minutes, we had excised the terror from an entire group of words that you and Rosie, especially, had been avoiding.

That evening, when we traded information with each other from all the literature we continued to study, I could not help but notice you and Rosie now using words like "cancer" and "lymphoma" as easily and comfortably as you used expressions like "pass the salt." I loved watching you allow yourself, Pop, to become more engaged with the material, excited about certain treatment protocols, and then completely adamant against other methods. In contrast to our first days together, you now began to develop strong viewpoints quickly and express those viewpoints with growing conviction. Rosie, however, appeared more and more confused by all the conflicting information. As she advocated more natural, less intrusive regimens, you talked about feeling more and more comfortable with traditional medical practices.

The sharply conflicting recommendations being presented by doctors, researchers, and alternative health professionals added confusion rather than clarity to our discussions. Conventional medical opinion often presented scathing indictments of the anecdotal evidence and nonscientific methods of alternative therapies, supplementing their arguments with impressive statistics supportive of the effectiveness of their own work. The nontraditionalists presented hefty documentation of the adverse and oftentimes deadly ramifications of scarring surgery and poisonous toxins that make war on disease rather than attempting to enhance body function. They supplemented their arguments with in-depth studies and personal endorsements from patients about the efficacy of their less invasive procedures.

We reviewed bioenergetic processes as well as the possible value of meditation, visualization, and mind-body methods. In the course of this discussion, you, dear father, in a major philosophical reversal, began to agree that attitude could have a meaningful impact on the course of this disease and your ability to heal. Even Rosie seemed startled by your flexibility to explore methods that you had previously dismissed. Was it the song we sang in the car? Was it a new ease and curiosity with areas that had seemed unfamiliar until you had a reason to seriously consider them on your own behalf?

The next day, we had two more consultations with noted researchers, which I had arranged before I left Massachusetts. We met for five hours, reviewing current medical protocols, with a specific accent on autoimmunology and biotechnology. Some of the studies had produced impressive data, yet no conclusive assessment could be made until further research had been completed. But the researchers gave us their recommendations, at times contradicting each other, and you listened, saying you found the entire discussion fascinating, though inconclusive. By late afternoon, you claimed your brain had turned to "mush" after being bombarded with all this information. I felt the same way.

In the end, no clear "right" or "wrong" path emerged. You and Rosie would have to make your best guess. When you asked Samahria and me for our opinions, we both tended toward the less invasive methods as the place to begin, though even we had differing opinions about which method to try first. Both of us encouraged you to acknowledge the mind-body connection and to focus on developing a positive attitude. We suggested that you could create beliefs to promote healing and to support any treatment procedure you chose.

By this time, Rosie was lobbying for a combination of alternative methods — such as herbs, nutrition, visualization, and immune system strengthening — joined with conventional protocols, even chemotherapy, if necessary. She had long ago introduced you to health food stores and to nutritional eating, helping you to develop a regimen of vitamins and herbs that I am sure contributed to your health and vitality. Pop, you had watched your seventy-something significant other doing yoga for years, so you'd seen firsthand an alternative method of maintaining physical vibrancy.

As we went back over some of the materials we had highlighted over the past few days, you acknowledged your openness to visualization and meditation. It made perfect sense to you to strengthen your immune system and design a diet likely to inhibit tumor growth. By evening, you had endorsed a plan similar to Rosie's, agreeing to consider alternatives if used in conjunction with standard medical procedures. You clearly did not feel any aversion to chemotherapy and/or radiation if they could be undertaken with reasonable assurance that such treatments would not undermine the function of your heart or remaining kidney.

Within twenty-four hours we found a facility in Tulsa, Oklahoma, that offered the best of both worlds: conventional medical procedures such as surgery, chemotherapy, radiation, hormone blocks, and red and white cell enhancement therapies, as well as less conventional methods including nutritional guidance, pastoral counseling, visualization/meditation classes, and patient support groups. Rosie had seen a commercial for the same facility on CNN and sent away for a brochure. Unlike the several hospitals you had already visited, this facility assigned each patient to a care group that would assist and advocate for that patient throughout diagnosis and treatment. Rosie and I spoke with the people from the facility, the Cancer Treatment Center of America, separately and at different times. We found that these professionals wanted patients and their families to be partners in all decisions, and they sought to be supportive and respectful of the patient's wishes and to make people seeking their services feel honored and welcome. They demonstrated a personal care and concern that had been absent from our visits to specialists and their affiliated hospital diagnostic centers. You both seemed truly excited about the place. And that excitement would be the key component of any healing process, enabling you to walk as successfully as possible along the path that both Rosie and you had selected.

The method of treatment any of us picks for ourselves can be extraordinarily important, whether it be chemotherapy, macrobiotics, or sitting on a mountainside in the Himalayas. What's most important is our belief in our chosen treatment. I knew that if you chose chemotherapy, Pop, then you would want to believe wholeheartedly in its usefulness — not to fight it, but to welcome it; not to fear it, but to love it. If you chose meditation or designing healing thoughts, then you would want to believe in the power of those thoughts, which express themselves continuously throughout the body on a biochemical and electromagnetic level. I didn't want you to simply adopt my perspective on your cancer and possible treatments; the most important and beneficial perspective would be the one you adopted for yourself. Samahria and I applauded your decision, and we also wanted to do everything we could to support the next step in your adventure. But when I offered to assist financially with the costs of the trips to Tulsa, you refused.

"I have my own money, thank you. We pay our own way... well, with the help of Medicare and some insurance." You smiled proudly. You had retired almost a quarter of a century ago and managed to maintain your financial and physical independence clear into your eighties. You would not compromise your integrity, your achievement, or your sense of well-being now.

"Fine," I said easily.

"Are you open to gifts on occasion?" Samahria asked.

"No," you said flatly. "No gifts. And no arguments."

"We got it." I touched your shoulder gently with my hand. "Always remember that we're here for you."

"You don't have to remind me. Look what you and Samahria have done just this week!" In an uncharacteristically gentle expression, you reached out and stroked my cheek with the tips of your fingers.

SEVEN

$\int$amahria fell asleep quickly, but I lay awake for almost an hour, reviewing the events of the days we had spent with you and Rosie here in Florida. We had come such a distance within this short time. No walls separated us now, Pop. God, how full and grateful I felt! Maybe I had needed to truly let go of my dream of having a relationship with you in order to have a relationship with you. When I no longer needed you to know and love me, only then did I become more adventurous and daring in trying to create bridges between us.

As I stared at the ceiling, I remembered Samahria, Rosie, you, and me strolling along those country roads that meander through the ninety-five-acre campus of the Institute about seven years ago. I had just finished teaching a program entitled "Empowering Yourself," a feisty, challenging, weeklong workshop encouraging participants to clarify what they want and then take steps toward getting it. As we walked together, I thought about the program and then thought about what I wanted in my relationship with you. I could hear myself say, "I want more love, more intimacy, more sharing." For me, meaningful love relationships began with and thrived on open, honest exchanges between those involved. I wanted to try yet again, Pop.

With you, though, I always seemed to put my foot directly into my mouth. What I taught in classes appeared, at first glance, outrageous in interactions outside of class. My problem, Pop, is that I've made my entire life a classroom. I feel like a child, so incredibly curious about people and events and our environment — thus my very direct questions. When people outside of a seminar or group program get angry in the face of a question (indeed, some get angry even in classes where the mandate is to ask questions and explore personal issues), I oftentimes feel totally surprised and clueless — like I've just hit another one of those invisible walls that folks do not want other folks to cross. Although I have mellowed, I still tend to push at the edges. Some people love that aspect of me, while others would prefer I disappear.

I thought that if you hadn't been my father, you might have also wished me to disappear. In the last few years, I've tried to contain my desire to nibble at the edges while in the presence of others, including my siblings, who give me "go away" messages when I question them too closely about their personal lives.

But that afternoon seven years ago, while you still viewed straight talk as impolite and unnecessary, I was determined to push at the borders of our relationship, to find a way for us to know and love each other more. I wanted much more traffic (information, thoughts, feelings, desires, dreams) on the bridge between us.

I am sure you remember this exchange:

"Pop, if you entered a room filled with people you know, including me, and you were asked to pick one person to be your friend and live with you on a private island without any other human contact, would you pick me?"

You stopped in your tracks. "There you go again. How could you ask me such a question? I am your father. It's ridiculous to pose such a question. You're my son."

"Yes," I said. "But, even so, would you pick me to be a friend on that island with you, given what you know about me — how I think, what I value, the ridiculous questions I seem to ask? Maybe the answer could help us know more about how we feel about each other. If you were going to pick one person, would you pick me?"

"I just told you. I won't answer that question. And that's final."

"Okay. Fair enough," I said. "Pop, I'm going to reverse the question and ask it of myself. If I entered a room filled with people I know, including you, would I pick you as that sole companion on that island?" I walked along in silence for a few moments. Samahria glanced at me cautiously. Rosie didn't say anything. Then I stopped dead in my tracks and faced you. I took your hand, rubbed it gently, and said, "No, Pop. Unfortunately, I don't think I would pick you."

You stared at me, amazed at my words. You took a step back away from me, disengaged from my hands yet remained focused on my eyes. In that moment, I recalled an explosive interaction between us soon after my sixteenth birthday. You had refused to let me visit my friends in the city. I packed my bag anyway, and just as I was about to leave, you confronted me. You glared at me in the same way you'd just done, then punched me squarely in the chest. I asked you if hitting me made you feel like a man and suggested, sarcastically, that you try hitting me again. You raised your fist a second time. At that moment, Mom interceded, grabbing your arm. Your face reddened.

"Abe, you're going to get yourself sick," she cautioned you.

Her words scared me at the time. I thought you might have a heart attack and it would be my fault. Although I pushed hard against what I experienced as your tight-fisted rule, I never wanted to hurt you. I backed away and left the house without saying another word. Now, as I looked at you, your face did not redden. In fact, your expression softened suddenly and your shoulders relaxed.

"Well, to tell you the truth," you said gently, "I wouldn't pick you for a friend or an island companion either."

We both started to laugh. I reached over to hug you, a hug you returned robustly. Then, we walked arm in arm, smiling and chuckling at each other. At one point, you leaned over and kissed my cheek, a rare occurrence at that point in our lives. I thought about the man with the wide-brimmed felt hat on Seventh Avenue with whom you had exchanged kisses. I could hear his words, Pop: "That's your father, Mr. Integrity. I love this man!" You and I had finally built a narrow pathway of authenticity across the bridge between us. I felt more warmth exchanged in those moments than I had experienced collectively over the entire previous three decades. Masks had been brought down. Our roles didn't matter; we talked straight to each other — and the straight talk had been acknowledged by each of us as a true gift.

Several weeks later, you astounded me by asking if you and Rosie could attend one of the programs at the Institute so you could get to know more about the work Samahria and I did — work we had been sharing and teaching for almost eighteen years by then. We arranged to have you participate in the Happiness Option Weekend Program. I felt so pleased. I understood what a gigantic step you had taken in my direction. Previously, you had dismissed our seminars and programs as collectives for self-indulgent chatter and unnecessary forays into people's problems. To smooth the way for you and Rosie, I asked the other program instructors and facilitators to give you as much space as you required so that if you did not want to participate actively, you would not be pushed. Well, you did it the best way you could! You sat outside of the circle in the back of the room, did not participate at all, and just observed. I understood what a stretch it meant for you to be among folks working on their "issues" and "difficulties" in a rather intimate but public forum.

When I taught the group on Saturday morning, I noticed how attentively you listened. I noted all the times you smiled, even the several occasions you laughed aloud. I so enjoyed watching you enjoy yourself. Rosie sat behind several other participants at the back of the room. Only much later did she tell me that she had cried at different times throughout the morning as she watched some of the participants find the courage to make changes in themselves as they confronted dramatic and even painful events in their lives. To her surprise, she found the environment very safe and accepting. And yet, watching perfect strangers open up their lives to each other in such detail and so quickly still seemed barely comprehensible.

On that Sunday afternoon, you told me you'd found the workshop interesting, even fascinating. Of course, you assured me, you did not have the issues or traumas other people discussed, but you noticed how many people reported being helped and supported by their experience in the program. I think you wanted me to know, for the first time really, that you thought our work had value...for others, if not for you.

My memories of our walk by the pond and of all your reactions during the program were quite vivid, and this startled me. It still does. Now, as I write, I can still feel your presence beside me. Sometimes, when I hit the keyboard, I am aware that my tears have blurred my view of the computer screen.

I pounded on your door for decades, but you kept so much of yourself unavailable. Sometimes, I felt like a little boy facing a ten-story door that had been cemented shut. Your armor against expressing feelings and private thoughts sent multiple messages. Be strong. Keep a stiff upper lip. Grin and bear it. Don't let anyone know what's going on inside! If you can, hide it even from yourself. As I type now, I experience a replay of another keyboard, one I tapped at over thirty years ago. I had been enlisted to help care for Mom during the last years of her illness. Jessica, married with a baby and pregnant with her second child, could not participate. Kenny still attended high school. Although at the age of twenty-one I had recently graduated from college and worked sixteen hours a day writing a novel and play simultaneously, you viewed me as unemployed and my endeavor as child's play; thus, I was available to help Mom. Often, you asked me when I would be getting a "real job" and going to work.

When I proposed to Samahria, I gave her a package of ten poems to express my love. No diamond ring. No gift of material worth that she could show her family. Her grandmother, who befriended and always welcomed me, gave me one of her diamonds and told me to make a ring for her granddaughter and never tell anyone that she had given the gem to me. She wanted me to be held in high esteem, knowing that poems written by a bearded, starry-eyed idealist might not make a favorable impression. Although I was dedicated to my writing, Pop, I agreed when you asked me to drive Mom into the city three days a week for radiation treatments and care for her at home on the other two weekdays. In addition to helping Mom, I wanted to be viewed as an upstanding person in your eyes.

Every time I entered the radiation department's waiting room at Memorial Hospital, my stomach would knot. People in various states of despair, some without hair, one without an arm, and another missing a portion of her face, waited their turn to be radiated. Mom, increasingly hunched and swollen as her disease took its course, would look around with empty eyes. I wanted to talk to her, but I never knew what to say. I wanted to comfort her, but I didn't know how to reach out. I watched you and tried to mimic your style. Often I said nothing, and at other times, I lied to her, telling her she looked great when, in fact, I could barely recognize her distorted face, swollen as a result of the radiation treatments and various medications. We never made it home without stopping on the shoulder of the highway by LaGuardia Airport, where I would swing the back door to the car open and help her crawl along the seat until she could position her head near the curb and vomit. The planes whizzing above our heads softened the throaty, choking sounds that she made. She kept apologizing for being sick. Although I would smile and reassure her, I wanted to jump out of my skin. I did everything I could to camouflage my feeling of helplessness as I watched her suffer, yet deep down, I knew she could detect my charade.

At home, I would change the bandages covering her mastectomy, which had left an oozing, gaping wound from her armpit right down to her stomach. I moved my hands very, very gently, trying to avoid the little tubes protruding from her chest so I would not cause her pain. Inevitably, she would wince, reassuring me at the same time. "I'm okay. You're doing just fine," she'd keep repeating like a chanted mantra. However, her facial expression said, "I'm not okay. This is terrible for both of us. I'm so sorry."

Did I read her expression correctly or did I feel the sorrow myself, wanting to apologize to her for seeing her so exposed and so scarred? I knew not to draw attention to such thoughts. Sometimes, after cleaning the wound and applying new bandages, I would sit alone in the bathroom, crying and vomiting at the same time. But then, according to our venerable family tradition, I would get my act together, push my thoughts and feelings into a lead-lined hot box inside and return to her with a big smile. And she would smile right back at me. We were both frauds, and we knew it. My anguish had intensified beyond what I could tolerate, so I tried to hide from myself. You see, Pop, I didn't know then what I know now. I couldn't help her in the way I've been allowed to reach out and help you.

You then asked that I work for you in your office, which I did as a way to support you during Mom's sickness. You had one of your partners place me in front of a keyboard to type invoices. I had been writing bills all morning when I noticed the paper below me getting wet. I kept watching the drops hit the words and smudging them. I looked up at the ceiling to see if a pipe was leaking. Suddenly, I realized my cheeks were wet and the drops of water were my tears. I had been thinking of Mom without even realizing I was crying.

Now, all these years later, I realize that in essence your request for assistance had called me home, giving me an opportunity to be with you differently than you and I and all of us had been with Mom. My mind fills with so many images of our interactions together. Days, years, and decades play together on an internal movie screen, which pays little homage to chronology; instead, scattered memories bubble to the surface as if obeying some deep urge to reappear.

For every memory of discontent that surfaces, I replay one of miracles and wonder between us. I know I write about us with a clear intention to celebrate our love. Perhaps a ghostly guide selects from the mass of historical data in my mind, pinpointing and spotlighting those incidents that define the separation as well as those that reveal the common ground we have created. My memories reveal you and I, a father and a son, a parent and a child, struggling to understand and accept each other and, finally, learning to express warmth and caring toward each other.

EIGHT

My mind felt so alive that I barely slept most of the night. Cancer did not seem like an enemy but a friend that offered us an opportunity to find more of each other and, in the process, more of ourselves. At about four o'clock in the morning, I got up to stretch and walk around. As I entered the living room, I could hear you and Rosie talking in bed. I ambled over toward your opened door and knocked gently.

"It's me," I announced.

"Come on in," you said playfully.

"If you're having a private discussion, I don't want to disturb..."

"No. No. Come in."

"You can't sleep, either," Rosie noted.

"My mind is whirling — but in a good way." I said.

You both looked extraordinarily cute. You wore striped pajamas, the exact style of nightclothes you owned when I was a child. Rosie wore a robe with a colorful floral pattern. Your heads were propped up on pillows with the blanket drawn up to your chests. Together, you could have been an uplifting advertisement for a spunky senior couple aging gracefully in an environment that appeared safe and inviting, blissfully unaware of the realities we had all dealt with during the day.

"It's cold," you said, moving closer to Rosie. Patting the mattress beside you, you added, "Here. Come. Hop in, it'll be warmer for you."

I slipped beneath the blankets beside you in disbelief. The ease and casual quality of your invitation disarmed me completely. Within a few moments, we heard new footsteps in the living room.

"Samahria?" I called.

She arrived at the doorway, looked at all of us together in the bed, and smiled. "I leaned over to hug you, Bears, and realized your side of the bed was empty. So I came looking for you."

"Good," you said to her, adjusting your position again. "So come on. We'll make room for you, too."

Awesome! A couple in their mid-fifties having their first pajama party with their seventy- and eighty-four-year-old parents.

"We have so enjoyed this time with both of you," I said, realizing that Samahria and I would be returning to the Institute at the end of the following day.

"Dad, I loved how we operated as a fine-tuned team," Samahria said. "I feel like this is a new beginning; we all got to know each other in a much deeper way."

"Pop, for me, this has been a special gift," I said softly.

"More for me and Rosie than you guys. You kids did all that work," you insisted.

"Can I suggest something?" I asked. Everyone nodded. "If

you don't want to tell your friends or neighbors about your medical condition, fine, but I would like to lobby again for sharing what's happening with Kenny, with Jessica, Alan, and David and their families. Pop, they love you. They're your children, Rosie's children. They care about you. Wouldn't you want to know if any of them had a serious medical problem?"

"Your father doesn't feel he can handle all the distress that everyone will have once they know."

"Wait a minute, Rosie; I can talk for myself. Like I told you before, Bears, I'll have to repeat all the information, over and over again, until I'm blue in the face. I don't want to talk all day about what hurts, what tumor is getting bigger or smaller, or what the doctors say about my condition. Everything can remain the same with them."

"Well, not quite the same, Dad," Samahria offered. "You will be going to Tulsa, maybe often. Your life will definitely change."

"I know, honey. But I'm not referring to that sort of change. I don't want to be treated like an invalid or a sick person where all anyone talks about is the disease. I don't want people checking up on me, which will happen if they all know. We talk to all the kids on Sunday mornings and that's the way I like it!"

"How about if you explain your feelings to everyone — tell them that although you now have cancer, you don't want the style of interactions, phone calls, and visits to change in any way? Everyone will understand," I suggested.

"Why are you trying to talk your dad into this?" Rosie asked.

"Because I believe they all love both of you and would want to know and support you. I feel honored to be here and to help. They'd probably feel the exact same way."

"You're different," Rosie said. "They'll get upset, and that's hard for your father. Besides, we don't need any more help, since we've decided what to do."

"The problem here, Rosie, is that you'll have to lie to them all the time — about how Dad's feeling and about any trips to Tulsa," I noted.

"I don't want to have to deal with all the craziness that will go on. I have too much to think about right now," you insisted.

"Okay. I have a suggestion," I countered. "How about I make the phone calls initially? So, if they get upset, I can give them time to absorb the information, and then you can get on the phone. You won't have to go through the same story over and over again. I'll fill them in on everything that's happened. Then you can get on and just tell them how you're feeling and what you want."

"What happens if they want to fly down immediately?" Rosie asked.

"Rosie," Samahria said, "then you just explain that's not what you want."

"It's not that easy," you said.

"Well, Pop," I suggested, "maybe that's because we haven't had much practice in saying what we really think in this family and then asking for what we want."

"What's that supposed to mean?" You looked at me a touch intensely.

"There's never been much straight talk in this family and not much tolerance for honesty," I suggested. "And you've been at the center of the game, Pop. And we've all been playing it for years. What about no more omissions or misinformation? Say the truth and ask for what we want! At least, in the end, we can feel clean by saying what we really think and feel. Here's our chance to start cleaning it up with our family."

"You know, Abe," Rosie added, "you don't tell Kenny certain things, sometimes, because you believe either he'll be hurt or he's not strong enough."

"Maybe you do the same thing with me as well, although you really do bitch a lot at me," I laughed. "So I assume you talk about me that way behind my back as well. And, if so, that's fine. At least you're consistent and real. I just hope you're getting it all out and, at the same time, getting it over so we can move on." I paused as I looked at your face. I could not detect any resistance. "I have been totally straight with you for years, and I think you've become that way with me. I love it, Pop. So opening up about your illness to everyone might start to change the 'don't tell' games in our family."

As the early morning light filled the bedroom, I noticed your eyes flitting back and forth as you considered what position you wanted to adopt.

"Bears, you will make all the calls, explain everything, and then I talk. Yes?"

"I would be happy to do that for you. Sure."

"And you'll explain that I want everything to remain the same — no extra phone calls, no extra visits."

"I thought you'd be the one to say that, Pop," I said. "I think if they heard it directly from you, they would comply with your request more easily."

"Fine," you responded. "But how about you explain what I want, and when I talk to them, I'll let them know these are my wishes? How does that sound?"

"If that will make this easier for you, fine." I agreed.

"Rosie, what do you think?" Samahria asked.

"I don't know if this is going to be so easy. Whatever your father wants is fine with me. I just don't want him to get upset."

"Understood," I responded, turning toward you. "Pop, you're in charge of your 'upsetness,' so you can decide that no matter what happens, you're going to have a good time and be open, loving, and direct. But, remember, none of us can predict how your other children will respond to this news."

"Dad, you'll be able to handle it. You'll do just fine," Samahria said. "I think this is definitely the way to go."

"Okay," you said. "But, Bears, you handle the first part of the phone calls and tell them what I said."

"Yes, I will do my best," I tried to reassure you. "If any of my siblings gets upset, I will try to talk them through it...and then, I'll hand the phone over to you. How's that sound?"

"Good." You paused thoughtfully. "Bears, I won't be able to handle everyone crying. That's part of what you do in your profession, right? So you'll handle it, right?"

"I'll do my best. I promise."

Four hours later, I made the first phone call. Kenny listened in silence as I detailed your medical condition and the results of our research during the past week. At various times, his voice quivered.

"Can I help in any way?" I asked.

"I need a couple of moments to digest what you're telling me."

"Sure, Kenny, take your time."

At that instant, as I spoke on the telephone in your bedroom, you passed by the open door and pointed to yourself. I shook my head and put up five fingers, gesturing to you to wait about five more minutes. You walked away, looking somewhat nervous.

"Why am I talking to you and not him?" Kenny asked me.

"Pop didn't feel comfortable dealing with a lot of emotions. He'd prefer talking to everyone once they've settled into the situation. He also didn't want to have to repeat this story over and over again, so I'm trying to help him out."

"I'd like to come down and see him," Kenny said.

"Sure, I understand, but, uh, that's another wish of his... that nothing change. He didn't want all his children and grandchildren rushing down to see him. It's very important to him to have everything remain the same, Kenny. If there have been planned visits, great, but no specific trips because of the cancer. He doesn't want to be treated like a cancer patient or a dying man. Right now, he's doing fine."

"I don't like this. Sure, you're there, so it's not a problem for you." Kenny stopped talking and then said, "I'd like to speak with him."

"Sure," I said. Then I signaled for you to pick up the extension. You gestured to me to stay on the line.

"Kenny, how are you?" you began as if you were beginning one of your typical Sunday morning phone calls.

"I'm fine, Dad, but I'm concerned about you."

"Nothing to be concerned about. We got everything under control."

"I'd like to fly down in the next few days," Kenny said.

"No. Bears explained it to you. No extra visits. I want everything to remain the same."

As Kenny pumped you for more information, I could feel your voice tightening. "Bears explained it all to you. I heard him. I don't have anything else to add. Look, Kenny, if you want more information, please call Bears. He will be the one who will let everyone know about my condition and what's happening. Okay, so you talk to him. With me, we'll talk about other things. That's the way I want it. Okay?"

"Okay," Kenny said tentatively in a low, breathy voice. He

seemed displeased with your edict. Whatever feelings Kenny had, I found your decree disconcerting. You had appointed me, without my consent, to what I guessed would be the thankless job of press secretary. What a reversal of previous roles! Suddenly, the sibling everyone viewed as the outsider had become the insider. In our family, such a turn of events would not be a cause for celebration. After Kenny hung up, I walked into the kitchen and looked you right in the eyes.

"Hey, Pop, what's this about? We never discussed my disseminating information to all my siblings on a regular basis."

"I know," you said reflectively. "I didn't know what else to say. He kept pressing me for more details, and I just didn't want to get into it all again." You walked into the living room. I followed. "Look, Bears, it would really be helpful if you did fill everyone in about this situation. This way they could call you. Besides, you're good at explaining things. They'll be satisfied, and I won't have to go over all this stuff again and again. With this pain, I am not up to it right now. The more I keep talking about cancer and tumors and hospitals and biopsies, the more it takes over my life. You're strong. You can handle it."

"If it will help you, I will do it," I said. "You know I'm not the most popular brother in this family, Pop. I'm not sure any of them will be thrilled to talk to me, except perhaps David, who has always been so sweet and cordial. But even though everyone might get a little nuts about this, if that's what you want, I will make peace with whatever comes with this territory." I sighed and then smiled a smile of resignation. "I'll do everything I can to be here for you, including being a conduit for your medical bulletins." I could not quite believe the agreement I had just made with you and the questions that now emerged for me.

In one of our training programs at the Institute, we ask

participants to make a list of intentions by which they mean to live their lives. We call it "A Vision to Live By." This exercise creates a meaningful focus of attention for participants, enabling them to practice clarity of purpose and conviction in all their actions. I, too, have developed a personal vision to live by, Pop, one that enabled me within seconds of that first phone call announcing your condition to pointedly choose to love and serve you as my first response to your situation. Having such a vision allows me to enter unpredictable and unexpected situations and find a centered, peaceful place inside. Am I 100 percent successful? No, but now I feel so much more in charge of how I choose to be from moment to moment.

Years ago, I might have walked into a room filled with people and found myself tossed in the wind emotionally as I responded and reacted to many different stimuli without any clear intentions. It never occurred to me to set an intention before walking into such a room and to create my experience by living that intention. What would I make all-important to me? Approval? Success? Being clever? Receiving an invitation to return? Being happy no matter what anyone might say or do? Or deciding, in advance, to love others even if they might judge or reject me? I like the two latter intentions most.

I composed my own vision to live by over twenty years ago; I discovered the list buried beneath a pile of papers in a file cabinet only a short time before we came down to Florida to be with you. One intention, far down on the list, after "Prioritize happiness and love" and "Live your life as if there are no wrong moves," was this: "Invite into your life only what you want in your life." I like the openness of that intention much more than the many "shoulds," "have tos," and "supposed tos" that people use to guide their life choices.

Now you had invited me fully into your life, Pop, probably for the first time ever! And I responded, not from obligation, but from a deep yearning to make my love tangible to you so we could know each other and enjoy each other. Now, in my agreement to be the informational oracle, I had just invited all my siblings into my life, perhaps on a frequent basis, believing they would likely see me as an unwelcome intrusion or a wall to climb over rather than a user-friendly resource.

Later I returned to the phone for another call. Jessica sobbed loudly as I informed her of your condition. I know you could hear her cries from the receiver. I talked with her much longer than with the others.

Finally, after composing herself to a certain degree, she said over and over again, "This is awful. This is awful."

"I understand, Jessica. Why don't I give you some more time to absorb all this. Okay?"

"It's awful," she repeated, more forcefully than before.

"This might sound crazy, but we're all trying to look at it differently," I offered.

"What are you saying?" she queried, raising her voice noticeably. "Am I supposed to think it's good that our father has cancer and he might die soon? What kind of person are you?"

"Nobody wants Pop to have cancer, but since he does, maybe we can find a way to make it an experience that ennobles, not diminishes, him. In the last few days, Pop and Rosie have been able to find a way to be easier and clearer about what is happening and about what to do. We even sang songs using the word 'cancer' to defuse the tragic and catastrophic associations with the word."

"Well, I'm just not there, brother. And if that doesn't fit your schedule, tough luck. I'm flying down tomorrow."

"But you know he really doesn't want you to do that."

"Everything's gotta be his way...or is it your way? Well, I have feelings, too." Her voice began to break. "I have needs, too." Jessica began to cry again. "I'm not ready for him to die."

"Jessica, he's not dying."

"How does he look?"

"Good. Actually, great," I volunteered. "He looks no different than when we all saw him during the summer."

"Is that the truth?"

"Absolutely."

She cried again. I waited until she had finished expressing her feelings and was somewhat calmer. I described my experience with you during our first phone conversation in which you shared your news with me. I told her that I had made your interests my interests as a way to honor you and be helpful to you.

"I'm just not there! I don't even understand what you're talking about. And I don't want to understand either. Let me speak to him right now! Do you hear me?" Her voice had become more intense.

"Sure I do," I said in a very soft voice, trying to de-escalate her distress and soften her adversarial stance. "Do you feel ready to talk to him?"

"What? Who are you to ask me if I'm ready?" she yelled.

"I am just trying to help Pop. He said he'd feel more comfortable talking once everyone has calmed down after hearing the news."

"Well, then I'm calm now," she continued, her voice trembling. "So, please put him on the phone."

"Sure, here he is."

Since you had just walked into the room and stood anxiously beside me, I handed the phone directly to you. I could sense your annoyance as you asked her several times not to come down to see you. Ultimately, you prevailed.

Our conversation with Rosie's son, Alan, proceeded much more smoothly. At first, he sounded startled. His voice quivered, and I could hear him cry. After discussing your situation and your wishes, he said he felt left out. My presence at your home sharpened his sense of alienation. He talked about his own father's death from leukemia and his awareness that he could now lose his second father.

"Two times," he said quietly. "That's more than I can take." He stopped speaking for a long period of time.

"Alan, are you still there?"

"Yeah," he sighed. "Yeah, I'm here. Well, is there anything we can do? I'd like to come down with Margie, but I understand he doesn't want us to do that. So where do we all go from here?"

"He'd love to talk to you. I'll put him on."

You picked up the extension and gestured to me to stay on the line. In the midst of your reassurances, you said, "And don't worry, Alan; I haven't changed a bit. This cancer hasn't made a difference; well, a little pain but no big deal. I'm exactly the same."

From my end of the line, I interjected, "Pop, I am going to disagree with you. Alan, I think this experience with cancer has definitely changed him. I don't ever remember him so open, so sweet, or so gentle as I have seen him this past week. Pop, you really wear your cancer well."

"Do I?" you asked, truly amazed. I could tell by your tone of voice that you accepted the comment as a compliment. "Well, you heard him, Alan," you said with vitality. "I'm wearing my cancer well."

He responded limply to your enthusiasm, possibly recoiling from our casual use of the word "cancer."

I placed the final phone call to David, who immediately put his wife Eileen on the extension phone. After I had reviewed all the information with him, he responded in a singular fashion. First, he thanked me and Samahria repeatedly for coming immediately to your aid. He said that it made perfect sense that you and Rosie had called me.

"Hey, Bears, I'm with him and with you all the way. Whatever he and Mom want. That's it for me. It's their life! If they don't want visits or extra phone calls, great! I've got no problems with anything you said. I just hope he's going to be okay, that's all. If I can help you, him, or Mom, whatever, you just call and I'll be there!" Later, he repeated his commentary to you directly. I watched your face as you listened. You appeared more relaxed and at ease while talking with David than during any of the other phone conversations we had made. David had no pretensions; he was just an incredibly sweet guy, who expressed so much love to you and to Rosie. Eileen's embrace of you during that conversation seemed just as warm and sincere as David's.

NINE

So much transpired between our visit with you in Florida and our flight from Alaska almost two years later. As I sat at your bedside in the New York hospital you had been taken to, I anticipated the arrival of Kenny, Denise, and Jessica — all of whom had visited you on previous days. Although at your request I had spoken to each of them about your illness on the phone many times in the preceding twenty months, I had not seen them in person for as many as four or five years. How starkly my separation from them contrasted with the warmth and affection we had all shared years ago!

Jessica had been one of my best friends when we both attended college. Do you remember, Pop, when I would sit on the floor beside her bed and talk with her into the wee hours of the morning about all those pressing big issues — like life, love, death, God, and especially anthropology (she was going to be a champion for the indigenous tribes around the world while I would write books)? You would come by in the midst of those starry-eyed conversations and do the fatherly dance by telling us to go to sleep. Our spirits had been ignited by youthful dreams to change the world with our ideas: there was her initial foray one summer into the Amazon area in South America, and then her involvement with organizations dedicated to the preservation of primitive cultures. Often, as I left her room, my mind was tingling with diverse utopian images of possible futures not yet even clearly conceptualized. I wanted to do great things in the world; so did Jessica. We juiced each other with our ambitiousness and our idealism. I would write the great American novel. Jessica would help educate the world by teaching people to go back to their roots. Think expansive! Reach for the stars! Then, suddenly, everything changed. Jessica married Frank and changed her career orientation immediately, becoming a part-time human resources administrator for a major retail corporation. Soon after, she became pregnant with the first of her three children. We drifted apart.

What happens with families, Pop? Many tend to dysfunction more than function. They create explosions instead of responses, offer judgments instead of forgiveness. They cut off communication instead of talking through opposing viewpoints. In our work, it has become quite apparent that altering any family's dynamics requires a passionate yearning for change or an earthshaking event that forces a fundamental reassessment. So far, your cancer had not pulled down the pillars of our dysfunctional family dynamics, though it had certainly stimulated fundamental realignments in my relationship with you. Sometimes, Pop, one person taking action in a family can make all the difference. And then again, some families armor themselves against or even ostracize a family member who threatens the established groove or network of interaction.

I had tried years ago to challenge our family's dynamics, defying the rules "Say nothing" and "Be polite." Instead of effecting change, I found myself being muzzled by everyone, Pop, including you. Rather than being included, I found myself excluded. In response to those patterns, I encouraged "radical authenticity" as a way of life with my own family. Not all my ideas have been overwhelmingly popular with my children, but thankfully, they have worked reasonably well, and sharing honestly and from the heart has become an underlying principle of interaction between most of them and Samahria and me.

I have always found it important to stand up for what I believe, even if that means standing alone. But that's me. I understand that not everyone thinks the same way.

Like Jessica, Kenny, too, had once been a major presence in my life. After Mom died, both Samahria and I kept a watchful eye in his direction. For instance, one afternoon Kenny drove his car to a repair shop, with Samahria following in our car. He changed lanes, inadvertently cutting in front of another vehicle. The other driver, enraged, swerved ahead of Kenny's car and slammed on the brakes, blocking the road. He jumped out of his car and moved aggressively toward Kenny's vehicle. Trying to be accommodating, Kenny stepped into the street and began to apologize. But the man, towering over Kenny with his tall, broad form, began to wave his arms threateningly. Samahria bolted from her vehicle and threw herself between them, facing the stranger with her fists raised in the air.

"Don't you dare touch him!" she said protectively as she moved forcefully toward the angry man despite his large frame and her diminutive size.

"Okay, lady," he answered, startled by her assertiveness, and put his hands in the air as if to signify his surrender. He began to back slowly away from her. "I don't want any trouble, lady. I'm out of here. I'm gone." Turning, he walked quickly to his car and drove away.

I asked Samahria later that evening whether she had been frightened during the skirmish on the road.

"Nope," she said matter-of-factly. "Too busy taking care of your brother, who's like my brother. I wouldn't have let anyone hurt him."

When Kenny married Denise, Samahria and I did all we could to support their process of creating a new home. I assumed the big brother role fully, easily, and actively, for I had developed a genuine attachment to and affection for him after Mom died. Although separated by a six-year age difference, Kenny and I became more than just brothers; we created a sweet friendship.

As young married couples, Samahria and I and Kenny and Denise spent many evenings as well as vacations together with our growing families, and we shared many ideas and ideals. Kenny attended graduate school in the evenings, earning a master's degree and then a Ph.D. in economics. Samahria and I traveled a very different route, finally studying the power of beliefs and its impact on human behavior, then going further by exploring and expanding a method of personal transformation we call the Option Process. I came to believe in the liberating power of choice — the freedom to investigate, change, and choose or re-choose our essential beliefs and the feelings that flow from them. As a result, both Samahria and I were convinced that all people have the power to re-create themselves and not be victims or prisoners of the past. In contrast, Kenny, perhaps as a result of his growing involvement in the world of investment banking, began to subscribe to a vastly different model of the human condition, viewing genetics, the environment, and chance as significant factors determining human behavior and interaction. We challenged each other's perspective in feisty, playful late-evening discussions that I found exciting and stimulating.

Denise and Samahria solidified a very warm and affectionate friendship. They became pregnant at the same time and gave birth to boys within weeks of each other (Denise with her second son, Samahria with her third child, Raun).

Then, rather abruptly, Samahria and I experienced a profound change in our lives. After their son and ours celebrated their first birthdays, Raun began to exhibit bizarre behaviors. By eighteen months of age, he spent all his waking hours flapping his hands in front of his eyes, rocking back and forth on the floor, refusing all physical contact, and avoiding eye contact with everyone. Those changes occurred in the winter and spring months, which you and Rosie spent in Florida. The ultimate diagnosis for Raun was classic autism, severe neurological impairment, and functional retardation with an IQ under thirty.

Rather than share such information in a telephone conversation, we waited until you had returned to your New York cottage for the summer to speak with you and Rosie in person. When we explained the situation, Pop, I could see pain in your eyes. You had a tough time, not only with the diagnosis but also with the prognosis — an irreversible, lifelong, incapacitating disability eventually requiring some kind of institutionalization. This was our son. Your grandson. Although you meant to be supportive, I could hear the condolences in your tone of voice — no different, Pop, from the despair apparent in commentaries from our friends, as well as the professionals we encountered.

Kenny and Denise seemed uncomfortable in Raun's presence — perhaps because their son, the exact same age, had no problems; perhaps for other reasons. They curtailed visits to our home, finally withdrawing from our lives. Although Jessica and I would talk from time to time on the telephone about Raun, she, too, kept her distance. Suddenly, while confronted with the biggest challenge of our lives and seeking support, Samahria and I felt very much alone. Nevertheless, we had developed understanding, principles, and ways of being in our own lives that guided and helped us through this challenging isolation.

During the years prior to Raun's slide behind the invisible veil of autism, we had begun to work with individuals and small groups, sharing methods for discovering and changing limiting beliefs while creating positive attitudes of strength and confidence even in the face of adversity. Could we apply and really live what we had just begun to teach others? Pop, Samahria always felt as if God had looked down at us and said, "Okay, so you think you got it together; well, here's a mountain to climb with your son. Let's see what you do."

We contacted resources around the globe, reading dozens of textbooks and consulting top medical and educational professionals. Even you recoiled when we told you about the still dismal prognosis and some of the abusive behavioral tech- niques (slapping, hitting, shocking with cattle prods) that we found were used to "train" children like Raun to develop simple skills, like eating with a fork or learning to use a toilet properly.

Going the conventional route meant treating our son in ways we refused to even consider. Instead, we took the heart and soul of what we had been teaching and applied it to help ourselves make sense out of this trauma. First, we refused to institutionalize our son. Second, rather than assess him as bad, terrible, and a tragedy (words others and, indeed, most of my family used to describe him), we made up our own perspectives about him. Our son was special, wonderful, and an opportu- nity. On that hopeful and optimistic foundation, we created our unique home-based program, built on the attitude of love and acceptance that grounded our work with adults. Instead of trying to make Raun participate in a world that seemed so incomprehensible to him, we joined him in his unique uni- verse, spinning in circles, rocking back and forth, flipping our fingers in front of our eyes, and mirroring him passionately, joyfully, and without judgments. Samahria, working with him tirelessly twelve hours a day, seven days a week, during the first six months, innovated and established our initial break- throughs with him. We spent each evening analyzing every minute detail of his interactions and actions, sometimes setting up new strategies to try the next day.

Slowly, Raun began to acknowledge our presence and to bond with us, allowing us to construct a bridge for him to cross back into our world. Eventually, Pop, as our success became more apparent, you became more and more interested, asking questions and even complimenting our willingness to defy cur- rent wisdom about our son's condition. Although you tended to dismiss our focus on attitude, you enjoyed hearing about the high-stimulation educational methods we developed. That first Son-Rise Program, which has become a model for the way we teach families to reach, love, and educate their special-needs children, consumed all of Raun's and Samahria's waking hours and a good portion of my time during those first months.

We needed all the help we could get: Support for our program. Assistance with our two daughters. Some friends and neighbors as well as local high school and university students came to our aid, several offering to be trained in our program and to work directly with Raun as part of a cohesive volunteer staff. Others would make meals for our family or help by taking the girls on special outings to the park. Oddly enough, this group of folks, a few of whom have become lifelong friends, did not include a single member of my own family. Given the growing "heart" distance between Jessica and our family in general, her lack of interest in our situation had not been especially disconcerting. But Kenny and Denise surprised us. We would have treasured them as supportive partners in our efforts to save our son. Several years later, Denise told us that it had been difficult to see Raun so impaired and so bizarre in his behaviors. She had stayed away, she said, because of the pain she felt on our behalf. Their distance at this time provided me with a profound lesson: pain and unhappiness can often overwhelm even the best intentions to provide caring and support to those you love.

You cheered, Pop, when Raun evolved finally into a highly extroverted, bright youngster with a near-genius IQ, bearing absolutely no traces of his original condition. I know the pride you felt when he became an honors student in high school and graduated with a degree in biomedical ethics from an Ivy

NO REGRETS

League university. You showed interest in the results of our efforts, though you still resisted any sharing about the underlying principles that comprised the path Samahria and I had now chosen to walk.

The lessons about family dynamics continued. We began to adopt other children who came from circumstances of extreme deprivation and abuse, as a way to express gratitude for Raun's healing and for what we had come to know. You questioned the wisdom of these adoptions, at one time saying, "What are you doing? Looking for trouble?" After each subsequent adoption, you appeared unenthusiastic. When inquiring about our growing family, you would ask about each biological child by name and then pose a generalized question about the "others." Finally, I confronted you about it.

"Pop, I have six children. You always remember the names of three, but you group the others together. You did it just now. In fact, you inquire about them in that same manner most of the time. How come?"

"It doesn't mean anything. You have all these kids. I'll be on the phone forever if we have to talk about each one, every time."

"Fair enough. But then, how come you don't sometimes specifically ask me how is Sage or Ravi or Tayo, by name?"

"Here you go, making a big deal out of nothing."

"Not nothing. You always ask about Bryn, Thea, and Raun by name and not the others. I really want to understand. We choose the words we use for a reason. Please, think about it for a minute."

A full minute passed before you spoke. "Maybe you're right. Maybe there's something to this. I guess I feel, um, I'm not sure what the right word is — maybe closer, more involved with your older children."

"How come?" I asked.

"They're yours."

"Pop, they're all mine."

"I know that. It's not what I meant. Bryn and Thea and Raun have my blood in them. That makes them closer."

"Why? What does blood have to do with this?" I asked.

"I don't know," you said. "It just does."

"What about David and Eileen's adopted son, Stevie? Do you feel less close to him than their other son, Danny?"

"No, of course not. Rosie and I are very close to Stevie. We love Stevie and Danny equally," you said.

"How come, Pop, given what you just said?"

"There's a difference. Maybe, well, maybe, it's because David and Eileen could not have children at the time and that's why they adopted Stevie. With you and Samahria, you already had three children. You were just doing your 'make-a-difference-in-the-world' thing. David and Eileen desperately wanted a child. They didn't have any."

"Okay, Pop. If we adopted our children to help make a difference in a child's life by creating a home for them and loving them and David and Eileen adopted their son because they wanted a child for themselves, to love that child and begin a family, why would those differing motivations make you feel closer to one grandchild than to the others?"

"You raise a good point," you admitted. "Good point. I'll think about it."

I came from the cradle of your world and yet I have chosen to carry such different beliefs than you have. I didn't distinguish between my children based on blood or the different colors of their skin or their varied religious backgrounds. All of them were children of my heart, children both Samahria and I chose to parent. There's the operative word for us — choice!

For me, a parent becomes a parent not simply because of shared blood but because of the choice to love and support a child. A family becomes a family not simply because of shared genetics but because two or more people choose to bond, pursue a common vision, and act in a loving, supportive manner. If blood alone made such a difference, why do some moms abandon their babies and why do some children disown their parents? Why do brothers and sisters make war on each other? And why, Pop, if blood and genetics make all the difference, did my own blood family members disappear when we needed help with our son?

Those folks who held hands with us in a circle of healing around Raun became our family. Strangers entered our home and became our brothers and sisters, not because of shared fluids circulating in our bloodstreams but because of their loving behavior and their choice to help. I no longer measure the quality of a family according to its origin or duration but according to the manner in which an assembly of people, small or large, choose to be with each other.

Samahria and I have been blessed to have had many families. Some endure, others do not.

TEN

There was a time warp in my mind. Incidents and conversations spanning years melted into one another. Streams of consciousness flowed into other streams of consciousness. And yet, as I sat there, only just that morning arrived from the ship off Alaska, the pieces of my life with you were beginning to make more sense, and I was grateful.

The muted green walls of the hospital room encapsulated us in a cubicle technologically outfitted to support you medically but without personal touches such as curtains on the windows, an area rug on the floor, paintings on the walls, or photographs decorating countertops with visual representations of you and those you love. Instead, a bland anonymity of gurgling, clicking, and beeping sounds serenaded us. An antiseptic smell of iodine and alcohol permeated the air. You looked much different in this environment — thinner and smaller, more vulnerable, your skin a pale, milky, yellow-gray color. You appeared so different from those days in Florida when you had insisted emphatically that life should remain exactly the same. Instead, everything had changed as a result of your trips to Tulsa and the continued choices we had to make regarding your ongoing treatment. For a long while, you certainly did get your way — no extra visits from children or grandchildren, no avalanche of phone calls from worried relatives, just trips to the clubhouse every day, workouts at the gym, bridge, Ping-Pong, ushering at the theater, summer in New York near your children and grandchildren. But now, Pop, had we run the race almost to the end?

When you cried earlier this morning and pleaded to die, I wondered why God and the universe would allow or in some way support such a difficult dying after these past years of dignified living in the shadow of death's door. This was the same question I had asked when my mother died. But we had all come light years since her disappearance from our lives. This time, with you, I felt grounded, with clear intention and a defined purpose. I knew, as I had known when I had first arrived at the hospital, that I wanted to remain a force of nature in your life, guarding you when you could no longer provide for yourself and ensuring, as best I could, that you have every possible opportunity to feel our love and to find peace, even as you confronted distressing upheavals in your own body.

The last dosage of medication, combined with your own fatigue, had allowed you to sleep for almost an hour. At times, Samahria, Raun, Rosie, and I talked quietly. Occasionally, we would stop speaking and instinctively turn toward you — admiring and loving you as we watched you breathe. The rising and falling of your chest told us we had more time with you. During one of those expanses of our silent reverence, you awoke, opened your eyes slowly, and scanned the room. A weak smile creased you face.

"What's the matter?" you asked. "You all don't have anything else to do except look at me?"

"We like to look at you," Rosie responded.

"Hey, you're the man of our dreams," Samahria added.

"Some dream," you whispered.

I rose to readjust the pillow behind your head. You tapped my hand appreciatively. "Anything else we can do?" I inquired.

"Sit. You had a long trip. Didn't you just come from Alaska?"

"Absolutely," I responded.

"You get crazy in a place like this. One day melts into another. You sleep, you get up, you sleep more — sometimes it's light, sometimes dark. What day is it, anyway?"

"Saturday," Rosie said.

"Holy shit! How long have I been here?"

"Three days, Abe."

"What did you say? Will you talk louder?"

"Pop," I interjected in a booming voice, "can we put in your hearing aid so it's easier for you to hear?"

"I hear good enough. Just talk louder."

Rosie increased the volume of her voice as she repeated her previous comment. "Three days, Abe."

"That's better," you said, nodding your head as you winked playfully at Samahria and Raun.

At that moment, the door to your room opened. Kenny, Denise, and Jessica entered slowly, each of them glancing at us casually and avoiding eye contact as they looked around the room. Initially, they went immediately to your bedside, appearing genuinely concerned about your state of health. They noted that today, happily, you appeared considerably more comfortable and bright-eyed than you had during any of their previous visits over the past few days. Fortunately, they hadn't seen you earlier this morning.

Kenny looked much older than I remembered him from five years ago. He had a ponderous, professorial manner, perhaps a reflection of his role as senior economist and financial adviser. Although I had heard he'd become an expert tennis player, he nonetheless moved his body slowly and cautiously. Remarkably, Denise appeared nearly the same as I remembered her from encounters long ago — trim, well groomed, youthful — her body movements distinctly more energetic than her husband's. And Jessica — well, Jessica's face had a rounded appearance, with dark creases etched at the corners of her eyes. I peered intently into all their faces, searching for signs of who they had become.

I recalled the old adage: God gives us the face we were born with, and we give ourselves the face that we die with. As I looked at their faces, I thought about my own. The lines etched across my forehead, the creases carved at the corners of my eyes, the turnup or turndown of my lips, the crevices indented around my mouth, even the manner in which I hold my head, all tell a story about who I am and how I have lived my life. What story does my face tell? What attitudes or beliefs have I etched into it? And yet, in an instant, I could override the message of years of sculpting and communicate warmth or disdain, love or hate. I wanted to communicate a welcome, although my fascination with their physiology left me feeling curiously out of my body, as if while I observed them, I also observed me observing them. I smiled.

Clearly, Pop, neither my siblings nor Denise, as they came

into your hospital room that day, wished to use their faces as an invitation to connect with Samahria, Raun, Rosie, or me. Although our presence in the room could not be easily ignored, they continued to avoid eye contact with any of us, nor did they acknowledge our presence in any other way. No conventional expressions made their faces friendly; neither did they make their faces appear unfriendly — they were more like inscrutable "poker faces."

Kenny angled his head slightly downward so that he peered out at the world from beneath bushy eyebrows. He held his lips tightly together. Denise's face seemed curiously unlined, as if still waiting to be formed. Dark eye shadowing highlighted the intensity of her eyes, which jumped from object to object as if alert to danger. Jessica's facial expression reflected her phone voice, oftentimes raspy and strained. I didn't know if her current demeanor and the slight squinting around her eyes reflected her response to your critical condition, the need for eyeglasses, or a more general pessimism about life. Directing a commercial real estate office for years and dealing with local politicians about zoning issues on a continuous basis could have dampened her innocence and optimism. And yet, in our limited telephone interactions, she had talked enthusiastically about her profession.

After greeting you, Kenny sat down, nodded politely to Rosie, looked at me blankly, then tipped his head to Samahria and just peered curiously at Raun. Jessica mimicked his behavior, except that she ignored Rosie but did reach out to touch my arm. Denise, in turn, ignored me, hugged Samahria, touched Rosie lightly on the shoulder, then acknowledged Raun, saying, "You must be Raun."

Maybe they did a superb job of tolerating my presence,

given their history with me. Interestingly, I felt pretty soft and easy inside. I walked over to hug Kenny, who put one arm up stiffly to acknowledge my gesture, though he remained seated. Then I hugged Jessica and Denise. Though Jessica appeared responsive to my overture, Denise seemed almost as rigid as her husband. What struck me most, Pop, was that none of them greeted Rosie with any warmth or intimacy, at least not that I could see. Their overt gestures indicated clearly that they cared for you deeply, but Rosie did not receive the same attention. Perhaps their inconsistent greetings reflected their concerns about your condition.

The nurses administered more medication. You drifted into a fitful sleep.

I wanted the energy around you to be soothing, so I turned toward my siblings and Denise warmly, asking them questions about their lives and their thoughts about seeing you so sick. Initially, their responses were brief and unrevealing. Raun, however, participated in the conversation with great charm, talking animatedly about himself and his ten-month stay in England and Ireland. After his sharing, Denise and Jessica appeared more relaxed and a touch more forthcoming. Kenny remained quite distant. Samahria, exhausted by our exit from Alaska, climbed up onto the empty bed next to yours and promptly fell asleep.

Later, as you napped again, Rosie and I took yet another walk. We spent the next hour, Dad, discussing her feelings, most specifically her discomfort with Jessica.

"I know she doesn't like me," she said emphatically. "And you — you have been so nice to all of them since they've arrived, but they don't give anything back to you. I feel bad for you."

"Don't! Why put an ounce of energy into feeling bad? It

won't cure what's happening and it won't make you feel very good inside. Believe me, I'm fine," I said. "I don't require them to love or even acknowledge me to feel fine. Rosie, let's go back to what we talked about in the hallway — why do you believe Jessica doesn't like you?"

"I can feel it, Bears. You can feel those things."

I thought about my sister's greeting to Rosie — more correctly, about her lack of a greeting — and I recalled that she had continuously given me the distinct impression during our telephone interactions that she had issues with Rosie. When I encouraged her to talk with you, Pop, and with Rosie, she became evasive. I saw that family trait again and again: Say what you really feel about someone behind that person's back but never to that person's face. Inauthenticity ruled. Walls of silence prevailed. Misinformation, rather than straight talk, remained a major currency within our family.

Years ago, I judged you for not telling Jessica, Kenny, other family members, and me what you really thought. Finally, however, I came to understand the rules or standards that guided you in interpersonal relationships — civility always meant more to you than honesty. Oftentimes, you suggested that my commitment to authenticity seemed self-indulgent, and perhaps it was. I wanted to get everything off my chest and wanted others to do the same. In contrast, you demonstrated much more self-control. I know now that you withheld your thoughts and feelings for the best of reasons, including self-protection. We just have different brands of integrity. However, my recent experiences with you reconfirm the value of the authenticity I cherish. Pop, I got to know and adore you only after you let me inside, sharing yourself more openly and honestly with me. What do I say now to Rosie when she believes she can feel

Jessica's dislike of her, even when that supposed dislike has not been expressed directly? What do you think, Pop? When I talk to her, do I let your standards guide me, or mine?

"Rosie, I have no idea what Jessica really feels about you, specifically. My impression is that she has issues with you." I walked over the line you had set up for yourself, Pop, and said what I knew, which at this point, wasn't very much, anyway. "I asked Jessica to talk with you and Dad about her concerns. Did she?"

"No, Jessica never tells you what she feels unless, of course, she gets real angry about something. Then she finally tells you what's on her mind. She was very upset once when your father sold a silver serving set he and your mother had owned without consulting her. She has so much anger toward us, especially toward your father. Bears, it's nice of you to suggest we all talk, but your father doesn't need these kinds of outbursts in his life right now."

"Okay — then what about you, Rosie? What do you need? How about telling her that you believe she doesn't like you?"

"Listen, Bears, the most important person now is your father. He's very sick. He needs everyone's support. If Jessica has problems, she'll have to deal with them. I don't have time for that now."

"Yeah, I hear you, but if you don't have time for that now, what are going to do about feeling uncomfortable around her?"

"I'm not going to feel bad any more. Especially now that I'm aware of it. I'm going to focus on your father. That's it. Done." For a moment, Pop, she sounded just like you. "Done." "That's it." Not important. Move off the issue and back to what counts!

I liked it. I didn't always like it, of course. I used to call that kind of thinking "unconscious" and "unreflective." To me, it implied shallowness. Now, I liked it: It was the ability to form clear intentions and then act on them. Clarity of purpose! Action! Rosie had put you back exactly where she wanted you — at center stage.

"And another thing," she said. "I'm going to tell Abe he can leave this world . . . but I won't mean it."

I laughed. Rosie gave me a shove. "He'll know," I said. "Don't say it if you don't mean it. Do what's in your heart. If you're not ready, if you don't want him to die now, that's totally okay." We stopped walking and hugged each other. "Do only what you really want to do," I said softly.

We began strolling again, this time in silence. Rosie appeared busy with her thoughts. As we rounded yet another corner and approached your room, she touched my arm firmly and said, "I'll do it. I will!"

Before I could ascertain whether she meant it or not, we entered your room and found you sitting in a chair, asking for food, and talking animatedly to the nurses as well as Kenny, Denise, and Jessica.

"I want everything on the platter, especially the dessert," you asserted strongly. When the attendant wheeled over the tray, you surveyed its contents with real interest, delighted to see the chocolate pudding. You pointed to the dessert and said, "I'd especially like another helping of that."

"Abe," Rosie responded, "first eat what's in front of you, then we'll get you more." She didn't miss a beat, jumping back into your world at the very place you had entered it again.

You bowed your head toward her sweetly and respectfully, then looked at all of us, acknowledging our presence, as you started eating. Rosie and I exchanged wide-eyed glances. Just as she was about to reassure you that you could die, you appeared very much alive, wanting sustenance to continue living your life.

Pop, you surprised us all. Although markedly thinner and weaker, with a fluctuating fever, you had caught a second wind by late afternoon.

"It's been a very good life," you reassured all of us as we sat in an informal circle around your bed. "Can't complain. Almost eighty-six years old, and until last week, I exercised just about every day. Yes, sir, almost every day. Why I've had more energy than all those old farts at the clubhouse in their sixties and seventies. Ask Rosie; they can't keep up with me." Rosie nodded at you adoringly, although a cloud of sadness darkened her expression. I wondered if you were doing a "last hurrah." You stared off at some unknown distant point. "I have been very blessed. Your Mom and I had a good life together." You paused and in the silence acknowledged her passing many years ago. I admired the way both you and Rosie could talk about your deceased spouses so easily and openly in each other's presence. "And Rosie had Norman." You looked in her direction, smiled, and talked to her as if the rest of us had disappeared. "Rosie, honey, we've had a wonderful life together." Your eyes softened.

"C'mon, Abe," Rosie protested, "stop getting yourself upset."

"I'm not upset," you insisted, even as your eyes filled with tears. "This woman," you said to all of us while you looked only at her, "this woman is the reason I'm still alive. She makes me take all my medications, my vitamins — keeps me on track and watches me like a hawk. And she loves me, loves me a lot. I've been very fortunate." The intensity of your feelings disrupted your sharing.

"Abe, that's enough," Rosie said, trying to protect you from acknowledging and, perhaps, confirming an awareness that time no longer stretched out expansively before you.

"It's okay, Rosie," I suggested. "This is good for him, good for all of us. This is better for him than any medication he's taking."

You took my hand as I sat in a chair beside your bed and nodded, then you reached over and took Kenny's hand. We were your sons, Pop, vastly different from each other, living separate lives, yet joined in this moment to love and support you. "My kids are here," you said with delight, glancing at the two of us as well as at Jessica. "Well," you remarked with a smile, "not all of them are here right now," referring obviously to Rosie's two sons, Alan and David, who had become much more than stepsons over these past three decades — you had given them a place in your heart. Then you turned your head and acknowledged Samahria, Denise, and Raun graciously.

This unfolding event could not have transpired twenty years earlier, ten years earlier, or even two years earlier. This illness, this cancer, a curse in the lives of so many people, had inspired you to open your heart, and as a result, it allowed you to create the world anew. During these last two years, Kenny and Jessica had protested the brevity of their phone conversations with you. David and Alan had responded similarly. I kept telling them that you had become more open and forthcoming than ever before in your life. I encouraged my siblings to tell you what they felt and ask for more from you, but Jessica and Kenny thought I was merely being presumptuous about your willingness to share with me. Pop, I even conveyed their complaints to you in the hopes that you would choose to alter your interactions with them. My impression was that neither they nor you wanted to take down the walls between you. Knowing this made it especially wonderful to watch you now being so gentle and self-revealing in their presence!

Before we left for the night, Samahria, Raun, and I sat with Rosie on chairs beside your bed and watched you sleeping. You awoke as if you sensed our presence, looked right at us, and smiled.

"Hey, we're going home. You did great today," I said.

Samahria hugged you. "Dad, I probably won't be back tomorrow. I'll come in a day or two."

"Don't come," you said weakly. "You take care of yourself. Rest. This had to be very hard for you. Don't come back soon. You rest."

"I will rest...and I will come back soon," Samahria laughed, patting your hand.

Raun walked over. "'Bye, Grandpa. Feel better. I love you." He bent over and kissed your forehead.

"I love you, too," you said back to him with another smile. "I love all of you."

ELEVEN

When I arrived at the hospital the following day, your energy had dissipated and the pain had increased, especially in your lower back. The doctors had increased your dosage of pain medication, and you appeared irritable and listless. Once again, the pressure of the blanket against your skin made you very uncomfortable. The side effects from the operation the week before, in which the stents to your kidneys had once again been replaced in order to keep the ureter open, still disheartened you. Your urination continued to be irregular and inconsistent. Despite your intake of food and liquid, blood tests still showed you to be dangerously dehydrated. Obviously, the lymphatic tumors throughout your abdominal cavity and groin continued to grow. You appeared ambivalent about chemotherapy and asked us to decide about administering more. I asked Rosie to support me in delaying more chemotherapy. I felt you couldn't take any more assaults on your body just then, Pop.

Ironically, a new doctor, an associate of the oncologist handling your case, lobbied for a new, more intense protocol of "chemo," though one possible side effect was respiratory distress and possible respiratory failure. How could we subject you to such a possibility?

Although Rosie had some doubts about our joint decision, we refused to let the hospital administer a new round of chemotherapy. Rosie wanted to save you. I wanted to make your comfort a priority and then, if possible, to save you. Nevertheless, Rosie and I continued to make a good team, and I always remembered your directive that in the end, no matter who held what opinion, Rosie was to decide. In order to honor this directive, I kept reminding her that, even if we differed on what direction to take next, in the end, I would go along with her decision and support her fully.

By the afternoon, your state of health deteriorated further. You floated in and out of consciousness. I talked again with the doctor, who now agreed that your condition had eroded further. He withdrew his suggestion to prescribe the more aggressive chemotherapy at this time.

Rosie and I sat with you most of the day. From time to time, we took walks through the hospital corridors, talking endlessly about our thoughts and feelings. Whenever she would keep herself from crying, Pop, I'd encourage her to express her emotions so she could look at them and, perhaps, find a more peaceful place inside.

As the evening hours approached, you began to slap the bed with your hand and shake your head. The pain had grown more intense. We asked the nursing staff to give you more medication. They resisted, claiming they had set amounts they could give you at set times. Rosie and I asked them to shorten the time between doses, given the agony you were experiencing. The desk nurse said they would need the doctor's permission; thus, at our request, they paged him. It took almost two hours for the doctor to respond. Meanwhile, you lay in your bed, unable to even sit up without assistance, held captive by the complexity of the bureaucratic process that appeared so insensitive to your difficulties. Rosie and I tried to locate the doctor ourselves, without success. Like you, we had to wait. But unlike you, we did not have to endure the screams of our nerve endings registering razor-sharp eruptions of pain.

Another nurse entered the room and began her ritual medical routine without ever addressing you.

"Nurse," I said, "he's in a lot of pain. Could you go real easy with him, please?"

"I know what I'm doing," she retorted. "Most of the patients on the floor are in pain."

"Still, please be gentle with him."

She whipped out a hypodermic needle and, without warning, plunged it rudely into your arm. You winced, probably more from the surprise of the assault than from the pain. Several times, she huffed impatiently.

Shocked by her insensitivity and longing for you to be treated with care, I followed her into the hallway.

"Excuse me. Can I talk to you for a second?" She stopped, tapping her foot noisily on the tile floor. "I know you might have a lot on your mind with a very intense schedule here at the hospital, but I'd like to ask you to be more gentle with my dad. Also, I think it would be more respectful if you greeted him when you came into the room and then explained to him what you intended to do before doing it. Could you do that please?"

"Listen, mister, I am always dealing with someone's father or mother or brother or wife. I worked the night shift last night. I'm tired. And I cannot spend time pampering one patient when I have to take care of so many others." What a difference between this hospital and the Cancer Treatment Center of America in Tulsa.

She turned and began to walk away from me. I followed.

"I know you work real hard. But what if you took just a little extra time anyway to pamper every patient, including my father?" As my words fell on deaf ears, I imagined my daughter Sage advising me, "Oh, Popi, get real, they'll never listen to you!" Yet I knew, in that instant, I would go for broke. "Maybe," I persisted, "pampering and loving all these patients would have as much power as any medication you might be charged with dispensing. Honestly, if you were sick and in pain, wouldn't you want to be treated by a nurse that felt like a loving, caring, and dear friend?"

"I don't have to continue this discussion with you," she barked, then skidded around athletically on her heels, changed direction in an artful fashion, and disappeared behind a door marked "Medical Staff Only."

Pretty powerful lady. Imagine what she could accomplish if she took all that energy and channeled it into loving acts toward you and every other patient in the ward. I located the floor supervisor, asked the name of the nurse I had just spoken with, explained our experience with her, and then requested that she no longer administer any services to you ... and, perhaps, not to anyone else, either. The supervisor acknowledged my request in a perfunctory manner.

Another nurse, standing nearby, said she would personally check in on you, Pop, and treat you like a visiting statesman.

"Thank you so, so much," I exclaimed. Overwhelmed by

appreciation for her, I asked, "Can I express my appreciation by giving you a hug?"

"Sure," she said with a giant smile. I will always remember this woman, the tall nurse with the John Lennon glasses — sweet, motherly, yet no-nonsense. I could tell you liked her because you flirted with her every time she entered your room. Indeed, she always treated you with respect and kindness.

As we hugged, the floor supervisor who had watched us frowned and sighed. Having communicated her disapproval, she refocused her attention on the papers piled on her desk. This is about people, I kept thinking. People first — then the papers, then the procedures.

When I returned to your room, I watched Rosie encourage you to sip more water from the cup she held. You gave her one of those "leave me alone" looks. However, she persisted.

"Abie, you've got to drink more water. Cooperate! Don't be so stubborn." You turned your head away from her and saw me standing by the door. I pointed at the cup of water.

"All right. I'll take a sip," you whined.

Later, I urged you to participate in another visualization with me. You refused. In addition to the physical trauma in your body, I suspected some additional distress, which I could not quite define. I sat beside you again.

"Hey, Dad, you look pretty miserable. We want to do every-thing we can to help you. Is it the pain?"

"Yes . . . and no."

"What do you mean 'no'?"

You hesitated.

"Don't hold back. What are you thinking?"

Again, I could see you withdrawing from my question. I encouraged you further.

"Pop, c'mon. You do great with questions now. As I always tell you, you don't have to answer any questions I ask. However, you've been answering many of them lately and I think it's been useful. So what about it? What are you thinking?"

"I hate being in the hospital. They wake me all the time, put needles in me when it doesn't matter, take my temperature, check my blood pressure over and over again as if I've got a heart condition, which I do not. But when I want help with this damn pain in my back, nothing — only rules and regulations and, sometimes, a lousy temperament."

"Pop, the folks here have the best of intentions, even that unhappy nurse who just visited you. Really, you have to admit that some of these people have been very sweet, very helpful; and some, well — they do their misery and dump it on others. But I'd like to think the bottom line is that everyone follows these procedures with the best of intentions."

Earlier that morning, I had suggested to Rosie that she take you home. I remember thinking, "Don't ever let anyone you love die in a hospital." But Rosie refused to remove you from the medical facility, and I decided to try to support her and help you make the best of it. For the moment, I wouldn't press the issue.

"Bears, I've been in this damn hospital too long. I'm not getting any better. I feel so lousy, and being here makes me feel even worse."

"I hear you. Let me talk to Rosie."

In the hallway, Rosie and I continued the discussion we had had before lunch. "He hates being here, Rosie. You know that. What about taking him home?"

"No," she insisted. "We already discussed this. I can't take him home."

"Why not?"

"Here, we have all this help. The doctors. The nurses. If we need extra medication, we can get it. No, he has to stay here."

"Rosie, we can get all kinds of support at home. A full time nurse, even..."

"He'd hate that, too. You know how independent he is!" Her voice quivered.

Aware that she was masking something, I asked, "Is there something underneath your resistance to him leaving the hospital?"

"Nothing. This is the best place for him to get help. What about his chemotherapy?" She turned away from me. I could see the tears flowing down her cheeks. "If we take him home, that means it's over. His only chance to live, to get better, is to stay here."

"I don't agree. You don't have to give up if you take him home. Quality of life, Rosie. Please, look at him; he's suffering here. He doesn't want to be here. Let's take him home where we can create a loving environment, give him back his dignity, and not push and poke him if he doesn't want to be pushed and poked."

"I get to decide, right?"

"Absolutely," I agreed.

"Then he stays here where he can be helped."

On my drive back to the Institute that night, I kept picturing you pleading with me to help you leave the hospital. You could no longer get yourself out of the bed to execute your own wishes. With your personal power and liberties extraordinarily curtailed, you had to ask, even beg, others and then hope they might support you. I found your circumstances intolerable.

By the time I drove across the New York and Connecticut

borders into Massachusetts, I knew I couldn't let you languish in the hospital. I wanted you to be free to live these last days as you wished. I realized I would do whatever it took to give you that opportunity. Once I arrived home, I told Samahria about my day and how I wanted to bring you home to our house to live with us. I felt compelled to do it as soon as possible.

"We'll do whatever it takes," she said without the slightest hesitation. Tears filled my eyes. "What's the matter, Bears?"

"I'm overwhelmed by you," I said, embracing her. "You always support me. You're always there for me. And now you're there again for Pop."

"He's become my father, too," Samahria insisted.

"I know. I still feel, well, this huge sensation inside…like it's bigger than my body and I can't quite hold it in. So much gratitude, Samahria, for you, for these two years with Pop. Thank you. I can't wait to get that man out of the hospital."

"We'll make this a wonderful time for him…for all of us," she whispered. "You know, you've been so focused and so dedicated to him. Just remember I'm still here."

Her comment jolted me at first. But then I considered how consumed I had been with you, Pop. "Samahria, poke me if I look like I am passing you by. Juggling the Institute, the kids, the staff, the program participants, the publication of my new book, and Pop's situation feels like a round-the-clock treadmill. I know it's the treadmill of my choice and I love it all, but I also know that I do sometimes take you for granted…um, maybe more than just 'sometimes.' Just whack me on the head when I do because when all the dust settles you are the most important person in my life." She turned away with a skeptical smile. "Hey, wait a second, I'm serious. Do you know you're number one?"

"Sometimes. And sometimes I'm not sure."

I drew her close to me again. "Be sure. Either I'm loving you so it's visible or I'm brain-dead. And when I'm brain-dead, wake me up. I want to be awake, always, to you, to what matters."

"Fine. But when I come knocking on your door, don't become defensive. Just wake up. Okay?"

"You got it. A deal!" I hugged her tightly. "Aren't there always opportunities at our doorstep?"

"I guess you mean we're engaged in another outrageous event, like what we're doing with your dad, which I'm totally with you on. That's a really wonderful opportunity for all of us. And then there's you getting yourself in trouble by saying too much or being too damn forthright. So yes, I agree, there are always opportunities and never a dull moment living with you."

"And never a moment without love, living with you," I said. "Do you know after all these years, whenever I come into a room and you see me, your eyes light up? Thirty-six years and you still get so excited to see me. I guess I never believed anyone would ever care for me as much as you do. Thanks, babe. I feel so blessed."

"Me, too," Samahria added. "Even with constant pain in my back and my joints, I still always appreciate what we have."

With Samahria's help and the support of our dear friend and colleague, Zoe, we managed to locate a hospital bed, an eating tray, and other accessories. I explained to both of them Rosie's resistance to removing you from the medical facility; thus, all our efforts to find this equipment might be just a quick spin of our wheels. We all agreed not to let this daunt our enthusiasm.

When I arrived at the hospital early the next morning, I found you staring at the ceiling, your eyes glazed. Your depression had deepened. When you saw me, tears filled your eyes, though for very different reasons than tears had filled mine on the previous night. I could not contain the intensity of my gratitude; you could not now contain the intensity of your despair. I wanted to hug you and hold you, but I knew you did not want to be touched. Your entire body had become abnormally sensitive again.

"Pop, I love you." You acknowledged my words while the tears kept flowing. "You don't have to answer, but I'd like to know why you're crying so I can help you."

"It's more than I can take, Bears," you said in a raspy voice, parched from dehydration. "I'm so sick, and I can't stand being in the hospital." A nurse cut our conversation short as she adjusted your intravenous tubes and began to do a complete check of your vital signs. You turned away from the young woman, not wanting to be rude as you tried to maintain your own space and freedom. She rolled you quickly to the side in order to check your back. You moaned audibly.

I realized that Rosie had been watching from the doorway.

"Where'd you come from?" I asked her. She didn't answer. I could see she was about to cry. I left you, took her outside, and told her about my idea to take you both home to my house and care for you there.

"He'll die if we take him out."

"But can't you see?" I countered. "He's dying right now before our eyes. The situation here is profoundly different from his other hospital experiences during the last two years."

"I know. I can see he's so uncomfortable." Rosie acknowledged.

I wanted what we all wanted for you, Pop —for you to be surrounded by dignity and love. "Can I make the proposal to him?" I asked her.

"Yes," she said, surprising me with her lack of resistance.

"Wow, what made you change your mind?" I asked.

"I was afraid to take him to our home," Rosie admitted. "We're all alone. Most of the neighbors have left; the summer season's almost over. If something happened in the middle of the night, what would I do? How could I help him? I was scared I couldn't handle it by myself…and I couldn't. But with you there, I know we'll be fine. Go ahead. Present it to him. See what he says."

I returned to your room as soon as the nurse had completed her medical service. She had propped you up slightly on a pillow. You welcomed me with a slight dip of your head, obviously in pain and still in considerable distress.

"Pop, I have something to ask you. What do you say to the idea of you and Rosie coming to live with Samahria and me in our home at the Institute? Rosie likes the idea and we would give you our favorite room in the house, the guest room with the curved wall and a sensational view. We'd love to have both of you."

You relaxed back into the pillow. Your eyes sparkled for the first time in days. "Wow, that's a nice offer," you said, the master of understatement. "Actually, it's a wonderful offer. You'd really want that?"

"Absolutely." I touched the center of my chest with both hands. "From the heart, Pop, I would consider it a privilege to have Rosie and you stay with us. Samahria and I would love to have you. And so would Zoe and Bryn. You'll get to see Tayo, probably a little bit of Raun and Sage, and then, of course, little Jade — another great-grandchild for you and Rosie to enjoy. In addition, Kenny and Denise, Jessica, David, and Alan and their families could visit you whenever they want — we'd give them total and complete access to the house. Pop, it'll be fun for you.

And I think we can make you much more comfortable than you've been here."

"What do you think, Rosie?" you asked spiritedly.

"I think it's a beautiful offer. Bears has been there with us every step of the way. I think going to his home is a great idea."

"All right," you said, mustering up that authoritative voice. "Then that's it. The answer is yes. We'll come live with you."

"Great. I'm going to go down to the phones and start the process immediately."

Samahria responded with obvious excitement, harnessing all her energy to support your move into our home even while she continued to negotiate with her own physical pain and work at the Institute. Zoe cheered, offering immediately to use her lunch hour and evening time to help get everything ready. "You tell me how I can help," she said easily, "and I'm off and running." Although many of the Institute's eighty staff members exhibited sincere dedication and caring when giving to our clients and to each other, Zoe had a particular quality of heart and fire in the belly that made her a true "force of nature" in her personal relationships and in my life.

"You are truly one of the most giving people in my life," I said to her.

"No," she insisted. "I do what I do because I love this work and I love you and Samahria. Look at all I've learned. I am just giving back a little piece of what I've been given."

"Take it in, Zoe; whether you recognize it or not, you have the biggest heart," I said. "And you deliver like no one I know."

That evening, Zoe worked the phones, trying to locate whatever paraphernalia we needed to revamp the guest room for your arrival. Together, with the support of other friends, she and Samahria prepared our home for its new occupants.

Hopefully, we could have the bed and everything we required delivered within twenty-four hours. I hoped to bring you and Rosie home within the next two days.

When I returned to your hospital room, you appeared to be in extreme distress again. Rosie said they had moved you, causing pressure on the tumors against your spine. Clearly, you were in great physical torment. However, you told me you could handle your pain for another two days, knowing now that you would be leaving after that time. In that moment as you spoke, I realized that I could not leave the hospital without you tonight, that I could not leave you there for even one more day.

"Today, Rosie. Let's take him home today."

"I agree," she said haltingly. "We can't just let him suffer like this."

"Pop," I announced so you could hear me. "Pop, we are going to engineer your escape today. You're coming home with us today. Okay?"

You didn't answer. You nodded appreciatively.

"You hang in there because this might take us a few hours. Okay?" You dipped your head again.

I called Samahria to tell her I would be coming home with you and Rosie. She understood the reasons immediately, telling me that she and Zoe would do their very best to make the room ready. I informed the nurses at the central desk about our plan to leave. They said we required a doctor's approval. I explained that we would be happy to comply; however, if we couldn't get one of their attending physicians to come soon, then we wanted another doctor, any doctor, to authorize your departure. More rules. More regulations. The supervisor informed me that that would not be possible; only the attending physician could authorize your release in writing.

"Not so," I said. "If you can't get the attending physician here in the next hour or two, we're taking him home whether or not you approve. This is a hospital, not a prison. When we're ready, you can either help us or watch us prepare my father to leave." I couldn't let anything stop us.

I called Kenny to inform him of our decision and tell him about the action we planned to take. No one answered his phone, so I left a message on his answering machine. I then called my sister, explaining Pop's condition and what we wanted to do. I also told her that she and my brothers would have complete and absolute access to my house, day or night. They could come at any time and visit for any length of time. I wanted her and my brothers to feel totally welcome; I would even give them keys. No one had to call and check with us first; they could just come and be with you, Pop, whenever and for however long they wished. Jessica didn't say anything after I finished speaking.

"Jessica, are you there?" I asked.

"Yes!" A pause. "This is the way it's been for two years, ever since Dad has been sick. You decide and then tell us."

"Listen. If you have a different idea, tell me," I said to her. "We can talk to Rosie about it."

"You mean you can talk to Rosie about it, don't you?"

"No. If you want, I'll put her on the phone. She's standing right here."

"Don't you dare."

"Then Jessica, what do you want me to do?"

"Ask me my opinion when it counts, not after you've made your decision."

"Well, okay, I hear you. Pop's still in the hospital. Nothing has changed yet, so truly, your opinion does count."

Silence.

"We haven't moved him. That's the truth. Let me explain the current situation to you and then you tell me what you think. He's in the same intensity of pain and distress he had on the weekend, when you, Kenny, and Denise visited. His condition has not improved. In fact, he's deteriorated. We can't let him die in the hospital; he hates being here."

"So he should go to *your* home?"

"Is that what this is about?" No answer. "Okay. Make an offer," I suggested. "Are you willing to take Pop and Rosie to your house?" Again, no answer. "Why don't we call Kenny and Alan and David and ask them if they're willing? Then we can take all the offers to Pop and Rosie and let them decide. How does that sound?"

"Everything's moving too fast. I'm really, really upset. I just can't pop out quick answers."

"Then take your time," I suggested. I knew if I asked Jessica any questions to help her investigate or resolve her discomforts, my overture would be greeted yet again as presumptuous and unwelcome. Rather than appear adversarial, I waited quietly, without speaking.

In recent decades, Jessica has tended to close down rather than be exposed and self-revealing with me. Although prior to your illness, Pop, we had many cordial telephone conversations, Jessica limited herself in those calls to sharing topical news about jobs and children rather than sharing about feelings and nitty-gritty challenges in her life. Sometimes, if I shared my inner thoughts or reflections, she would acknowledge my meandering without much comment. Whenever I would ask questions she deemed too personal in nature, I sensed a tightness in her voice. Frequently, she would say that certain areas of her life were "personal," a diplomatic way of saying, "Hands off."

Had she created, I wondered, resources within her own family, with her children, her friends, or even with a counselor to air and explore her issues? I could understand how she might feel because, years ago, I too resisted disclosing my feelings and inner thoughts out of fear of being judged. I felt grateful that I now lived on a daily diet of self-exploration with program participants, my staff, and my family, which taught me that the judgments made by others are only valid if I give them power. This awareness enabled me to be comfortable and nonjudgmental as Jessica sat silent on the other end of the telephone line.

I closed my eyes and visualized a peaceful, loving energy enveloping her.

"Are you still there?" she called across the wires.

"Yes, I'm still with you."

"I still don't feel connected to what's going on," she said. "I don't want to be called after the fact."

"Jessica, this is not after the fact. If you want to be connected, you have to do something to be connected." I paused. "What do you want to do?"

"Why are you putting me on the spot?" she protested.

"You are — 'on the spot.' So am I. So is Pop and Rosie. The man is suffering, really suffering. We can't continue to discuss this situation combatively; we have to talk with the clear intention of devising an action to help him. So, again, what do you want to do or want us to do as a family about his situation?"

"Like you're in charge and I'm supposed to submit an offer."

"I'm doing the best I can, honey. I know you have difficulty with me. Can you put it aside for a couple of minutes and just focus on what we can all do that would be best for Pop?"

The conversation ended abruptly with Jessica hanging up. The truth was I did feel better equipped than any of my siblings to care for you. I called each of my brothers separately, told them about my proposed plan and gave them the same offer of complete access to my home and to you and Rosie. Additionally, I suggested, they could offer to take Rosie and you to their homes. To my surprise, they all loved the idea of Samahria and me taking you and Rosie to the Institute. David, who had been especially gracious and appreciative throughout this entire adventure, wanted to drive up to the hospital from Long Island immediately to assist. I thanked him, explaining that by the time he arrived we hoped to be gone. Additionally, Kenny, who I anticipated might possibly have a reaction similar to Jessica's, surprised me pleasantly and supported the idea vigorously. Like me, he wanted you freed from your sense of imprisonment in that facility.

As I waited in the hallway so that Rosie could spend a few moments of private time with you, I took an internal inventory. Although I championed an accepting attitude as the crucial component of personal transformation, I had often felt driven, at the same time, by a deep yearning to take immediate action if I believed that I could make an immediate difference. Responding to your cries with a definite act satisfied that yearning. Yet I wondered if I had acted too quickly.

Six months earlier, I had tripped on my own expectations to be useful and effective with both of you and Samahria. You had undergone stent replacement surgery in the Tulsa medical facility in order to keep the ureter to your one functioning kidney open. Rosie had telephoned to say you had tremendous back pain after the operation, even as the physicians experimented with different pain medicine. She had asked me to talk with your doctors, which I did. The urgency expressed in her voice lingered with me as I guessed at the level of agony you might be enduring. About an hour later, Samahria, who had traveled halfway around the planet to receive treatment for her illness, telephoned to discuss her concern that her pain had not abated and her physical maladies continued. We talked for almost an hour during a break between my classes.

Immediately following my next seminar presentation, I attended an Institute board of directors' meeting. Someone inquired about Samahria's condition. I kept thinking about how her voice had quivered with pain throughout our phone conversation. I kept thinking about Rosie pleading with the doctors to get more help for you and begging me to intercede and make the difference. I kept thinking about you, Pop, lying in total agony in a hospital bed in a strange city. Instead of responding to the question about Samahria's condition, I flooded my mind with an avalanche of distressing thoughts. I felt an explosion of sensations from those thoughts throughout my body. I started to speak, but in midsentence I heard the trembling in my own voice. Instead of continuing, I put my hands over my face and started to cry. The room fell to absolute silence. I knew all eyes focused on me as I did something I had never done before, something I had never dreamed of doing in a professional setting.

Suddenly, I heard someone ask if she could help me and then someone else ask, "What are you feeling, Bears?"

Rather than answer, I said, "I can't do this right now. I'm sorry." I stood up and left the room.

I retreated to our bedroom and stood alone silently in the center of the room. Bryn, who had attended the board meeting, knocked on the door.

"Popi, can I come in?"

I hesitated for a moment and then said, "Yes. Sure."

Bryn walked in and seated herself on our bed. I began to walk in a circle around her as if partaking in some unspoken ritual.

"So, what's going on?" she questioned.

"I love both of them so much. Mom's still in pain. My father's in agony right now. I just don't want it to be so hard for them."

"Why the tears, Popi?"

"I'm believing that their pain is terrible. Knowing all that I know, why would I perceive their pain as terrible — and feel so awful about it?"

Bryn smiled. "That's a good question. Why are you believing their pain is terrible?"

"I guess to motivate myself to know what to do and do it more a lot more quickly. I feel like I have to find the way out of pain for both of them."

"I know you want to help them, Popi, but why do *you* have to find the way out?"

"Because nobody else is, Bryn." I took a deep breath and reconsidered my thought. "Wait! Wait!" I said, putting my hand in the air and pausing in the middle of my third lap around the bed. "I have always been able to reach into my bag of tricks and find something to make things better — for Raun with his autism, for you with your heart, and for Grandpa during much of his bout with cancer." I could feel a constriction in my breathing as I continued. "But now, right now, as I reach inside, I can't see any way to make things better — there's nothing there."

"How do you feel about that?" Bryn asked softly.

"Not very good. There must be something else I can do."

"Like what?"

I closed my eyes, hoping for some illumination in the darkness behind my lids. Nothing came. "I'm giving myself a hard time, honey. I guess I believe I'm supposed to save them. No, that's not it. I want to save them. Do you remember the night your heart arrhythmia became so intense that you thought you were going to die?" Bryn recalled this incident. "You didn't want to go to the hospital yet again and spend another night in the emergency room. There was severe pain in your chest and that scary feeling of suffocation. You were frightened and daring at the same time. You kept asking me to help you, so I stayed with you most of that night, peering intently into your eyes, hoping our eye contact would somehow help keep you alive." I paused and touched her arm. "We talked. We searched for meaning in your experience. We did breathing exercises, meditations. Remember?" Bryn nodded again as I continued. "I massaged the muscles that spasmed in your neck and shoulders. I held your hands. We smiled at each other, even laughed a few times. Although you had almost died several times from this condition, I thought of nothing but being present and using each unfolding moment to help you, to love you. In the end, with your heart still fluttering through its irregular rhythms, you were able to relax and dismantle your fears, falling asleep eventually with a soft expression on your face. I was able to make a difference that night."

"Popi, what does that have to do with Mom and Grandpa?"

"I can't make the difference for them. I don't know what else to do to help them right now, Bryn. I ... I don't know how to make it so they're not hurting, not suffering." As I vocalized that thought, I sat down on the edge of the bed and cried. I could feel my body shaking. Bryn told me later that she had wanted to reach out and touch me but instinctively knew to allow me space. I had to move myself through this process. Yet I could feel her love and hear her crying with me.

"I want to continue," I said, finally regaining my composure. "Why am I doing this?"

Bryn, wiping the tears from her face, stayed right with me. "What's your answer?" she asked immediately.

"When I consider what's happening to Mom and Grandpa and see it as bad, I start to see myself and them as victims, and then the universe looks pretty darn hostile." I closed my eyes for a moment. "So, right now, thinking this, I feel weaker rather than feeling empowered."

"So why are you creating a perspective that results in your feeling weaker?"

"Good question, Bryn. It wasn't my intention to feel weak. I guess it comes back to motivation. Like I see others do in our seminars, I started to believe that my unhappiness means I really care and that it helps me find a solution. But, as you and I both know, the result is just the opposite. Misery is the great distracter. It disables rather than enables, and all I'm doing right now is sitting here crying and not coming any closer to finding a solution. I teach that point all the time. So I guess I have to remind myself of what I know." I shook my head and smiled. "It's a lesson to be learned hundreds of times."

I began pacing around the bed again. "Okay, I got it. I can ask myself to search for every answer, every miracle possible, but I don't have to get unhappy in order to do it. I'm going to call Mom later tonight and go further with our discussion, injecting hope and optimism into the conversation. And I'm going to visualize that the new medication I discussed with the surgeon has diminished Grandpa's pain, even as we speak. It doesn't matter whether that's true or false; it just makes a whole lot more sense to construct my universe from that perspective. But I'll still check in on my dad just in case we need to use another medication."

"Don't forget you're the one who told Grandpa and all of us that he had just begun a great new adventure with his cancer. See, I listen," Bryn said. "Popi, are you sure you're okay?"

"I'm fine now. Thank you for helping me . . . and for all your questions. This dialoging 'stuff' is pretty swift, isn't it?"

"It's amazing," Bryn answered.

"And now I have one question for you. Why did you cry when I cried?"

"I kept thinking about that as I did it. I don't remember ever seeing you upset like that. I was just loving you, Popi, and I didn't know how else to express it." Bryn laughed. "So, like a fool, I joined you in your actions, like we do with the kids in The Son-Rise Program, so you'd know I was there with you."

"Not like a fool," I suggested. "Just a very caring, wonderful daughter."

I hugged her tightly as we exited the bedroom to rejoin the board meeting. I felt drained and invigorated at the same time. The next day I received a note from Bryn.

Dear Popi:

I really appreciated that I had the chance to be with you and support you yesterday. Thank you for not pushing me away and letting me help. I love you. I love all the many sides of you.

Your grateful daughter, Bryn

P.S.: What did you think of my mentoring skills? Good questions, eh?"

TWELVE

Rosie and I drove back to your tiny, three-room cottage, clustered together with other similar structures adjacent to a central grassy field and a swimming pool. This modest relic of the nineteen-forties once housed urban dwellers with children and modest incomes who used such bungalow colonies to retreat from the heat and humidity of the city. Now this enclave housed seniors like yourself who had bought shares of ownership in what became a cooperative, providing inexpensive summer housing in a simple, relaxed, and safe environment. As we walked down the path toward your little abode, I smiled at the plastic windmills that you and Rosie had placed near the flowers you had planted along the walkway.

Never looking up or around, Rosie bent her head downward and watched only the segment of ground in front of her as she moved. She wanted, almost at any cost, to avoid interacting with your friends and neighbors. She knew they would ask about you with sincere concern and interest, and she anticipated that she would break down in front of them, unable to speak. Although I offered to answer the questions of anyone who might inquire, Rosie preferred invisibility.

Once we entered the front door, she stopped, almost breathless, then scanned the living room as if taking mental inventory. I noticed her reviewing the photos, cards, and drawings you'd received from both your children and your grandchildren, which you had posted on a small bulletin board. She glanced down at the old couch that in recent months had become a resting place for you while we and others visited. Funny, Pop, you always asked permission to lie down, knowing that once you put yourself in a prone position you would more easily fall asleep during conversations. Actually, I found it touching that you would allow yourself to be so comfortable and relaxed that you could just dose off while conversing with us. Rosie began to shake her head. She touched the arm of the couch adoringly. She knew, Pop, that you would never be returning to this home with her.

"Do you want to talk?" I asked. "We could just sit a while. Take some time if you want to."

"No. Let's just get it done."

With Rosie in the lead, we went right into your bedroom and opened the clothes closet door. She surveyed your hanging shirts, pushing one aside, then another, and then yet another in an attempt to decide what would be useful to retrieve for you.

"Are these all his?" I asked finally. She nodded. I stepped in front of her and grabbed all your shirts off the rack.

"We don't need so many shirts," she protested.

"Rosie, it doesn't matter."

She ignored my comments and flipped through your shirts as I held them. "Oh, he loves this one. And the flannel one, that's his favorite." She held back her tears.

"Go ahead, cry. I know this is hard for you." As tears flowed, she grabbed her throat, trying to hold back and release her emotions at the same time. "Why don't you just point and let me do it?" I offered.

Rosie shook her head forcefully, went directly to the bureau, opened the top drawers and tried to select from among the neatly folded garments.

"Here, let me do it," I said, swooping up most of the contents of the drawer. "If we do this fast, I think it might be better for you...and for him. We'll get back to the hospital sooner. Okay? You with me?"

"You're right. Take whatever you want. I don't care."

"Also, Rosie, I don't see you taking anything for yourself. You plan to wear one outfit day after day...or you going to strut around naked?"

A little smile curled at the corner of her lips. "I don't need much. Don't worry, I'll make sure I take clothes for me, too."

She allowed herself now to be somewhat less discriminating as she placed piles of clothes on the bed. I packed the back of my van and returned to find Rosie filling plastic bags with vitamins, soy milk, and breakfast cereals.

"Excellent," I said. "What do you think? Are we almost done?"

"I know I'm going to forget something."

"That doesn't matter. We can buy what we need at my house...or I can send someone here to retrieve anything important we forget."

We drove by the pharmacy to renew your prescriptions and doubled the amount of pain-killing medication. I could feel my heart pumping rapidly in the midst of what I now characterized as a rescue mission. I knew I would be taking you home to die, Pop. Although I had not planned any specifics, what I wanted most for you was a sacred dying...a "good death."

THIRTEEN

As Rosie and I returned to the hospital and rode the elevator up to the third floor, I thought about the past two years, amazed at how quickly they had raced by. Although I could recall vividly our week together in Florida and details of subsequent conversations in which we set directions for treatment while sharing so many sweet and tender moments, I had not anticipated that the very end of your life might be marred by the kind of suffering you currently experienced. I knew that if we could dare to take total charge of your environment, we could ease your anguish and, perhaps, help you have more sweet and tender moments.

Just as Rosie and I exited the elevator, I took her hand energetically and smiled at her.

"We're going to do this, Rosie, you and I! I am so excited." Tears started to gush from my eyes. I had hoped, in those early days after your diagnosis, that you would never be limited and confined as you had been recently. Maybe I had a silly vision of your falling over one day after doing fifty sit-ups and that would be it. Pop, I did not think your integrity or stature as a person was diminished one iota by your weakened bodily condition and ever-increasing frailty. In fact, the quality of your character shone even brighter these days. But I did so want to ease your suffering.

Now we had come to set you free. The discharge papers had still not been signed and it had been two hours since our request, so I told the nurses that I intended to disconnect all the wires and tubes immediately — they could help or just watch me do it. The nurses at the counter backed away from us and our request. However, one young nurse, listening to us in the hallway, smiled at me then followed us into your room to assist. Within minutes, the doctor arrived. He signed the discharge papers quickly and gave me additional prescriptions for medication to help you handle any pain that might break through your current pain levels. Although he lobbied lightly for keeping you in the hospital, he altered his position once he understood your wishes and ours. He appeared genuinely concerned about your discomfort and wanted to support whatever decisions we had made. I gave him a big hug. He smiled and patted my back gently.

The pain had abated somewhat since early that morning, although the gnawing ache in your back made you wince as the attendant and I moved you from the bed into a wheelchair. Rosie acted quickly to gather up your clothing and toiletries. As I placed your feet on the chair's platforms, I could feel the edges of your bones at the surface of your skin. You had become malnourished as the rapidly growing cancer cells consumed what little nutrients you could bear to take in. The severity of the dehydration also continued, weakening all your bodily functions as well as putting excessive pressure on your kidney and further compromising its ability to function. And yet, Pop, as we lifted you into the chair, you smiled broadly. Your body relaxed noticeably. Your wish to leave the hospital had come true.

We wheeled you through the front doors of the medical facility, stopping momentarily in the warm summer sun. You looked up at the sky, closed your eyes, and drew in a long, deep breath. Another smile exploded on your face. You took my hand and exclaimed, "Wow, does this feel good!" Even in your weakened condition, your eyes sparkled.

Once we had loaded you into the front passenger seat of my van, Rosie hopped into the rear seat and off we went. We lowered the back of your seat to minimize the pain as I drove north toward Massachusetts.

"How are you doing?" I asked.

"Don't worry about me. I'm fine," you lied.

"Pop, I want you to be more comfortable, so I will drive more slowly and more conservatively than I have ever driven before." I laughed. "This will be a challenge for me, but I'm up for it. I'll do my best to make sure the turns, the stops, and starts are easy on you. And please let me know if you want me to pull over and stop the car at any time."

You nodded. Later, as I drove north on the Taconic Parkway, you reached out and touched my leg. "You know, Bears, you treat me much better than I've treated you in the past."

"Hey, you did the best you could," I countered. "It would be great if all my children believed that about me as well — that I do the best I can, and with the best of intentions."

"I am not talking about doing the best I could." You paused to draw in a breath and summon up additional energy in order to continue speaking. "You have been wonderful to me, much more wonderful than I've ever been to you."

Rosie, sitting directly behind you, gestured her concurrence.

"I hear you, Pop," I acknowledged. "But you know, when I was young, I challenged you at every turn. My God, you had your hands full. Do you remember — I must have been in my mid-twenties — when I started my graphic design company in the motion picture industry, enrolled in graduate school, and began psychoanalysis all at the same time?" You nodded. "I claimed I did the therapy only to supplement my course work, but really, I felt so darn confused and unhappy, I just wanted to straighten my life out. God, it was like spending hours, weeks, months, and years dancing with the skeletons of the past, trying to pin my despair and anger on old inequities and disappointments." I smiled. "I wasn't ready to take responsibility for my thoughts and feelings because that therapy didn't encourage me to see myself as the architect of those thoughts and feelings. Instead, I found a scapegoat to blame for my discontent. You, Pop." As I stopped for a traffic light, I looked into your eyes.

"Should I go on?" I asked.

"Yeah, go ahead," you said in a raspy whisper.

"We lived on Princeton Street at the time," I continued. "I invited you over for dinner. Before the meal, I asked you to take a walk with me. Remember?" You shook your head; no, you didn't recall. "If I go further, I'm sure the memory will come back to you, even though this happened thirty years ago. You and I walked around the block, circling the neighborhood for at least an hour while I kept blaming you for making me an angry, unhappy person." You tipped your head and now smiled faintly. Ah, now you remembered. "I itemized every incriminating action that I could remember, since I had reviewed them ad nauseam in therapy, especially a particular incident about my attendance at military school. I had wanted to go there in the first place. I think I had John Wayne on my mind. You cautioned me not to go. However, when I left, armed with my trumpet and saxophone, having received a musical scholarship, you agreed not to stand in my way. Six months later, after being brutalized physically by some aggressive upperclassmen, I begged to come home. I sat at the kitchen table on a weekend pass, choking with distress as I described to you how I had been systematically punched and kicked and how dead rats had been sliced apart and placed between my bed sheets at night while I fulfilled an obligation of my scholarship by playing taps throughout the campus every night. You listened without apparent emotion and gave me two clear messages. First message: Be a man and stop crying. Hello, John Wayne. Quite a message for a skinny thirteen-year-old who had mistakenly registered for two semesters in hell. Second message: I'd made my bed, against your advice, so now I had to sleep in it until the end of the year.

"During that period of 'blame and complain' therapy, I used that example and a lot of others to abdicate responsibility for the feelings I had created, and just pointed to you. I'm sorry for it now, Pop. And you were so damned surprised and sweet during that walk. You kept shrugging your shoulders, saying you never meant to hurt me; you just wanted to teach me to be responsible for my actions. I remember wanting more from you. I think I wanted you on your knees. I ragged on you rather mercilessly and didn't feel any better afterwards. So, Pop, we can trade apologies. If I am treating you better now than you ever treated me, it's because I've dumped all those beliefs that left me a victim. It's the old story: If I'd known what I know now when I turned twenty, I could have treated you this nicely starting way back then! Wouldn't that have been a kick?" I tapped your hand, smiling broadly at such a possibility. "And if you'd known, Pop, what you know now, right now — if you'd known all this 'stuff' years ago — you would have probably been a lot easier with me as well. We're both growing."

"Well, one of us has a lot more life in them than the other," you said.

"Hey, the spark of life burns brightly in you. Check out those eyes," I noted, glancing at you.

"How come you make everything sound so good?" you asked.

I laughed. "That's my job."

You smiled at me, then gazed off thoughtfully. "Your grandmother once said that when she looked at a tree at ninety years old it still looked like the tree she saw at twenty years old. Her eyes, what they saw, didn't get older. Sometimes, when she looked around, life seemed timeless. But when she looked at her hands, wrinkled and arthritic at the knuckles, she had no doubt about her age. 'These are my hands?' she said once. 'How did I get so old?'"

You surveyed the passing landscape visible through the front windshield and sighed audibly. "The sky and the clouds out there, they're like the sky and clouds I saw as a boy. They're beautiful," you said. "But when your body starts to give up, you don't quite enjoy them like you once did."

"Are you enjoying them now?" I asked.

"Now, with you here, with Rosie — yes, I am enjoying them now," you chuckled.

You dipped your chin, squinted your eyes in an exaggerated

gesture, and said, "Are we having one of those deep conversations?" You paused thoughtfully, as if awaiting an answer to your question. "Doesn't matter," you concluded suddenly. "We're having a real nice talk. Besides, it keeps my mind off the pain."

"Abe, do you want some water?" Rosie asked. When you nodded, she placed the straw in your mouth, and you sipped some liquid from the container. "Good, Abie! Take a little more." You pulled in a few more sips, then waved to indicate that you had had enough.

"Do you want to sleep?" I asked.

"No," you said matter-of-factly. "You keep talking. I'll listen."

"I have an idea," I suggested. "In the hospital, you couldn't do what you wanted and get what you wanted. You lived in accordance with someone else's rules and standards. Well, at our house, the world will operate quite differently. You get to do whatever you want, and you don't have to do anything you don't want to do. Maybe I can convince Rosie to cut down on the amount of vitamins she gets you to consume throughout the day. What do you think, Rosie?"

"Abe, I know you don't like taking the vitamins, so how about if I just reduce them to the essentials?" Rosie offered.

"Great!" you said.

"Okay," I continued, "now to the menu. What about you eat only your favorite dishes. We can all help — every day we'll round up portions of what you like to eat most. So what do you want?" I didn't know how you would respond to this. I knew you hated being pampered, but I also realized that you had never been so sick.

"Listen to him, Rosie," you said playfully.

"Hey, you have to humor me so I can humor you!" I said quickly, not wanting to break your apparent enthusiasm.

"Okay, I have a pad in my pocketbook," Rosie noted. "I'll be the stenographer. I'm ready to take your order."

"I can't do this," you asserted suddenly.

"Yes, you can, Abe, if you want to," Rosie insisted. "I get to put some of my favorite foods on the list, too. I'm ready."

"The lady's waiting, Pop."

No one spoke for almost a minute. Then you blurted, "Hot and sour soup!"

"Excellent choice. We have a great new Chinese take-out restaurant, which makes the best hot and sour soup!"

"What's next?" Rosie barked like a drill sergeant.

You licked your lips as if sampling another flavor. "Barbecued ribs!"

"Chinese or American?" I inquired.

"He likes any kind of ribs," Rosie noted, wincing as she wrote this item on the paper. Both of you were about to abandon a twenty-five-year commitment to health foods.

"In luck again, Pop. There's a place near us called The Woodland. They make the best, most sumptuous ribs in America."

"Hey, I thought you were a vegetarian," Rosie said.

"Not any more," I smiled. "Okay, Pop, let's keep going with more of your culinary favorites."

"A good roasted chicken hits the spot." You smiled. "I also like shrimp in lobster sauce."

"No problem. We get that at the same place we get the hot and sour soup," I added. "What about smoked salmon?"

"It's not good for you," Rosie protested. She glanced at me in the mirror, then laughed. "Okay, Abe, that's probably not any worse than barbecued ribs. Some smoked salmon, yes?"

"Absolutely," you responded in a voice noticeably stronger than when you left the hospital. "What about dessert?"

"For you, we can always include dessert," I said. "You like anything chocolate, right?" You smirked mischievously.

"Seven layer cake," you announced proudly with a wink. "You know, Bears, you don't have to go to all this trouble for me," you offered.

"This is not trouble. This is joy. You're going to have the best of everything you want. Maybe I'll get to eat some of it, too. Rosie, what do you think?" I asked.

"Don't ask me. You're the crazy one here."

You drifted off to sleep for the remainder of the two-hour trip. When we arrived at our home at the Institute, I woke you gently.

"I can get a chair and some help and we can carry you in like on a throne. What do you say?"

"I say I can walk," you snapped.

"Then let's walk." I came around to your side of the vehicle and gave you my arm to lean on. You took it gracefully. With Rosie at your other side, we walked very slowly toward the house.

Although we had to cover a distance of less than two hundred feet, you stopped several times to rest. You gazed at the main building, then turned to look at some of the other structures nearby, finally scanning the meadows, valleys, and mountains in the distance.

"Beautiful. Just beautiful. It's good to be here."

"It's good to have you and Rosie here, Pop."

As we walked around toward the front door, Zoe met us. She hugged you like a daughter and welcomed you warmly. You tapped her shoulder and kept calling her "honey."

Samahria walked determinedly through the doorway. "Dad,

we are so excited to have you here!" she said. "We fixed every-thing up for you. Zoe helped do the impossible. Your room is completely ready."

"You're kidding," I said, surprised and impressed. "I thought you needed twenty-four hours to get everything delivered."

"Not with Zoe. She sweet-talked everyone, and, voilà, the room is fully equipped and ready."

"Pop, do you want to go upstairs now or wait till later?" I inquired.

"Now, Bears; I don't feel too good."

Once we entered the house, you paused to look at the signs hanging by the fireplace that had been made by your grand-children. Bryn and William had made a poster announcing, "We love you!" in huge, colorful letters. Tayo, Sage, and Raun had created an artful sign welcoming "the greatest grandpar-ents in the world." Your eyes became misty as you read their messages; then you grabbed the banister to the staircase and tried to pull yourself up one step.

I positioned myself behind you and gave you a continuous supportive lift that allowed you to negotiate the entire staircase while stopping every three or four steps. On the top landing, you tottered backwards, but Samahria and I steadied you as you paused to rest once again. All of us walked across the balcony together until we arrived at our special guest room. When you looked inside, your eyes opened wide. In addition to a queen-sized bed that awaited you and Rosie, a special hospital bed had been positioned near the windows. An adjustable food tray stood nearby. Flowers had been placed on top of the bureau, and a box of fruits and snacks had been put on one of the night tables. Both beds had been turned down, hotel style, awaiting your entrance. Another welcoming sign had been taped to the top of one of the windows. I felt myself fighting the tears filling my eyes. So many people had made so much effort to make you feel welcome and treasured. "What do you think?" I asked.

You couldn't speak. I could see your bottom lip trembling.

"You don't have to say anything, Pop. The adjustable bed by the window might be more comfortable." You shook your head and pointed to the queen-sized bed. Samahria and Rosie helped you remove your jacket. Zoe ran to the bathroom, filled a tall container by your bedside with fresh water, returned it to your room, and then discreetly disappeared. I removed your shoes and supported you as you eased yourself into the bed. You moaned from the considerable pain you experienced with each movement. "Time for some medication," I said to Rosie, who handed me a container of capsules. You took the two pills I gave you without questioning the timing or the dosage, then sighed noisily.

"Would you like us to leave you alone for a while?" I asked.

"Yes, but first…" You stopped mid-sentence. Tears started to cascade down your cheeks. You scrutinized the room again, then reached out to take Samahria's hand and my hand, a touching ritual that you repeated many times over the next four weeks.

"Abe," Rosie said softly, "don't get yourself upset."

"I'm not upset. I'm happy." You took another stab at trying to control your emotions. "You two are really a blessing for me." You started to cry again, Pop. Samahria and I smiled at you through our tears. Rosie held her throat, turning away to hide her face from you.

"We're the ones who are blessed, Pop," Samahria said. "Maybe God's smiling on all of us right now." You nodded your head and closed your eyes.

Samahria and I stood at your bedside until you fell asleep. Your presence had altered the character of this room and our home. These walls now enclosed a sacred sanctuary from which one day soon you would take flight. None of us anticipated, at that time, your dazzling walk back from death's door to give yourself, Rosie, Samahria, and others you loved four more precious weeks together. The next twenty-eight days would bestow on me one of the most poignant, spiritually fulfilling experiences of my life.

FOURTEEN

Evening came quickly. As you slept, Rosie, Samahria, and I joined Tayo, Raun, and Sage in the kitchen. The kids greeted Rosie with sweet smiles and warm hugs. Raun slung his arm around his grandmother's shoulder and leaned against her, casually, like a sports buddy.

"Hi, Grandma!" he said affectionately.

"Hi, Raun," she answered, a bit subdued.

He removed his arm from around her shoulder as his expression turned more serious. "How's Grandpa doing?"

"Not that good," Rosie said matter-of-factly.

"Is it okay for us to go to his room and visit him?" Sage asked.

"I am sure he'd love it," Rosie said. "Only right now he's sleeping."

"We didn't come up because we didn't want to interrupt or disturb him," Sage continued. "When we realized you had already taken him upstairs, we thought it would be best for us to wait here."

"That was very sweet, honey," Samahria said. "So, while Grandpa sleeps," she continued, "we can whip up something to eat. Tayo, how about you setting the table?" He nodded and headed for the cabinet containing the dishes and glasses. "Sage, you can start with the lettuce for a salad. Popi and I will chop some onions and mushrooms." Rosie offered to cut up the tomatoes. Raun grabbed some cans of tuna from the pantry, then some mayonnaise from the refrigerator.

Funny, Pop, how life rolls on.

Although the room hummed with our spirited food preparation, the conversation turned back to you quickly. What could we do to make you more comfortable?

"What about contacting hospice?" I offered.

"No hospice," Rosie declared.

In order to involve hospice, we would have to formally stop any further treatments that might save you, Pop, and get an attending physician to sign a document attesting to our decision to take that step, one Rosie still refused to initiate.

"Hospice will help us make him more comfortable, Rosie," I suggested, "and — this is the key factor — they will allow us to take charge of his medication so we can make sure he's not in pain. As it stands now, we have to call the doctors, wait until they call us back, convince them he needs more or different medication, then hope it's during the day so a pharmacy will be open to fill any new prescriptions. Hospice would allow us to cut through that cumbersome process and help Dad on a moment-to-moment basis, especially with the pain. They said they would be available by phone twenty-four hours a day and would come to the house whenever necessary, even in the middle of the night for an emergency. I've spoken with them several times; they sound like caring people."

"I appreciate the calls and all your research, always; you know I do," Rosie responded. "But I want to ask you something else. Okay?"

"Sure."

"You said Zoe had found an oncologist who agreed to see your father and take him on as a patient. Right?"

"Yes," I answered.

"And you checked the man out and thought he was good. Highly recommended. Yes?"

"Yes."

"Then that's what we do," Rosie declared. "I know it doesn't look good right now, but maybe in a week he'll get his strength back and he can have more chemotherapy. Bears, it's his only chance."

"I hear you. But even if he did start to feel better, I'm not sure his body can tolerate that kind of treatment anymore. And Rosie, the new chemo protocol, well, you know the possible side effects." I considered using the word "gruesome," but I realized Rosie had a clear grasp of the possible debilitating and life-threatening complications that could arise. "I'm sorry if I sound like a broken record, but I don't want us to put him through all of that unless — well — unless he really wants it. Does that make sense?"

"Yes," she acknowledged.

"When I saw Grandpa in the hospital," Raun added, "he looked so much weaker, so much thinner. And real tired. Grandma, he looked very, well, um…very different." Sweet Raun — to the point but always the diplomat. Tayo and Sage, who had been listening attentively to our conversation, watched Rosie's face for a reaction to Raun's comments.

"I know," Rosie said in a hushed voice. "He's been through so much. This has been a terrible week. Too much. I'm..." Her voice quivered as she stopped speaking and stopped breathing. She put her hand on her throat in a gesture she had made several times before when she felt a surge of emotion.

Sage watched Rosie, then glanced at Samahria and me, finally looking back urgently at her grandmother. "Are you okay, Grandma?"

Rosie walked to the other side of the kitchen, trying to regain her composure. She held her hand in the air, like an umpire, standing purposely apart from us and signaling for more time. We all stood quietly, respecting her request. Finally, she sighed, releasing the block in her vocal cords, and said, "Your grandma is okay, Sage. Just tired, like Grandpa."

"And maybe holding back a little, too," Samahria said gently. "Any time you want to talk about what's going on inside, we can. Just let us know, okay?" she asked.

"I'll be fine," Rosie answered.

"I have no doubt you'll be fine. That wasn't the question."

"I know what your question was," she said. "I'm just avoiding it."

"Fair enough. We don't have to continue talking about this if you don't want to," I suggested. "Hey, we could bring up other less controversial subjects to ponder, like the origin of life, the nature of family relationships, or speculation about the hereafter. Or what about the mating practices of elephants on the Serengeti savannas in Tanzania?"

Rosie slid a batch of scallions across the counter, shoving them purposely in front of me. "Here, Bears, cut these for the salad and give your head a rest."

I laughed, as did Samahria, Raun, and Sage. Tayo, counting napkins for the table, either missed or ignored Rosie's humor.

"Salad and sandwiches," Samahria remarked as she unwrapped a loaf of bread. "If there are any objections to this gourmet meal, find another restaurant."

"Feisty, aren't we?" I noted.

Her expression changed suddenly. "Rosie, I'm sorry to go back to this, but Bears, do we have enough medication to help ease Dad's pain if it got worse tonight?" I nodded affirmatively. No one spoke for a few minutes as each of us digested the challenges you might face tonight, Pop — challenges that we would face with you.

"Will Grandpa be coming down to eat with us?" Tayo asked.

"Not tonight. He's too weak," I said. "And he probably wouldn't be enticed by a sandwich and definitely not excited by a salad! However," I said with a flourish, unveiling the favorite food list we'd created with you in the car, "this magical list contains all the dishes your grandfather truly adores."

Tayo eyed the piece of paper as I placed it on the counter. He laughed. "A lot of Chinese food and ribs. Ugh, chicken. Salmon. Bagels. I like salmon and bagels."

"Hey, Tayo, that's Grandpa's menu, not yours!" Samahria noted.

Tayo laughed again, not a belly laugh but a few short grunts that sounded much like his "Ay" hellos. "Just checking it out, Mom," he said. "You know, the Chinese take-out is still open. I can drive over and get him hot and sour soup in case he gets hungry later."

"I don't think he'll be wanting to eat later," Rosie said. "Sit. Have dinner. You don't have to go now."

"I want to go. It's not a big deal. I want to help, too."

Samahria eyed Tayo thoughtfully, then threw him a set of car keys and gave him some money. He left the kitchen immediately.

"He didn't have to do that," Rosie observed.

"Yes, he did," Samahria countered. "Rosie, that was his way of helping his grandfather and being part of what's happening in his home."

I checked on you before we began to eat. You continued to sleep, your mouth slightly ajar. Your body made pronounced, concerted efforts to draw in each breath. Your facial expression, more chiseled in appearance than ever before as a result of your weight loss, seemed tight and strained, as if even in sleep you experienced an underlying exhaustion. Several times, when your body twitched, your face cringed in response. I considered waking you to see if you wanted more pain medication, but I didn't want to disturb your slumber.

I said a prayer for you as I stood by your side. Then I placed my hand on yours, closed my eyes, and visualized sending you my love. Although you did not acknowledge my touch, I decided that somewhere inside, you would feel my presence and my caring.

When I returned to the kitchen, Samahria, Rosie, and the children sat patiently at the table, awaiting my report about your condition.

"He's still sleeping. He looks totally exhausted, but he's resting more comfortably now," I assured everyone. No one appeared very eager to start eating.

"What do you say we eat like hogs," Samahria offered, "making sure that all of us, especially you, Rosie, stay strong so we can all help Grandpa?"

"So now we're going to give our meal a special purpose?" Rosie asked.

"Seems like a great idea," I laughed. "Hey, we can ascribe a wonderful purpose to everything we do."

I extended my arms to the right and left of me, reaching for Samahria's and Rosie's hands. For decades, Pop, when you had visited our home, you joined our ritual of holding hands before meals with great hesitancy. In fact, you poked fun at the communion we tried to create with our children around the dinner table, sometimes waiting a trifle impatiently until we had concluded our comments or moments of silence. However, since you had been living with cancer, you had softened your contrarian position, oftentimes taking the initiative by grabbing my hand or one of our children's hands at the table and then waiting expectantly for others to follow your cue. Every time you did it, Pop, I could feel myself melting inside. Although you might not have agreed with all the principles by which we lived, I experienced your willingness to accept, even participate in, such simple moments of communion as signs of your sincere stretching and giving of yourself. This night, I missed your cantankerous presence at our table.

Responding to my outstretched arms, Rosie smiled, clasping my hand on one side, then taking Raun's on the other. Once we had all created an informal circle at the table, holding hands together, we spent a few seconds smiling at each other. I love taking some moments each day, whenever possible, to notice and appreciate each other.

"We're so glad to have you and Dad here," Samahria said to Rosie.

"And we appreciate being here," she responded.

"If all of us together surround Grandpa with our good feelings and our love," Samahria added, "that's going to help him and make a difference. We can do it when we're with him, and we can also do it now in our hearts."

"Let's spend a few moments, each of us in our own way,

being grateful that we're together, that we're sharing the gift of this meal, and that we have the privilege to have Grandma and Grandpa here with us," I suggested as we continued holding hands.

We all closed our eyes. In my mind's eye, I brought you to the table, Pop. I visualized you enveloped in a soothing and healing yellow-white light, not necessarily to magically effect a cure — no, more as a way to ask God and the universe to provide you with a cradle of warmth and wonder in which to spend your remaining days. I said a prayer for Rosie, then one for Samahria, then another for our children, and a finally one for all the folks and creatures that share this planet with us. Although I had an impulse to direct God (Do this! Do that!), especially on your behalf, Pop, I reminded myself to trust the wisdom of events taking place around me, events that I did not direct, and to do the best I could when I had the opportunity to make a difference. I used these moments to feel and express gratitude for the abundance around me and for your presence, Pop, in my life.

Suddenly, I heard footsteps behind me, marking Tayo's return. When he stopped short, I knew he realized we were in the midst of our gratitude circle around the table. To my surprise, I heard him move toward me and take a position quietly beside me, then felt him place his hand on my shoulder. Ordinarily if he arrived late, he would stand apart and wait, not very interested or excited to be part of this family tradition. This time, however, he apparently wanted to join us, perhaps to express his love and caring for you.

Once we had reopened our eyes, I turned toward Tayo. "Hey, that was nice, really nice. I liked having your hand on my shoulder."

Tayo acknowledged my comment with a purposely dead-pan expression, and then, in a fashion distinctly his own, his mouth formed the sweetest little smile. "Here's Grandpa's food," he announced as he placed a large bag on the table. "They had all his favorite dishes."

"Excellent," Samahria said. "Thanks for going, Tay. I know Grandpa will appreciate it."

"Ay-Tay, I appreciate it," Rosie added, mimicking Tayo's familiar greeting of a grunted "Ay." He nodded sweetly. Tayo knew something in his home had changed profoundly with the arrival of his grandparents. In his eyes, I could see a softening as if he had shed his sometimes tough football-player exterior in order to open himself more to both Rosie and you, Pop.

"Tayo, come, sit down," I said. "There's more than enough for you." I rose from my chair. "I'll be back in a few moments. I want to check on Pop. You can start eating without me."

"You sit," Rosie directed as she jumped to her feet. "I'll check on him."

"It's not a problem for me to do it," I insisted. "I'd like the exercise."

"Why don't you both go?" Raun laughed. "You could keep each other company."

"A great idea," I bellowed, putting my arm out to Rosie as one might do with a date upon entering a formal party. Instead of responding to my chivalry, she pushed my rather ample form aside decisively, moved in front of me like a competitor in a race, and took the lead by walking determinedly toward the center hall and up the staircase to the second floor.

As soon as we entered your room, you opened your eyes and gazed at us with a weak smile.

"Abie, how do you feel?" Rosie asked.

"Not too good, but better. Better to be here than in the hospital."

"Pop, do you want some water or a little something to eat?" You squinted your eyes as if seriously pondering the possibility. "Hey, what about some absolutely delicious hot and sour soup?" You managed another smile and nodded your head. "Okay. One hot and sour soup coming up!" I called Tayo on the intercom and asked him to bring a bowl of soup to your room immediately. He arrived with Samahria within two minutes.

While I lifted your upper torso and head, Rosie repositioned the pillows, enabling you to rest in a partial sitting position. You watched Tayo appreciatively as he handed the soup proudly to his grandmother.

"Abe. Look what Ay-Tay got you."

"Hi, Tayo," you said to him in a weak, raspy voice.

"Ay," he grunted. We all laughed.

"Thank you, Tayo. You kids, all you kids," you said, including both Samahria and me with the kids, "you make a fellow like me feel real special." With a mischievous smirk on your face, you peered down with mock curiosity at the bowl that Rosie held near your chest. You raised your hand slightly to take the spoon, then, too weak to complete the movement, you let your arm drop limply back to the bed. Rosie grabbed the utensil immediately, filled it with soup and brought it to your lips. You sipped the liquid into your mouth, swallowed it, and exhaled with a very vocal "aaah."

"Goooood. That's very good soup."

"Only the best for you, Dad," Samahria chimed.

"You always say that to me," you noted.

"Because I mean it. I want the best for you. We all want the best for you, and we're willing to show you." She flashed you one of her radiant smiles.

Your eyes became misty as you looked at her, then you dipped your head thoughtfully. "I can handle it." Samahria adored you, Pop, and I knew you knew it. She has a wondrous ability to put so much warmth and love into her smile that anybody she looks at could easily imagine themselves to be the most important and special person on the planet. Your face brightened as you gazed into her eyes.

"Are you feeling any better now?" Tayo asked, noticing the softness in your expression.

"Yes," you said slowly. "Thanks to you and the hot and sour soup you got me."

At that moment, I noticed Raun and Sage standing in the hallway, just outside of the room.

"Pop, can you handle two more visitors?" I asked.

You nodded. As Raun and Sage entered, you greeted them with a smile. Raun kissed you on the forehead. You kissed the air in his direction. Sage snuggled her face against yours, calling you "Grampy." You apologized for not having the strength to hug either of them.

"No problem, Grandpa. I feel that way every time my alarm clock rings in the morning," Raun commented.

Sage sat down on the bed beside you, taking your hand and patting it. You closed your eyes and sighed.

"Hey, Grandpa, if this is all too much, just tell us to leave," Raun said.

"Stay a little longer," you said, opening your eyes. "I like having my family around me. When I get too tired, I'll tell you — unless," you paused, taking another breath, "unless, you don't mind if the old man catches a nap, from time to time, in the middle of a sentence."

"Whose sentence?" I asked.

You laughed. "Could be yours. Could be mine."

"Well, that's the prerogative of the elder of the tribe," I assured you. "In this house, you have the license to do whatever you want. 'Appropriate' is out the window. Do what feels good. Your great-granddaughter Jade does it all the time — naps when she wants to, cries when she wants to — doesn't matter who's in the room or what's happening."

"Here, Abie, have another spoonful," Rosie said. "If you eat, you'll get your strength back." You sipped more liquid from the spoon while looking around at all of us.

Bryn arrived at the door and entered the room very cautiously. She had not seen you since her visit to you at the hospital only the weekend before, the visit that had provoked her urgent telex to me on the ship. Her face broke into a surprised grin when she saw you taking soup from Rosie, but then she stopped herself and asked gingerly, "Can I come in?"

You signaled to her with your hand, inviting her to come directly to you. She touched your face with the tips of her fingers, then kissed your cheek. As she moved away, you gestured for her to place her face near yours again, then you kissed her cheek gently. I felt as if time had expanded, stretching out before me like a choreographed dance intended to express the deepest human emotions. Each simple gesture between you and us took place before my eyes as if in slow motion. I could see the heart and soul of my children displayed on their faces as they greeted you. I witnessed a ray of palpable affection shining from your eyes each time you acknowledged one of them and smiled. I saw your tenderness and humanity embrace them when you moved your lips and made contact with their cheeks or even when you kissed the air between you.

Who was this amazing man before me? My father. Yes, you

had become the father of my dreams, strong, self-reliant, and dignified even in your current condition and yet open, easy, and loving. Though your body had withered, your spirit burned so much brighter.

Later that evening, after Samahria and the children had gone to bed, Rosie and I changed your clothing, which had become soaked with perspiration. Although you did not appear to have a fever, your skin would suddenly become covered with sweat. When that happened you'd ask us to remove the blankets from your body. At one point, you instructed me to remove your shirt and pajama pants so you could allow your body to cool in the open air.

The skin encasing your limbs appeared tightly wrapped around your skeleton, the fleshy mass of your arms and legs having diminished noticeably. Your pectoral muscles, always prominent as a result of daily calisthenics and workouts with dumbbells, stretched thinly now across your rib cage, the bony frame of your upper torso fully visible. What amazed me about your declining physical presence was the beauty and the lean purity of your form. I know that many people recoil in distress when they see dramatic changes in the physical condition of those they love, especially those weakened by severe illness. Miraculously, as I looked at you now, I had the opposite experience, Pop. Nothing about your condition made me want to hide my eyes. As I looked at you, as I held your hands or helped shift your body in different positions on the bed, I sensed a profound divinity about you — no longer a helpless soul amid high-tech machinery in a hospital cubicle but a sensitive, think-ing, feeling person embraced by a room redesigned specifically to honor your presence and support you in letting go of a body that no longer served you.

Lifting your arms, even turning your head, had become a chore requiring a concentrated effort. However, the intense pain you experienced in the hospital over the past few days had abated. You appeared much more peaceful, even relaxed at times. Nonetheless, you waved Rosie away after taking only about five spoonfuls of soup and resisted drinking any more than a single sip of water at any one time.

While Rosie unpacked your clothing, filling the bureau and hanging jackets, shirts, and pants in the closet, I lifted the con-tainer of water by your bedside and offered you yet another sip. You grimaced, nodded a touch defiantly, indicating an affirma-tive response only as an accommodation to me while putting me on notice that you might consider not taking in any more nourishment. I placed the straw in your mouth, enabling you to draw the liquid into your mouth. You took enough water to lubricate your tongue and parched lips, then shook your head, turning away from me.

A few seconds later, you took my hand. "Don't stay with me anymore. I know you have a large group of people here this week. I know you have to get up early in the morning to pre-pare your classes. Go. Rosie and I will be fine."

"I can't think of anything I would rather do than sit here, relax, and hold your hand."

"What did you say?"

"Selective hearing. Have you been hearing everything said tonight without your hearing aid?" Over the years, as your hear-ing failed, you refused steadfastly to utilize that very expensive equipment. If you had to choose between what you viewed as pride or a hearing aid, you would choose pride and deafness. And yet, you often reported hearing exactly what you wanted to hear when you wanted to hear it, no matter what the volume.

"I read lips," you assured us.

"No, you don't. When you don't hear, you make it up, right?" You nodded like a little boy with his hand caught in the cookie jar. "Can you hear everything I'm saying?"

"Just talk a little louder." You glanced at the clock on the bureau. "Bears, it's almost midnight."

"You noticed," I said, raising my voice considerably. "That's a good sign, Mr. Kaufman. It suggests your continued interest in worldly matters."

"Listen," you said in a softer voice than mine, "as long as I'm alive — and I'm still breathing and kicking, aren't I? — then I want to know what's happening and I want to have my say."

"Sounds fine to me. Anything you want to know about right now?"

"No. Anything you want to know about?"

I looked at your shrunken body and wondered how you felt about it. In the past, I knew you wouldn't want to talk about such matters — too private. Too painful, perhaps. We never, ever touched on this subject when Mom was dying — not in front of her, not even in her absence. So much territory had been roped off as taboo. But, now, you had initiated, hadn't you? "Yeah, Pop. How do you feel about your physical condition?"

You smiled at me warmly. "You jump right in, don't you, my boy?"

I nodded.

"Well, I know I didn't sound very cheerful when you first

saw me in the hospital. I hated for Rosie, for you, for anyone to see me like that."

"Like what?"

You looked off into the distance. Your eyes danced laterally, left to right and back again, as if reflecting an inner search for a word. "Unglued," you said finally. "In pain. Falling apart. Crying. Peeing into a pan or jar." You sighed and shook your head. "Bears, when you've been the man, the strong one, the person who handled your family's affairs, and then you can't do what you used to do and you don't even have the strength to get out of bed to go to the bathroom, or if you do, you need assistance — that's tough, real difficult."

I so wanted to respect you and to know you felt my respect. But at the same time, I wanted us to go further, to hold hands even more firmly. If I had been working with a client dealing with the final days of life, I would certainly want to ask more questions in the hopes of being more helpful and giving that other person lavish space to reflect and, hopefully, come to a place of resolution and peace inside. Suddenly, I remembered Bryn's dialogue with me and her persistence in asking the most helpful questions. In this moment, she became my inspiration. "Pop, here's one of those questions you may find a bit outrageous or insensitive, but I'm just trying to help you sort out what you're feeling. Why is what you described so difficult for you?"

You gazed up at the ceiling, then eyed me again. "Maybe because at my age, you don't want to be reduced to a baby. You want to live... and die, with dignity."

"Using your examples, do you think that it's undignified to pee in a jar or require assistance to go to the bathroom?"

You crinkled your forehead. "I guess so. But maybe, as we're talking about it, it's not undignified. When your grandmother was sick, I used to help her get around. She needed a bedpan. Once, I even had to carry her into the bathroom. I never felt that diminished her dignity. Not one bit. She was one tough cookie, that lady." You licked your lips and smiled again.

"Want some more water?"

"What?"

"Want your hearing aid?" You shook your head. "How come you heard the kids pretty well but now you appear a bit deaf?"

"I'm not going to answer," you declared.

"Okay, I'll just talk louder. How are you feeling now about not having the strength sometimes to do even simple tasks, like feeding yourself, or needing assistance, even a lot of assistance, as your own mother once did?"

"As we talk about it, I'm feeling better." Again you stared off at the ceiling. "Do you think I should just lie back and enjoy it?"

"What do you think, Pop?"

"I will consider the possibility," you declared, tapping my hand affectionately.

"Excellent," I said.

"Good." You took my hand again. "One more thing, Bears. Remember when I used to visit your grandmother after she starting losing her memory?" I nodded my head. "She'd call me Max, my brother's name, and I'd insist that she acknowledge me as Abe. Then she'd ask me whether I'd done my math homework, as if I were still in high school, and talk about dead relatives or friends as if they were alive. Every time I visited her, I'd leave totally upset. It drove me crazy. Then we talked. Do you remember?" Again, I nodded my head. "Boy, this goes back a long, long time. Anyway, you suggested that, given her life in a nursing home and confinement to a wheelchair, she might have dipped into the past to create a more palatable world.

Rather than fight her, you suggested I go along, support her, even join her in her make-believe world. I remember you said everybody's world is make-believe, anyway — even though you knew that I take exception to that perspective."

"Duly noted," I said, enjoying your recollection of a conversation we had had at least fifteen years before and delighting in the stamina that enabled you to note our philosophical differences despite the frailty of your condition.

"Well, I did what you advised the next time I saw her." You paused, looking off now to the right side of the room. I had the feeling you replayed the movie of you and your mom talking together. "Bears, we had a wonderful time. I didn't get upset. After a while, I really didn't care if she thought I was Abe or Max or her brother Louie or even Aunt Sadie. I never thanked you for your help. I just want you to know it worked — for me and, certainly, for my mother."

"I'm glad. But, Pop, you're the one who did it." I stood up and touched you on the shoulder. "Okay, sweet man, I'm going to say good night." I leaned over to hug you. I realized that an old assumption I had made about you had just fallen to dust. It wasn't that you never had sweet thoughts about us and our interaction together; it's just that you had never chosen to share them until now.

You grabbed my jacket, kissed me sweetly on the cheek, and whispered, "Thank you."

"Thank you, Pop, for allowing me to help you and Rosie." I turned to Rosie. "Anything else I can do for you?"

"Yes. Go to sleep. You have been running for us day and night since you came back from Alaska."

"Alaska. Feels like that happened in the last century."

"That's not a good sign," Rosie insisted. "We'll be fine for the night. If we need you, I know where to find you. Go." I hugged Rosie and left.

Two minutes later, I returned. "What about Pop's medication?"

"I gave him the last dosage about three hours ago. Abe, I can give you more now, if you want?"

"Okay," you said. "My back's starting to hurt more."

I waited until she gave you the pills, then waved to both of you and exited the room a second time. As I stood outside your door for several minutes, I had a peculiar feeling that everything in my home had, indeed, changed. Oh, yes, the smooth peach walls in the hallways, the huge photographs documenting the changing faces of our children over thirty-one years, and the translucent Lucite sculptures chiseled by Samahria decades ago remained the same. Yet, something less tangible, though more powerful, had shifted. Was it the very air we breathed? Was it the light filtering through the windows from a bright, moonlit sky? Was it your presence, Pop, yours and Rosie's, that enveloped me like morning mist? Or was it the specter of death, no longer at a distance and scary but yet another metamorphosis beckoning from the future? Perhaps, in fact, nothing had changed around me, only my state of mind. Perhaps I had learned to meet you, Pop, from a place inside, where I keenly feel the presence of God. Perhaps you had opened yourself to greet me from a similar place inside you.

Throughout the night, at intervals of an hour, I awoke as if some internal clock nudged me to roll out of bed to check on you and Rosie. Instead of feeling inconvenienced or fatigued, I felt exhilarated each time I walked down the hallway, experiencing the floorboards beneath my feet as hallowed ground. A compelling sense of purpose permeated my every move.

On most of these treks, I peeked into your room to find both you and Rosie asleep. However, on one occasion, at about five o'clock in the morning, I entered the room to find Rosie awake in bed. She looked at me and smiled. We whispered together, noting how peaceful you appeared. Apparently, you had slept for hours without requiring any additional pain medication. That landmark event, given your extraordinary difficulties in the hospital earlier in the day, delighted Rosie. She patted my arm affectionately.

"He's doing okay," I said in a hushed voice.

"He's doing great," she said, sighing.

"What's the sigh about?" I whispered.

"Relief."

FIFTEEN

At four o'clock in the morning, my eyes opened at full alert. The sensation, which I experienced almost hourly throughout the night, felt easy, almost natural. This was your first night in our home. I noticed the bed was empty beside me. I slide out from under the blanket to take my ritualistic solo walk down the hallway to check in on you and Rosie. As I strolled down the hallway, I encountered Samahria walking in the opposite direction as she returned like a congenial apparition from her vigil outside your room. We exchanged smiles and hugged a quick hello and good-bye as we passed each other in the night. After checking on both of you, I returned to my room and crawled back into my bed, only to awake in another hour.

At six o'clock, I walked alone through the house as a golden light from the soon-to-be-rising sun filtered through the second-story windows that faced east. The mist, encased in a midnight blue light at the base of the valley, sent swirling vapors like a thousand fingers reaching upward for the approaching daylight. I imagined your spirit reaching upward similarly for that final exotic moment of transcendence, Pop, when the life force evaporates mysteriously from the body and joins an unseen universe too mind-boggling for any of us to truly comprehend. Would today be that day?

Though you rested more comfortably here than in the hospital, your obvious deep fatigue, growing tumor cells, intensifying pain, and avoidance of nourishment or liquids left you hanging on to life by a thin thread. I kept thinking about how much life we had lived in the preceding twenty-four hours and how much sharing you and I had done in these past two years. More than ever, I wanted us to notice every smile, every touch of our hands, every word spoken and unspoken. I wanted to relish every thought I had about you, Rosie, Samahria, my family, my children, my work, life, death, love, and God. I wanted to heighten every sensation I conjured up inside, from the explosions of delight to the more subtle bursts of internal warmth or coolness that cascaded unpredictably through my body. I wanted to squeeze every last ounce of substance from each unfolding moment that you and I might yet have together.

It's funny, Pop, how most of us have conjured up the illusion of permanency in countless relationships and situations and as a result, have become complacent, maybe even insensitive to the wondrous ebb and flow of shared experiences. Like the crest of waves that dance in the sunlight only to be swept ashore and disappear among grains of sand, these rarefied moments would, I knew, endure for only an instant and then vanish. Now, when the days or even the hours of your life appeared numbered and no longer available in limitless supply, I allowed all the complexity of miscellaneous chores and minutiae to fall away, realigning my attention purposely with what I identified as most meaningful and important. What lessons we can learn if we treat each day as if it were our last!

I remember the phone ringing at three in the morning several years ago. The house had been very quiet, as it was now. Our bedroom felt like a black cave as I lifted my sleepy form from beneath the warm blanket to answer the telephone. A cardiologist, in an emergency room at a Boston hospital, announced that Bryn had been brought in by a friend and that her heart arrhythmia had worsened so profoundly that he feared for her life. Doctors had administered several series of medications intravenously without successfully reversing what had now become a life-threatening condition. Several times, Bryn's blood pressure had diminished so far that they could no longer palpate a readable measure. The physician explained that because my daughter had been first unconscious and later only semiconscious, the nurses had been unable, until just seconds earlier, to secure the necessary information about her family that enabled them finally to contact us.

At that moment, I thought about all the other "events" that had plagued Bryn for the previous decade as a result of this congenital heart condition, which caused erratic electrophysiological impulses to destabilize the normal pumping operation of her heart. As I pressed the physician for more precise information about the medications used, he responded impatiently, dismissing my probing and insisting he had to move quickly and experiment with another drug. In effect, he had called to ask my permission to continue a treatment that he resisted explaining and then counseled me to acquiesce immediately. Given that the other medications had actually caused her blood pressure to fall to this very dangerous level, why, I asked, would he believe at this critical moment that more of the same would save her rather than kill her? He claimed that he had no choice but to try another stimulant, even though previous "applications" had had an adverse effect. He kept citing his expertise as a specialist in this arena. I told him I wanted to share what he had said with my wife.

As I reviewed his commentary with Samahria while he waited at the other end of the line, I became even more doubtful about the merits of his logic. We had spent countless nights with Bryn in the past, endeavoring to help her endure episodes of disabling chest pain, shortness of breath, vertigo, and a foreboding sense of suffocation for hours, even days at a time. Hospitalization had frequently caused her further bodily trauma, so Bryn often elected to remain at home, during which time we would help her put her body into a state of deep relaxation and encourage her to send her heart meditative messages to correct its own rhythm. Sometimes, these efforts succeeded in breaking the arrhythmia. At other times, she had to let the chaotic heart irregularity run its difficult and at times frightening course.

Samahria listened attentively to my review of the doctor's perspective and then, like me, vacillated between agreeing and disagreeing with the cardiologist.

Finally, I blurted, "No! Please! We do not want you to give her more medication. We must give her body a chance to correct itself, not overwhelm her with more drugs."

"Sir, if this were my daughter, I would hit her with more medication right now. I don't know why the previous drugs haven't been effective, but we must try something else."

"I understand. But I still want us to give her body time to stabilize."

"We don't have that time," he insisted.

"Can you assure me," I asked, "that this next drug will not knock her pressure down further and throw her into cardiac arrest?"

"No, I cannot give you that assurance. The situation is critical."

"I hear you. So again, please leave her alone. Give her heart a chance to stabilize by itself."

"I'll follow your instructions, but I want you to know I disagree vehemently and so would any other attending cardiologist."

"Thank you." I paused to consider our next move. "We're three hours from Boston," I said. "We don't dare get into our car right now. We'll stay put, glued to this phone. I ask only that you call us in five or ten minutes to tell us how she is doing. Okay?"

He agreed and hung up the phone. As I sat on the floor in the blackness of the night, I realized that I had just made a decision that could result in my daughter's death. Had I let the doctor decide, whatever happened would certainly not have been my responsibility. I kept reviewing everything he had asserted. I questioned my own logic ruthlessly. Had I been presumptuous and dangerously shortsighted? Several times, I considered calling him back, but in each instance I resisted the temptation. I wanted Bryn to live and believed the elimination of more intervention by medication would give her the best chance, perhaps the only chance. In the end, Samahria and I stayed with that decision and waited by the phone. Neither of us ever turned a light on. Perhaps we both found serenity in the darkness.

About fifteen minutes later, the phone rang.

"She's stabilized just a bit. Her pressure came up enough to get a reading. Now, it's time to give her that additional medication."

"Sorry, Doctor, I draw the opposite conclusion. She's doing it on her own. Let's trust her body to bring her back, especially given the initial adverse effects of the medications. We're thankful for your caring and for what you're doing to help her. But, in this case, I believe doing less will be helping her more. Okay?"

"No. Not okay. I don't agree. But, as you've instructed, we will hold where we are and I will call you back in another ten or twenty minutes unless something critical occurs."

Again, Samahria and I waited in the darkness. I kept talking to God, intimating that I would be grateful for any sign or guidance. In the absence of any identifiable directive, I wondered what possessed me to hold steadfast even after the last phone call. It was logic, I decided finally. What I was doing just made good sense to me, and that would have to be enough, even if I stood alone in the face of much more seasoned and expert advice. I realized as well that if my conclusion proved faulty, I would have to live with the outcome the rest of my life. And what about Bryn? She had relied on us to help her.

The ring of the phone shattered the silence.

"Hello. How is she?" I blurted anxiously.

"Better yet," came the answer. "Her pressure is seventy-five over fifty-two and it's coming up. I think she's going to be okay."

To my surprise, the doctor counseled yet again that he administer intravenous medication. And again I vetoed his advice. Minutes later, Samahria and I jumped into the van and headed toward Boston, ultimately bringing Bryn back home the following day.

Throughout the entire process, Pop, I kept thinking that if Bryn died, at least we would have not left anything unsaid between us. As a result of her precarious physiology, we had always treated each moment with her as singular and extraordinary — saying each good-bye as if it could be the last. Consequently, we kept up-to-date, telling her, often copiously, how much we loved and treasured her in every encounter. Bryn helped us in a tangible way to learn and then bring alive one of the fundamental principles we teach in our programs: the importance and value of being present, mindful, and conscious in the moment.

The first sliver of sun had just appeared over the horizon, and I knew you might be waking soon. I leaned against the wood banister in the hallway, giving myself a few extravagantly extended seconds in which to deliberate on the many lessons I've derived from interactions with our children. Raun, like Bryn, has been a prodigious teacher. Initially challenged by autism, he taught me to notice and celebrate even the simplest of actions — such as looking into someone else's eyes, eating with a fork, verbalizing a single word and understanding its meaning, or just reaching out to hold another person's hand. For most of us, such actions represent simple, everyday occurrences. But for Raun, years ago, mastering each of these tasks required him to make almost superhuman efforts, reaching for the stars in defiance of his mysterious neurological malady. Every time I witness a child touch the face of her mother or father with apparent tenderness, I marvel at the complexity and magnificence of such an action. Whenever you have taken my hand, Pop, or permitted me to take yours, I have experienced a similar sense of awe and wonder.

Shifting my attention, I peered through the balcony windows at the rising sun. The molten, shimmering light danced like windblown flames, devouring the treetops until a sensuous golden ball, wrapped in a blanket of transparent clouds, made its full appearance above the tree line. As I watched, I realized that nothing remains static or at rest, that everything changes just as you and I do. In the distance, an array of reds, pinks, purples, and yellows died into each other and gave birth to an entirely new palette of subtle hues too numerous to categorize or name. Although I often paused momentarily to view the birth of a new day through these same windows in the early morning hours before beginning my daily exercise regime, your presence in my home inspired me to slow down from my usual fast-paced routines — to slow down, even stop, and open my eyes wider to the moment-by-moment unfolding magnificence surrounding me. Although I had slept only sporadically throughout the night, I felt energized and nourished by these quiet moments of reflection.

When I arrived at your room and gazed through the opened door, I saw both you and Rosie asleep on the bed. Time appeared at once seamless and endless and yet limited — so very limited. As I gazed at your face, I knew our time together was speeding to a close. I wanted to capture and savor each moment. I also told myself I had to let go of each of those moments at the same time. And yet, like a camera recording a special event, I tried to burn the image of your presence in my mind. I would not forget. I would always remember.

Rather than disturb either of you, I sat on the floor in the hallway and listened to you both breathe, your rhythms seemingly synchronized. I patterned my own respiration to match yours. With each breath in, I said a prayer for life. With each breath out, I whispered a prayer about letting go. I must have spent thirty minutes breathing in concert with both of you.

Rosie fractured the tranquillity. "Abie, what's the matter?"

I jumped up and knocked on the doorjamb. "Can I come in?" I asked.

"Yes," you answered in a breathy voice, moaning as you awakened.

"Are you in pain?" Rosie asked.

"Yes."

I moved quickly toward our arsenal of painkillers and removed two capsules for you. Rosie opened the water bottle and helped you swallow the pills.

"Twenty minutes and you should feel a difference," I assured you. Your eyes closed. "Do you want to sleep more?" I asked.

You patted the mattress beside you, gesturing to me to sit with you. I took your left hand with both my hands and squeezed it lightly. You pushed out a faint smile. Rosie rose from the bed, shook her head sadly as she stared at us, then walked quietly toward the bathroom. I asked your permission to talk. When you nodded your approval, I shared with you the reflections I had had in the hallway. You opened your eyes and smiled at me a second time, this expression lighting up your face much more than the previous one.

"Still got a bit of life left in you, huh?" I observed. As you started to move your lips, I could hear the suction made by your tongue as you released it from your upper palette. "Pop, your mouth is so dry. How about a little water?" You shook your head, declining my offer. "Okay, what about if I touch something wet to your lips and your tongue so you won't be so dry? It will help you be more comfortable." No reply. I kept searching for a way to make the intake of water or liquids appealing to you. "Okay, how about some hot and sour soup to moisten your mouth? You had a few sips yesterday. And, hey, you couldn't kid me — I know you liked what you tasted. What do you say? Two minutes and I could return." You surprised me by nodding. "Super!" I exclaimed, feeling I had hit the jackpot. "One hot and sour coming up. While I'm in the kitchen, what about some chocolate cake?"

Rosie, who had been listening to my commentary, re-entered the room and shot me a warning glance. Ignoring it, I asked playfully, "How about you, Rosie? Want some chocolate cake for breakfast?" She shook her head and went about the business of putting her clothes away in the bureau drawer.

When I returned from the kitchen, you had fallen asleep again. I stood beside your bed, soup in one hand, cake in the other. Rosie nudged you awake. "Bears brought the soup." As soon as you opened your eyes, you demonstrated genuine interest in my presence. We propped several pillows behind your head, and Rosie proceeded to feed you. You attempted to take the spoon from her but abandoned the effort when you realized how much energy was required to feed yourself. Rather than resist being fed, you smiled momentarily at her, raising your eyebrows to indicate your readiness to eat.

We both cheered each spoonful you accepted.

"You're doing great, Pop," I said. "A class act."

"Never mind the class act," Rosie interjected. "Abie, this will help you, make you comfortable and stronger." You peered at me as she finished her sentence, as if pondering her words. I believed that you wanted to be more comfortable, but I wondered whether you wanted to get stronger. Rosie lured you into consuming five full spoonfuls before you quit.

Moments later, I broke off a piece of chocolate cake and offered it to you. You declined by turning your head. "Then how about if I eat it?" I asked. You dismissed the cake with a wave of your hand. "I'll take that to be your approval." With mock ceremony, I fed myself the cake with obvious and sincere pleasure. I don't think I have ever before or since indulged myself by making such a sensuous dessert a breakfast appetizer at six-thirty in the morning. When you eyed me with obvious amusement and what I speculated might be curiosity, I made you a second offer. Any nourishment, even a decadent concoction supposedly so low on the food chain as chocolate cake, would probably be better for you than zero food and the starvation your body bespoke. Too weak to motion broadly to me, you cupped the fingers of your left hand affirmatively, glancing at Rosie, then winking at me. I deposited a modest piece of cake in your mouth. At first, you sucked on the cake like a lollipop; clearly, you enjoyed the flavors oozing into your mouth. Finally, you began to chew slowly.

"Want more?" I asked.

"No," you answered. Nevertheless, you accepted my proposal to drink some water to help you digest the cake.

"Wow, Pop, your first real meal in a week! I'm proud of you." You reached your hand toward me, but before I could grab it, you dropped your arm limply on the bed and drifted off to sleep. I took your hand anyway, although I don't believe you noticed. I flashed a "thumbs up" sign to Rosie, who shook her head, simultaneously approving and disapproving of the edibles you had just consumed. Obviously, she would have preferred for you to eat a plate of vegetables.

Rosie and I had different goals. Her goal was to get food into you so that you would live longer and keep death at a distance. I wanted to help you be as comfortable as possible. We both watched studiously for any signals you might make to indicate how we could best ease your physical distress. I laughed softly as I anticipated providing you with another culinary taboo later in the day — the infamous barbecued ribs.

At midday, I alerted Zoe and other staff members that

Kenny, Denise, and Jessica would be visiting. Because of the parade of people on campus attending programs, the Institute staff tend to be protective of our privacy and the area around our residence, and I wanted to ensure that my family members would be recognized and invited immediately into our home.

As I contemplated their upcoming arrival, I recalled the very peculiar conversation I had had with Kenny the previous night. Initially, I had explained that he, Denise, and their sons could visit at any time of day or night and stay for as long as they wished. I wanted him, as well as all my other siblings and their families, to feel warmly welcomed. Then I made a single request, which I had not anticipated would be controversial.

"Kenny, you refer to Samahria as 'Suzi,'" I began. "I understand that's how you've known her in the past. But for fifteen years now, everyone refers to her by the name she chose for herself. Here at the Institute and among all our friends, she's Samahria. I would very much appreciate your calling her by the name she cherishes."

"I'll think about it," Kenny said.

"Well, while you're thinking about it, I would be grateful if you called me by my name, Bears — Samahria's nickname for me for over a quarter of a century. It's the name that feels like home to me now. The name Barry only appears on my books these days. What do you think? Okay?" No response. "Kenny, are you still there?"

"Yes," he declared flatly.

"How's that sound? Especially with Samahria. I'd really appreciate it."

Another expanse of silence. "I guess you'll have to wait until we get there," Kenny responded, "and see what name I use to know what I have decided."

"Seriously?" I asked. "Why would it matter how you refer to us, especially if we've made the request?"

"Actually, calling you by those names would be like endorsing your work and what you do at the Institute. Frankly, I don't want to endorse or support anything you and your wife are doing."

"Wow!" I said, flabbergasted by his comment. "Kenny, I'm not asking you to endorse or support anything. I'm just asking for a personal courtesy, if not for me, then at least for my wife."

"As I said," he insisted, "you'll find out my response by seeing how I address you when I get there."

"Okay," I said, taking a deep breath while mentally instructing myself to let go of the discussion and any need for a positive response. "Frankly, I don't understand," I continued, "but I hear you. Hey, have a safe trip up and no matter how you choose to address us, please know you are totally welcome here." When I hung up the phone, I wondered if I had made "peace at any price." No, I reassured myself. Pick only the battles worth fighting. Let him call me whatever he wanted.

Kenny, Denise, and Jessica arrived early that afternoon. Zoe brought them into our home and alerted me to their presence. When I greeted them in the center hall, they appeared cautious, inquiring immediately about your health. How were you? Could they see you? None of them addressed me by name.

"Of course you can see him," I said. "As I mentioned to you this morning on the phone, he's still in pain but clearly more at ease than in the hospital. We're all just doing our best to make him comfortable. In fact, he winked at us this morning. I took that to be a hopeful sign."

"Also," I continued, "as I told Kenny on the phone, Samahria and I want all of you to feel totally at home anytime you're here. So know that you have absolute access, day or night. And I'd be happy to give you keys. If there is anything Samahria, Zoe, I, or anyone else can do to help make all this easier for you, please tell us."

"I love your father and mother," Zoe chimed in. "If you ever have trouble getting in touch with Bears, if he's teaching or doing a session, just call me. The office can always reach me."

Kenny dipped his head and murmured, "Thank you."

Denise added a word of appreciation as Jessica gazed toward the stairs. The three of them appeared attentive and courteous, but they cloistered themselves together by the door. Except for a brief time during Bryn's wedding, they had not visited our home in over a decade. In an effort to make my hospitality more concrete, I turned to Jessica first, opened my arms, and hugged her. She permitted my embrace, though her body stiffened. I smiled, trying to pierce the wall between us. She did not return the smile. Pivoting to the left, I embraced Denise, who angled her upper torso toward me for a few seconds and then pulled away abruptly. When I hugged Kenny, he patted me once on the shoulder, and then he, too, slid quickly from my grasp, all the while maintaining an intensely serious expression.

"Come on up," I said smiling. "I'll show you which room they're in."

Rosie, who had been watching from the balcony inside the center hall, greeted everyone from the top of the staircase. "Your father's been dozing. He just woke up a few minutes ago."

We followed Rosie to your room. Kenny, Denise, and Jessica gathered by your bedside. You looked up at them and nodded.

"How you feeling?" Kenny asked with warmth and concern.

"Better," you said in a faint, raspy voice. "Better than in the hospital. We've been treated like visiting royalty. Sit. Sit."

"Hi, Dad," Denise said, smiling brightly at you.

Jessica stood nearby silently, then kissed your cheek.

As everyone sat down, you closed your eyes and drifted back to sleep. Kenny eyed me with concern, then glanced at Rosie. Clearly, Pop, you appeared very fragile, more fragile than even a few days before, your breathing pattern more erratic as your visible life-form diminished. And yet at the same time, a sense of peacefulness pervaded the room in stark contrast to the blatant suffering you had endured while captive in that hospital chamber.

"He'll probably awaken in a few minutes," I speculated in a soft voice. "That's been the pattern yesterday, through the night, and this morning. I'm sure you'll all want some time alone with him, so I'll go now. Do you want me to get you guys some food or drinks?"

"We just had breakfast, but thanks," responded Kenny.

"We're fine," Denise agreed.

"In about half an hour, I have to facilitate a segment in one of the Institute's programs. But, until then, if you need me, I'll be downstairs in the office. Samahria and Zoe will be available, too. Raun will be back soon, and when Tayo comes home from school, he'll be happy to help. If you need anything, let him know."

As I exited, Rosie followed me out of the room. "Hey, you stay."

"I don't want to. Let them have their time with their father. I'll go downstairs with you."

We walked together down the hallway. "Something up?" I asked.

"No," Rosie said unconvincingly. "And don't ask me any more questions."

"Okay. No more questions for now." When I noticed Rosie's eyes filling with tears, I stopped and hugged her.

"You can cry," I whispered.

"I don't want to," Rosie insisted.

"Pop wouldn't mind," I maintained.

"I know. I mind," she said emphatically. "We have to be strong — for him."

"Crying doesn't mean we're not strong. It's just our way of expressing a big emotion, a big sensation. Remember when Pop first arrived here, he cried his appreciation. It was a powerful feeling for him, Rosie. Not weakness. Strength."

She glanced at me while wiping her tears. "You have a positive spin for everything, don't you?"

Her comment startled me. I thought about the menacing sense of pessimism and fear that I used to feel, like a personality bias genetically encoded during what I now identify affectionately as my formative years. I had worked on myself so intently these last thirty years, reeducating myself systematically as best I could in order to see opportunities where I once saw only problems and to ferret out the pearls and diamonds rather than focus on holes and injustices.

"Rosie, to me it doesn't feel like I have positive answers for everything because now it's my natural propensity. Purposely, with a biased intention, I now try to frame these kinds of events so that I can find the wonder in them. Sometimes I have to really stretch to hit the mark, and sometimes I miss it. With you, sweet lady, and with Pop, I'm going to do my best to hit the mark and see everything as an opportunity."

"Well, you're doing just fine — so far!"

After facilitating the afternoon class at the Option House (the Institute's principal teaching facility for larger groups), I jogged back to the main building, where we live and where over thirty staff members work. I entered our quarters and took the stairs three at a time in an effort to get to your side as quickly as possible. Kenny, Denise, Jessica, and Rosie sat near you as you slept.

"How's he been doing?" I whispered.

"Good. He talked a little. When the pain increased," Rosie continued, "I gave him more medication."

"Bears, is that you? Are you back?" you said, suddenly awake, a bit winded from the effort it took for you to speak.

I moved to your side and took your hand. "Yes, sir! I'm back. Couldn't keep away from you."

"How did your class go?" you asked.

"Hey, I'm impressed, Pop. You're still connected to the activities in the world around you. That's a good sign."

"What do you mean?" you said, a bit feistier than previously. "I may be sick — but, my boy, I'm not senile."

"So we've noticed." I kissed you on the cheek and then continued. "Class went well. Today we focused on authenticity, bringing down walls between each other, opening our hearts."

You signaled me deftly with your eyes, which I assumed meant that you wanted me to conclude my commentary as soon as humanly possible. Although throughout the past two years you had finally invited me to talk more about my work in our private conversations, I thought your expression indicated your growing concern about my sharing too much with my siblings present. After all, my last major "sharing" with all of them present had apparently violated family, and maybe even cultural, taboos so profoundly that our dynamics as a family had been fractured irrevocably.

SIXTEEN

It happened about eighteen years ago.

Out of respect for you and in response to your specific requests, Pop, one day each year, the day of our annual family gatherings, I would censor myself — omitting thoughts, observations, and questions I had in order to "keep the peace," as you had christened it. Be polite, chatty, and congenial; "do not question anyone about anything personal," you had decreed. "Do not talk about your work at the Option Institute. Do not discuss whether or not happiness and love are choices." You had been very precise in indicating all that you wanted from me, leaving me very few conversational options.

These annual gatherings meant so much to you. To me, they felt like contained volcanoes, with so much energy and so many issues boiling beneath a surface camouflaged by stylized smiles and frivolous chitchat. When I challenged the real worth of such conclaves and suggested these events could be wonderful forums for everyone to say what they felt (including you, Pop) and to get to know more about each other, you cut me short, insisting that I deliver on your emphatic and clearly articulated requests without further discussion. I acquiesced, attending as well as hosting those events within your guidelines as a way to demonstrate my respect for you. I did so, that is, until the infamous eruption.

We had congregated at Kenny and Denise's house. It was summertime, and all the families were in attendance — you and Rosie, Kenny and Denise with their children, Jessica and Frank with their family, Alan and Margie with their son and daughter, David and Eileen with their sons and, of course, Samahria and I with our brood of six critters. Most of the young children played in the swimming pool; Thea, Tayo, Ravi, and Sage joined them in water games. The adults and older children interacted informally around tables and on chairs set on the patio, as well as elsewhere in the house.

I listened as the conversation at my table focused on landscaping and furniture. During a lull when everyone sat around blank-faced, Kenny began talking about economic determinism. Within a few minutes, he and I had begun to discuss the difference between his worldview and the perspective that we explored and taught at the Institute.

Like a hawk riveted on its prey, Pop, you swooped right in, listened for a few seconds, then said to me, "C'mon, Barry, no talk about business. Or the Institute. Let's not create any conflict here; that's not necessary. Enough, okay?"

I looked up at you, smiled and said, "We were just talking — there's no conflict — at least not yet. But, sure, if you want, we can cut this discussion." I'm innocent, I could hear myself protest inside. I wanted to please you, but sometimes the dancing around real issues seemed unnecessary and silly. A kind soul at the table broke the awkward silence in the wake of your comment by introducing another subject. I stayed for a few more minutes, then excused myself. I strolled around, eavesdropping on other groups to see if I could find another place to involve myself. Finally, I decided to fill my empty glass with more soda from the kitchen. As I meandered through the den, I encountered Samahria, Bryn, and Raun sitting with Kenny's children, Craig and Lilly. I paused for a moment to listen.

Craig turned to me and said, "We don't feel that we really get to know each other when our families get together. We were just talking about it. This happens only once a year. You live so far away from us, so this is really the only time we see all of you. How can we get to know each other more?"

I remember a warning bell going off in my head. An innocent, curious teenager, Craig had just unknowingly violated your unspoken code and asked for substance. I smiled, sat down, and, unable to imagine how you, Pop, could ever view this interchange as controversial, ignored the cautionary chimes still ringing in my head and suggested we ask questions to find out about each other. Craig responded by expressing puzzlement as to why our two families, who used to spend weekends and vacations together, no longer gathered or interacted as a group except for this single day each year.

"I think the answer is rather complex, Craig," Samahria offered, "but I guess there were dynamics between us and your parents that led us to grow apart from each other. And when we moved away to Massachusetts, the opportunities to be together diminished."

"I'd like us to spend more time together," Lilly suggested.

"I used to love when we all went to that lake in Maine," Raun added, grinning about his memories.

"Given our work and the different viewpoints we live by, I'm not sure that what happened in the past will reoccur in the future," I said. "I don't know if we'll ever go to that lake again as we once did. However, we're all here right now."

Craig asked for an explanation about what we did at the Institute, unknowingly breaching yet another of your prohibitions. Nevertheless, Samahria responded cautiously but enthusiastically, giving him a brief overview of what we taught. I shared some thoughts as well. Bryn and Raun spoke about their experiences living on the Institute property, with staff and program participants housed all around them. Raun described the small herds of deer that often graze in the meadows at dusk, just outside his bedroom window.

During this exchange, I noticed Jessica's oldest daughter, Cynthia, a young woman in her early twenties, standing at the doorway, watching and listening for an extended period of time. Her continued presence surprised me because you had said, Pop, that you believed that Cynthia, like her mother, had adopted an antagonistic posture toward me, my family, and our work. My sole interaction with her had been limited to these infrequent, one-day yearly gatherings, during which time we barely spoke, so now I reconsidered that piece of secondhand information that I had heard from you and entertained the idea, as I gazed at her, that her lingering presence could suggest an ease and an openness to the discussion and to me personally.

"Cynthia," I asked, "would you like to join us?" She nodded casually and sat down next to me.

Since we had been talking expressively and personally about what each of us felt about our families and each other, sharing as well some sweet recollections of vacation highlights from past years, I searched for an opening in our conversation, wanting to invite Cynthia to join us.

"Any thoughts or feelings about what we're discussing?" I asked her.

"Why do you care?" she snapped.

Craig ignored her tone of voice. He claimed that we all cared and then, blowing me out of the water with his forthrightness, said, "I think it's fair to say we're all pretty uncomfortable when we get together like this."

"I'm not uncomfortable," Bryn noted. "I really like what we've been talking about today."

"Then how about we continue to learn more about each other as we've been doing?" I suggested. Almost everyone concurred.

Still wanting Cynthia to feel included and sensing tension in her reply to my last question, I asked, "Cynthia, how do you feel about me?"

At first, she did not respond. But then, within seconds, her face flushed rosy red and her eyes became bloodshot as she screamed, literally screamed, "To hell with you! And to hell with your questions!" Dumbfounded, I sat silent as she burst into tears and proceeded to cry boisterously. Within seconds, people had flooded the room, coming in from the yard, the kitchen, and the hallway. Raun, twelve years old at the time, surveyed all the action, grinning with excitement. He had always found the family gatherings dull, he later told me. Now, at last, he noted, something really interesting had occurred.

Cynthia rose from her chair, still crying, and dashed out of the room as everyone watched. Kenny stood by the kitchen door, visibly disturbed. David, more relaxed, stood near him.

Jessica rushed in past her daughter and glared at me antagonistically. Frank, Jessica's husband, who had been one of the first to enter the room, claimed an empty chair near Samahria and seated himself. You and Rosie charged through the hallway entrance. Alan, Margie, Eileen, Denise, and others arrived hurriedly. As the crowd grew in size, Cynthia returned to the room, still sobbing, her chest heaving up and down.

"What happened? What did you do?" you barked at me.

"I just asked her a question about how she felt about me because she seemed tense with me," I volunteered, wondering why you automatically assumed my involvement as a key figure.

"How could you?" you shouted. "We came to be together as a family. I thought you'd be big enough to respect my request and not get into these kinds of conversations!"

Jessica shook her head, narrowing her eyes. "How could you upset my daughter like this?"

I did not answer immediately. I scanned the room, wanting to stay open. "I'm not aware of having upset her," I responded softly, knowing that I subscribed to a perspective completely foreign to most of the others in the room. I believed each of us creates our own anger, frustration, or sadness. I would have loved for Cynthia to feel happy about our exchange. "I wanted to include her so she could feel a part of the conversation," I explained, "so I asked her a question, actually two questions. But apparently she didn't like the last question too much."

"That can't be the only thing that happened!" you said, Pop, shaking your head disapprovingly as you exited the room.

Rosie walked behind Cynthia and stroked her soothingly as she continued to sob.

"This is a family gathering," Kenny noted, still conspicuously distressed. "This is my house, not a place for you to do group therapy."

"Honestly," I said in a soft voice, "we weren't doing therapy; we just..."

"This is your profession," you interjected, Pop, cutting into my sentence as you returned to the den. "It's not fair of you to put people like us in this position."

"Forgive me, Pop, but I really don't understand what you mean."

Frank, who had been quietly observing, leaned forward and said, "We don't really know what happened. Why don't we give him a chance to tell us what happened?" Everyone, including me, appeared startled by his suggestion. He seemed calm, reasonable, and clearly at odds, perhaps purposely, with the current group logic. I wondered whether Frank knew more about his daughter's typical behavioral responses than anyone else in the room, except, of course, Jessica. In contrast to everyone else, he appeared neither surprised nor disturbed by what had happened.

I described the entire event from the very beginning. As I spoke, I thought about what we teach. Model the choice to be open and gentle even in the face of adversity, I advised myself. As the exchange progressed, I felt increasingly more relaxed and counseled myself over and over again, "Just love them. Have a clear intention to love them and demonstrate from that intention." After I had completed my explanation, Craig, Bryn, and Samahria concurred with what I had said, but their words had little impact on their audience.

Jessica's eyes suddenly became glazed. "You made her upset by asking her questions."

"I guess I'd have to say I don't see it that way. Questions

don't make people upset," I said. "We get ourselves upset for our own reasons. Apparently, Cynthia didn't like my last question. I had absolutely no idea — not in my wildest dreams would I have imagined Cynthia might respond in the way she did. I just wanted her to enjoy herself."

"But you did ask her a question!" you barked at me, Pop.

"Sure. I asked her a question. But that's very different than *making* her upset. If I get angry, I take responsibility for the anger. The same if I cry — because if I acknowledge that I did it, then I acknowledge I have the power to do it more or to change it. Rather than be a victim, that ownership leaves me in charge of what I think and feel. So in the end, I don't believe that I have the power to make Cynthia upset — only she has the power to do that . . . and to my mind, that's really a good thing. Otherwise, I'm in charge of her unhappiness, which leaves her with no real control over her own thoughts and feelings."

"We don't have to turn this into a psychology forum," Kenny said pointedly. "When I've finished my day at the office with my clients, I leave all that at the office. I don't take it home."

"Well, maybe that's the difference between us, Kenny," I suggested. "For me, what I live and what I teach are the same. I'm not one person with my clients and a different person at home. So in that regard, I guess I don't separate my professional life from my private life."

"Uncle Kenny," Bryn said, "Why are you rubbing your stomach?"

He glanced at her, then turned his attention back to me. "Because I'm upset, very upset. And Barry, all I hear about is what you're *thinking*. I want to know what you *feel* about all this."

"Okay, fair enough," I said. "Give me a minute to check in with myself." As I sat there, cross-legged on the ottoman, looking up at everyone, I realized I felt fine inside. No, more than just fine; I felt wonderful. Additionally, I realized that if I verbalized my internal experience, I would be damning myself as a thoughtless, uncaring person and would cross a line with my family that might be viewed as unacceptable. How could someone feel so good in the face of a young woman's angst and prolonged sobbing? Had I overdramatized the meaning of this event in my mind, or did I correctly assess the gravity and potential consequence of my response?

I knew the drill: if one person feels unhappy than all of us are supposed to feel unhappy to show how much we care. Although most of us want to be happy and feel a sense of peace, unhappiness (or feeling bad) rates much higher as the cultural symbol of caring and compassion. To violate such a primal principle of human decency could result in banishment. Feel bad, really bad, and maybe we'll forgive you. Feel good, especially when you're not supposed to, and, zap, we fry you! Although I wanted to respect my family, I knew I had to be true to myself and my feelings. I looked around the room slowly, even cautiously. And then, in a soft voice, I said, "In truth, I feel good, really good inside."

I could hear the moans around the room. Kenny grimaced. You shook your head disapprovingly.

"That's so insensitive," Jessica proclaimed. "What kind of person are you?"

Samahria jumped to her feet suddenly and addressed everyone in the room simultaneously. "You have never understood him. You have never appreciated him. And you will never really value and appreciate him. I have listened to you talk to him in this critical way for years. I, for one, don't want to listen to this any longer." She left the room, followed by Bryn and Raun.

"Well, it seems like my family no longer wants to be here," I said. "So I'll be leaving, too." I stood up and began hugging the people around me. Jessica walked away, as did Kenny and Denise. I walked over to Cynthia and took her hands. "I'm sorry this experience evolved as it did. I never had any intention of upsetting you or putting you on the spot. I wish you the best — and can I give you a hug?" She approved my request, though she held herself stiffly as I embraced her. I located Jessica standing alone outside. I shared with her what I had said to Cynthia. Making no response, she moved away from me. I thanked Frank for his evenhanded comment and gave him a hug. He gave me the warmest hug I had ever received from him.

As we began our long drive home, everyone chattered incessantly about their perceptions and feelings. Bryn said, "Popi, you looked so calm, and they looked so angry. I got real scared; I thought something bad might happen to you."

"You didn't have to worry," I responded.

"I don't want to ever go there again," she declared. "I don't think we should be with people like that; they were so mean to you."

Raun beamed. "I had the best time. I didn't get scared. I liked listening. Do you know what David said to Eileen in the dining room?" Samahria and I shook our heads. "He said that the whole thing was ridiculous, that everyone in the room wanted you, Popi, to walk on eggshells so they wouldn't feel uncomfortable. Even I understood what that meant."

"And do you know what Grandpa said to me when he hugged me?" Bryn asked. "He said he wanted me to know how much he really respected you, Popi."

"Wouldn't it have been nice for him to say that in front of his other children and grandchildren?" Samahria said. "Bears, how do you feel?"

"I feel good actually. I keep thinking about how they viewed everything. I'm definitely the bad guy, and I will always be remembered as the bad guy. Probably nothing I will ever say in the future will change that impression. I assume they're actively reinforcing that perspective with each other right now. So, I guess for me, the lesson is to let go. Being maligned..."

"What's that mean?" asked Sage, who had remained relatively silent during this conversation, having been swimming while most of this event took place.

"That was good, honey. Keep asking about words you don't understand. That's the way you'll learn English," Samahria said. Ten-year-old Sage, whose adoption had not yet been finalized, had come from El Salvador to live with us only about five months earlier. "'Maligned' is when someone says critical or judgmental things about you that you don't think are true."

"And in this case," I offered, "their view of me probably reinforced what they thought anyway but had never expressed. In ten years, in fifty years, or whatever, when they'll recall this incident, they'll most likely remember me as having done something terribly wrong. There's no way for me to reclaim my good name, so to speak. I knew I was digging my hole deeper every time I answered a question. My challenge from today is to let go and find a way to be totally at peace no matter what anyone made up about me."

Samahria touched my arm solicitously, tears filling her eyes. "I never, ever, want to sit and listen to people talk about you like that. They don't see you for who you are — and they don't want to, either. I am so sorry you had to go through that scene. I really wanted this to be sweet and easy. People have a lot of trouble with directness."

"I'm fine; really, I am," I assured her. "I'm afraid we don't just live in another state; we live on another planet."

Samahria relaxed back into her seat, exhausted, and closed her eyes. Within moments she fell asleep. We had talked for almost two hours. Everyone else, with the exception of Bryn, dozed as we headed out to open country and the Berkshire Mountains. During the remainder of our drive, Bryn and I talked more about "letting go." In fact, she mentored me, asking useful questions like the ones she had heard Samahria and me ask her when she had experienced confusion and distress. For the very first time ever, my daughter stepped forward and became a powerful friend and resource, helping me to sort out my thoughts. It would be the beginning of a lovely new dimension to our parent-child relationship.

Funny, Pop, years ago, when our family took extended car trips across the United States and through various European countries, Bryn would be the only one who remained awake to keep me company. As Samahria and the other children slept, we would have discussions about life, love, and world events, much like the conversations I once had with Jessica eons ago. Except that Bryn, soon to enter college, wanted not only to talk about everything on her mind and in her heart but also to know what others thought and felt.

The following evening I called you, jumping immediately into the subject I intended to address. I felt the line I had crossed with my family on the previous day had been the same line I had crossed with you. I had decided I did not want to ever again muzzle myself or disguise what I really thought or felt, even if that meant others might abandon me. If I could have pled with you, I would have asked you to simply love me as I am, not as you wanted me to be. If I could have begged, that would have been my prayer. But I knew I didn't want to beg. I wanted us to stand together on equal footing. Yes, of course, you were the father and I gave you my respect and loyalty as my father. However, I had to find a way to do that without giving up myself in the process.

"Pop, yesterday at Kenny's was a fiasco. I have truly, sincerely, with the best of intentions, tried to conform to your wishes — stifling myself, smothering my thoughts and feelings so you and others in our family don't get upset. I'm just not very good at it. And when I stumble over the line and get too personal or too real, everybody freaks out!" I paused to see if you had a response. "Pop, I want to continue talking. Okay?"

"Okay," you said.

"There's so much stuff beneath the surface, and my doing your version of 'best behavior' doesn't bring any of us closer together. Everything just festers beneath the surface. When I lock up my thoughts and emotions, I feel like I'm cutting out my heart at the same time. I just can't be part of that game anymore. It doesn't make sense. I'm totally authentic at the Institute, with friends, with my children, and the bottom line is that I am no longer willing to live any differently with you — you, specifically. So I want you to know that from now on I will say what I think, talk about what is meaningful to me, and ask questions when they come to mind. I guess you have to decide whether you want to see me and be with me as I am doing this."

There was no quick response. Then you cleared your throat and said, "I still want to see you. You be the way you want to be."

"Thanks," I said. "Actually, I wasn't sure what your answer would be." I felt relieved. I had made peace with giving up my siblings if they no longer wanted to be in my life, but I had not reconciled your absence if you had chosen to walk away. Although we did not develop an easy parent-child partnership over the next decade, we had, nonetheless, opened the doorway to more honest communication.

Now I sat at your bedside in my home, holding your hand during these final days of your life. Given our history, Pop, how amazing it was that you sought my assistance in the face of this life-threatening illness. How truly wondrous that you subsequently solicited and enjoyed the feisty, probing talks we have had. And, finally, Pop, how startling and delightful that you have allowed me to love you and provide you with this safety net.

I looked over at Kenny and Denise and Jessica. They did not appear any friendlier toward me now than they had at the end of that day almost two decades earlier. They just looked older and more tired. "Love them anyway." These words from a poem kept echoing in my head.

Kenny, Denise, and Jessica stayed at a local motel that night. After visiting with you again on the following day, they regrouped at the front door, about to return to their homes in New Jersey and Pennsylvania.

"Call us if he gets any worse," Kenny instructed, "even in the middle of the night. We'll come right back up. Okay?"

"Definitely," I assured him. "I know he looks terrible. I know there's the pain; it certainly hasn't gone away. And if he keeps refusing to take in food and fluids, then he can't last much longer." I paused for a moment, reflecting on my own

commentary. "But you know, since he's been here, I detect a different energy coming from him. More relaxed. More peaceful."

"We've noticed that, too," Kenny conceded.

"I don't know if that means he will live a moment longer,"
I added, "but at least it will be sweeter for him. I'm glad you
guys came. I know it means so much to him. I will call, and
you feel free to call as often as you want. Whenever you want.
It's no problem. Between me, Samahria, Rosie, Zoe, Bryn, and
Raun, there will always be someone here to update you. We also
installed a telephone in Pop's room. I'm sure if he's awake, he'll
want to talk to you himself."

After they had said their good-byes to Samahria and me, I
realized that the three of them had managed to address us on
numerous occasions over the preceding two days without ever
using our names. Without a doubt, that must have required real
effort and conscientiousness! After some reflection, I appreciated that effort, manufacturing a friendly version of the
unfolding universe: If my siblings and sister-in-law couldn't
give us what we wanted, apparently they had also endeavored
to steer clear of what we didn't want. I decided to go with this
"make-believe" and construe their avoidance of our names,
especially my brother's, as a step toward us rather than away
from us. I chuckled, aware that I had simply guessed, opti-
mistically, at what had transpired.

People often act without explanation. Even when asked,
people may lie about or deny their motives or secret thoughts
or the real meaning of their actions. I once taught an ongoing
seminar about self-empowerment to over fifty people who had
agreed that in the ensuing four hours no one in the course
would lie. They might choose to be silent, but they would not
misrepresent or be fraudulent in their communications.

Within the first two hours, we unearthed twenty-three lies told by twenty-one participants even though everyone, with sincere intent, had committed to saying only what they knew to be true. What folks discovered was their systematic training to lie, either to protect themselves or, a more kindly motive, to protect someone else from being hurt by their words or expressed thoughts (for example, telling people they are attractive or intelligent even though one secretly holds contrary judgments). Their transgressions exposed, the group howled playfully, then recommitted to truth-telling for the remaining two hours. Having been encouraged to challenge each other's statements, participants uncovered twelve more new tall tales told to the group in the next forty minutes.

Was this an unusual group? Not really. Were the lies the result of educational programming? Definitely. Systemic? You bet. People don't lie because they're bad. They lie with the best of intentions. However, the result is that all of this misinformation builds walls between people, between parents and children, between brothers and sisters.

In the end, we are left alone with our observations, hypotheses, and suppositions. I once consulted with the partners of a prestigious law firm who struggled uneasily with their awareness about jury trials: juries never pass verdicts based on what is true or what really happened; they pass judgments based on what they assess to be true (the *appearance* of truth) or what they *think* really happened. Thus, the innocent can be convicted and the guilty go free. We make up beliefs all the time, even what we hold to be true and what to be false.

When I asked my brother why he did not address us by our chosen names, I would never in a million years have predicted the answer he gave. After he explained that he believed acceding to my request meant endorsing our work, could I trust this communication? When he addressed me neither as "Barry" nor as "Bears" during his visit — did that constitute a compliment or ridicule? Will I ever get to know the truth? For the moment, I will ascribe to him the best of intentions until I know differently. But even if he shares with me at some future date another motive behind his leaving me with no name for two whole days, can I count on the veracity of that comment?

Why am I putting these musings in this book about you, Pop, and our relationship? Because after the "eruption," being authentic and sharing honest thoughts and feelings continued to be implicitly prohibited in our family. Although you had recently broken down your walls with me, my siblings had obviously kept theirs intact, at least with me, probably with each other, and most likely with you and Rosie. As a result, rather than conversing openheartedly, they engaged in conversational charades and verbal gymnastics, as Kenny did in that enigmatic telephone conversation with me.

I returned to your bedside after my siblings left and watched you sleep for several minutes, debating whether or not to wake you in order to offer you some water. As I turned to leave, you called my name.

"Bears."

"Hi. How are you doing?"

"I'm very tired. Have they left?"

"Yes," I said.

"Good." You paused, then sighed. "It felt like too much. Too much."

"Well, you can rest now. How about I give you some water, you take a nap, and then Rosie, Samahria, and I will come back?"

You nodded as I opened the bottle of water, lifted your head with my hand, and poured the clear liquid into your mouth. "Good," I said as you took a gulp. "You'll feel better if you're not dehydrated. How about another two sips?" You swallowed two more mouthfuls of water. "Fantastic," I said. "How about two more?" You pushed the bottle away, dropped your head back into the pillow, and closed your eyes. "Okay, Pop, I'm just trying to help." You nodded your head again. "I'm going to let you rest. Listen, if the water doesn't quite do it for you, we can try some of your favorite soup later. And, guess what? We have some ribs! Remember, Pop, this is heaven. And these ribs are the best ribs in the country. Just for you. You get everything you want here." I tapped your chest affectionately. My enthusiasm softened, melting into gratitude for your presence. "I feel honored to have you here, Pop; really, I do."

You opened your eyes, looked at me, and took my hand. As you touched me, I could feel a certain strength in your grasp. "I can't thank you enough," you said. Your eyes filled with tears. You looked off in the distance for a moment, then fixed your eyes directly on mine with notable determination. "We're still having our adventure, aren't we?"

"Yes sir, we're still having our adventure."

In the evening, you defied your profound exhaustion by allowing me to hold your head as you sipped some more hot and sour soup, then took three good bites off a succulent barbecued rib. Samahria cheered you. Rosie, perhaps clinging to a vision of steamed vegetables followed by a fistful of antioxidant vitamins and natural herbs, congratulated you in a subdued voice as she sneered playfully at the meat. Bryn, Raun, Sage, and Tayo visited with you in short bursts throughout the evening, each one expressing concerns about wanting to visit you without intruding.

While sitting beside you and stroking your arm, Bryn said, "Hey, Grandpa, I'm a grandchild, which means you can throw me out anytime you want. You don't have to stand on ceremony. You point to the door and I'm out of here."

You lifted your thumb and pointed it in the direction of the door. When Bryn jumped up, you grabbed her arm and said, "Just testing. Stay. I like it when you're here."

Rosie remained glued to your bedside throughout the evening — mother hen, knight in golden armor, and, most notably, your guardian angel. You appeared content, Pop, and more visibly interested now in the activity around you. Later, when Kenny and Jessica telephoned, you waved the receiver away, indicating you felt too tired to talk. I gave them each a complete update on your condition, highlighting your surprising willingness to ingest some liquids and solid food.

Samahria and I maintained our vigil through the third night. Every time I walked down the hallway, the moon outside the window lighting my path, I whispered a thank-you to God for giving us this sacred time with you.

When I entered your room at five in the morning, I encountered Rosie with her eyes wide open.

"Don't you ever sleep?" I asked her in a hushed voice.

"No. It's none of your business, anyway," she asserted with a smile. "He's sleeping more comfortably tonight. I think he's getting stronger. Bears, did you research another local oncologist to take him on as a patient?"

"Snagged an even better one today. Highly recommended. Zoe talked to him. She liked his style. Remember, she was a nurse, so she knows what questions to ask. Said he had a big heart. We only want people with big hearts around Pop. I will talk with the doctor myself in the morning."

"We have to start the chemotherapy."

"Rosie, sweetie, he's not ready. He couldn't handle it. He can barely move. And who knows whether he'd want it?"

"He'll want it!" Rosie declared. Such a force of nature! I knew she would fight the good fight right to the end. She loved you and would move heaven and earth to save you. I admired her spunk, Pop, and found myself touched deeply by her persistence in doing battle with your cancer.

"What if I make an appointment later next week? I promise to do this. Let's give it some more time. See how he does. See what *he* wants. Then we can go from there. What do you think?" I reached across your sleeping form and took her hand. "What about it? A deal?"

"A deal," she concurred.

We both looked at you simultaneously. Although your breathing seemed labored, I noted the relaxed expression on your face. Finally the medication, or the medication in conjunction with an attitudinally friendly environment, had succeeded in softening the impact of the pain, allowing you to rest quite soundly.

When I checked you later in the morning, to my surprise you were sitting in an upright position, leaning against a pile of pillows that Rosie had stacked behind you. Your eyes seemed clearer than in the preceding days. You said a sprightly hello.

"Good morning," I said. "You look like you slept better last night."

"I did," you said. "Could you help me with something?"

"Sure. What can I do?" I asked.

"I want to go to the bathroom."

Rosie beamed at your statement. You had not been out of bed for three days, using a bottle to relieve yourself.

"You got it," I snapped. "Let's see if we can guide your legs to the floor, then get you standing. Okay?" I slipped the blanket off your body. Your weight loss in the previous week had taken its toll. Not only had your legs narrowed, but the muscles of your thighs and calves had shrunk noticeably. The skin encasing them draped loosely over the bony portion of your legs, the elasticity now gone. It was hard to believe that just three weeks earlier, you had been pumping iron at the gym. "Here, put your arms around my neck, and when I stand, I'll pull you up." You followed my instructions and helped lift yourself, though you tottered once up on your feet. I slid around toward your back and put my arms around your upper torso. "Got you," I said triumphantly. Then I slid my feet beneath your feet. "Ready?"

"Yes," you responded, focusing intently on keeping yourself upright as we began to shuffle toward the bathroom just across the hall from your room. Each time I picked up one foot, you did the same.

"One step at a time," I said. "We're doing great." Slowly, we made our way across the six-foot expanse separating us from our destination. Supporting your weight, I realized, as I had realized earlier in our work with Raun, that even such a simple, everyday action as your walk across the hall, an activity most of us take for granted, requires strength, mobility, determination, and, in this case, a helping hand to accomplish. We were climbing Mount Everest, Pop, and I felt privileged to join you on the ascent. "Two more feet and we're there," I announced proudly. "You're doing it. You are one amazing guy... or, as Raun might say, 'one amazing dude.'"

"Some dude," you said, amused by the reference.

"Now, I'm going to turn you around by the toilet. Do you want to do this standing or sitting?"

"Standing."

We stood together and waited, and waited, and waited, but you did not urinate.

"Okay," I said with conviction. "How about both of us just stare at the water in the bowl and imagine a steady stream of liquid coming out of your body and cascading into the pool below, like a glorious fountain somewhere in Europe? Just keep visualizing this easy flow and the graceful splashing..."

"Wait," you said, turning your head and peering at me out of the corner of your eye. "How about you just shut up and let me pee?" We both laughed, and sure enough, you started to urinate.

Later, after you returned to your room, I found Rosie standing alone in the hallway. She stood with her back to me. I could see her body shake as she cried. I hugged her from behind.

"This is not right for your father. Where's the dignity?"

"Rosie, the dignity is in our hearts! I loved helping him. If he can feel our ease, our delight in assisting him, then he won't have a loss of dignity. He'll have only our love."

"Okay," she said, wiping her eyes as she heard you calling.

"We have to look for the beauty in what's happening. And there is beauty. When there's love, Rosie, there's beauty."

You slept for three straight hours after that massive exertion. Rosie joined Samahria for a morning walk as I left to teach class. Raun stood guard nearby. We all joined you for lunch in your room. When we presented you with a tray loaded with a plate of roasted chicken (another favorite of yours), a cup of soup, and an ice cream dessert, you did not protest. Actually, you ate a small portion of each item on the tray. I cajoled you into drinking half a glass of water.

"He drinks for you," Rosie protested. "But he pushes the bottle away when I offer it."

"You ready for some negotiation, Pop?" I asked, mystified by your increasing strength. "How about a half a bottle of water or half a glass every — well — every two or three hours? And you agree to accept that liquid from me or Rosie or Samahria." You looked up at Rosie and Samahria, flashing a grin at both of them. "Okay. We're all witnesses. We have a bargain. Yes?"

"Yes," you stated flatly. "A bargain. I drink. And you keep supplying all this great food. Maybe I'll even take a few vitamins each day. What do you think, Rosie, just a few?"

Rosie tried to hold back the tears that filled her eyes. I don't think she ever really believed that you would get out of that bed again, much less willingly agree to take vitamins.

Finally, Rosie stood up and held her throat, squelching her emotions. Barely able to vocalize the words, she said, "Okay, Abie, we'll start right now." Rosie secured three or four of her favorite antioxidants and gave them to you. Without an ounce of protest, you downed them with a flourish. Then suddenly you winced.

"What's the matter, Abe?" Rosie asked.

"My back. My back. Take the pillows away. I have to lie down." The lymphatic cancer had migrated and formed tumors that pressed against your spine. In some positions and only at some times, you were free of pain. In other positions, the pressure of the cancerous masses impinged on the nerves, sending bolts of severe pain through your system that could only be sedated by narcotics. Your entire demeanor changed as I placed my hands behind your back and slid you carefully downward until you rested fully on your back. Although you experienced some relief, the aftershocks of pain continued to thunder through your nervous system. Rosie gave you some more medication, and I offered to do a meditation with you. You agreed.

Everyone left the room as I sat on the floor beside your bed and encouraged you to follow your breath down into a quiet and safe place inside. Initially, you had difficulty concentrating, but then, very slowly, you relaxed your body instead of constricting your muscles when the pain assaulted you. I guided you to lift your finger should the discomfort become more tolerable. You lifted your finger. We continued the meditation for another thirty minutes until you drifted off to sleep. I imagined the medication had now begun to work. I kissed your forehead, left the room, and joined Rosie and Samahria in the kitchen.

"He's comfortable now. And he fell asleep," I told them.

"We have to do more about the pain," Rosie blurted out forcefully. "That's why he has to start the chemo. It will shrink the tumors. Talk to the doctor about radiation for his spine."

"I will. But, Rosie, I'm not sure that's the only issue to discuss. What about hospice? We'd get more assistance in making him comfortable," I offered. "I'd like to talk to Pop about it as well."

"No. You heard what your father said. He wants me to decide."

"Yes. And I will respect his wish . . . and yours. I'm only trying to put this on the table for discussion with you and with him."

Samahria put her arm around Rosie's shoulder. "I think it would be useful to talk about hospice, too. We'll still all go to the doctor together. You know another MRI has been scheduled. They'll also do a new blood workup. No one's giving up."

"Rosie," I added, "remember what Dr. Rubin said. No matter what the tests say, the most important indicator for treatment is how the patient feels and how the patient is doing. Back to quality of life. Admittedly, he's gaining ground. It's amazing."

"He'll come back again. You'll see," Rosie insisted.

"Hey, we're on the same team," I assured her. "There's a 'however,' though. This cancer and all the treatments to fight it have taken an awesome toll on his body. Even though he's feeling somewhat better, I'm not sure that he has the strength to endure another round of chemo. Nor do I believe it makes sense to keep him alive at any cost to him and his quality of life."

"But didn't the nurse say that we have to agree first to end all treatment or efforts to cure him, like chemotherapy or radiation, before the doctor will sign off in order for us to involve hospice?" Rosie asked.

"Generally, that's what I understood," Samahria noted. "But they could use radiation for pain control, just not for treatment."

"Essentially you're right, Rosie," I said, "it would be stopping any more attempts to cure him, acknowledging that his life is ending and doing our very best to help him be comfortable."

"I'm not ready," Rosie declared.

"What about Pop?" I questioned. "Maybe he's ready."

"Your father smiled more today than in the last week," she said. "He's eating, not much, but he's eating. And drinking."

"It's kind of mind-boggling, isn't it?" I observed. "And he's been so damned sweet, so openhearted. Except for the bouts with pain, I would say he's having a good time here."

"So do we quit now?" challenged Rosie.

"No. We don't quit ever," I answered. "But in the end, Rosie, he's the one to decide. If he wants to climb another mountain, we help take him over. He's defied all the statistics these past two years. But if he's too tired, if he feels done, I want to respect that as well."

SEVENTEEN

Our vigil the following night had a very different texture. On three separate occasions, you requested assistance to the bathroom. Rosie watched as I helped you; she no longer grimaced as we shuffled slowly across the floor. Each time we took the journey, you exhibited more vitality and strength. And each time I encouraged you to down some more fluids, you responded affirmatively. When I came to visit you before teaching my next class the next morning, you sat straight up in bed without soliciting or accepting any support.

"Is Samahria up?" you asked. I nodded, astonished by your energy. "Good. Can you get her? I want to talk to both of you."

"Sure, Pop. I'll be right back." When Samahria and I returned, we found you, to our delight, still sitting erect, braced against the headboard with pillows. Rosie sat beside you on the bed. You reached out to hold our hands in a gesture both intimate and affectionate.

"You two have done a wonderful thing for Rosie and me." Your voice quivered. "We know it can't be easy for either of you. You kids have been so fantastic with me...with us. We wanted you to know how we felt."

"We know how you feel," Samahria said. "Dad, every time you smile, we can feel your appreciation. We feel it even when you don't smile. We're doing this because we want to, because we love you."

I leaned forward to kiss your cheek. Just as I touched my face to yours, you kissed me back. I had always wanted to be your friend, like the man you kissed on Seventh Avenue, and now, in these precious moments, one of my dreams had come true. I could hear the camera shutter click in my mind. I knew I would never forget this moment.

"I can't say it enough, Pop," I added. "Having you here, having Rosie here — that's a blessing for us. It's like a special honor. And you have been the sweetest guy with all of us."

You started to speak but then stopped. At first, I didn't think you had allowed yourself to hear what I had said. But then, in a thoughtful pause, your eyes moistened. You smiled at me and said, "That's very nice of you to say that."

"He means it, Dad," Samahria asserted. You tightened your grip on our hands and fixed your gaze on us, lingering as you stared into our eyes. Pop, you gave us the best eye contact ever. Then, quite abruptly, you switched modes, assuming an executive manner and declaring, "There's more. Rosie and I want to contribute some money to the household. We want to do our share, pay our way."

"No, Pop. No way," I countered. "You're our guests."

You released our hands and altered your demeanor further as you challenged my statement. "We might be here a long time."

"Great. The longer, the better," I snapped.

"You're doing enough just having us here. We want to contribute."

"Pop, you are contributing. Just by being here. Money — no, not necessary," I insisted. "If you want to give, just be nice to me."

Samahria laughed. "That's what he always says to the kids when they ask what he wants for his birthday or on Father's Day."

"But I mean it," I protested amicably. "Actually, Pop, you don't have to be nice to me; it's just a request."

"We're off point," you countered. "We want to give you some money to take care of the expenses."

"Whatever you want to do, Dad," Samahria agreed reluctantly.

"Wait. You like to debate, Pop. What if you come up with a really good argument to convince us of the wisdom of taking money from you and we'll come your way on this? How about for now, we keep this arrangement. It's good for our souls. And it's good for your soul to take a little."

"A little?" you sighed. You looked around the room, peered through the windows, and then glanced back at us. "Bears, don't think Rosie and I didn't notice how nice you were with Kenny and Denise and Jessica. You didn't think I noticed, but I wasn't that cockeyed. Rosie and I talked about it after they left. We appreciated how you were with them."

"You were very sweet to them and helpful," Rosie added. "They didn't give you anything back. That was very obvious. I know you did it for us."

"Rosie, I also did it for them. Maybe there is more to this than meets the eye." I proceeded to tell both of you about my phone conversation with Kenny regarding our first names. "It can't be easy for them hanging out on my turf. Remember, only four months ago Kenny said he didn't want to talk to me anymore. He wanted all the medical bulletins about you to go to him through Jessica. Now he's forced to deal with me again. At least, for the moment, they're not adversarial. That's something to be grateful for!" I paused, considering other possibilities. "I wanted them to feel as comfortable as possible when they visited.

That evening, after I finished my mentoring sessions and consultations, you asked me to help you get down the flight of stairs to join us for dinner in the kitchen.

"But before we go, Rosie and I have something for you." Rosie pulled a piece of paper off the bureau and handed it to me. It was a generous check, a donation made out to The Option Institute International Learning and Training Center.

"I can't accept this," I said, handing it back to Rosie. She refused to take it. "Bears, if you won't let us help with the household, we want to help you with your work," you interjected. "We're living right here in the middle of the Institute property. It's like paradise, but not just because it's so beautiful — yes, it's beautiful — but because of all the help and love everyone here has extended to us. Zoe comes by every few hours. She's like an angel. The other staff members have been so kind to us. Let us do this." She folded my hand over the check. "Bears, take it. You'll use it to help other people like us. You take it for the Institute."

"We want to do this," you reiterated.

I put the check in my pocket, hugged both you and Rosie, then put my arm underneath yours, Pop, and walked you down the hallway to the staircase. Once I had secured my position on the stairs just below you, you grabbed the railing with both hands and eased yourself down, one step at a time. I caught a glimpse of Samahria, watching you struggle with each movement.

She applauded your efforts, as did Bryn and her husband, William, who had just entered the entrance hall from the office door.

Before we went to bed that evening, I showed Samahria the check. Her impulse, like mine, was to return it immediately. However, after we discussed the matter for almost an hour, I placed it in a box beside my bed, believing I would never turn it over to the Institute. Our giving had been a giving of the heart. Only later did I come to realize that your gift to the Institute had also been a giving of the heart. Indeed, in light of your doubts throughout the years about what we taught, this gesture represented an endearing statement of support for all that Samahria and I hold most dear. Thank you again, Pop.

Over the next several days, you gained even more strength, now walking down the stairs by yourself to join us for lunch as well as dinner. Additionally, you sampled smoked salmon on bagels, our special vegetarian burger, a roasted chicken, spaghetti, pizza, and various flavors of ice cream. With encouragement from Rosie, you nibbled on side dishes of vegetables but showed little enthusiasm for the salads we made for you. Each morning, then again at lunch and in the early evening, I extended my arm for support, taking you for short strolls on the Institute campus. Staff members would stop to greet us, as did some program participants. Pop, everyone talked with you so respectfully, genuinely excited to meet you.

You showed a special affection for Kate, a teacher in our Son-Rise Program, who hails from England and who, like Zoe, treated you like a visiting dignitary when she came into the house to visit us. Additionally, I know that you were a sucker for the King's English, and you enjoyed listening to Kate's accent and her more formal speaking style. One afternoon, when you met a woman from Holland and a gentleman from Kenya on our walk, you inquired more studiously into the origins of our program participants, genuinely fascinated to hear that folks from different countries and cultures could join together in exploring their beliefs and personal issues.

Kenny, Denise, and Jessica came for another visit. They had kept in touch with daily phone calls and expressed amazement at your progress. This time you greeted them not from your bed but from a chair on the front porch. I watched their eyes light up as they saw your new vibrancy and vitality of spirit.

Just before leaving, Kenny took me aside to ask for a more detailed update of your current medical condition and your upcoming appointment with an oncologist. He, too, voiced strong reservations, even objections, to bombarding you with more chemotherapy. I told him that I shared his perspective and appreciated our being able to interact more smoothly about issues regarding your health. Again, I assured him that I would keep him involved and abreast of any medical decisions.

"Thank you, Bears," he said.

I didn't miss the reference. "You're welcome. And thanks for addressing me by my name. I appreciate it."

He smiled.

Although your resurgence dazzled us, the oncologist viewed you as a very, very sick man. Based on your low blood counts, your general dehydration, and the diminished function of your remaining kidney, he did not believe you could tolerate chemotherapy. Nevertheless, he concurred with Rosie's specific suggestions about treatments that had strengthened your system previously and prescribed a bioengineered concoction to be given by injection every forty-eight hours in the hope of raising your blood count. Additionally, the physician believed you required much more fluid and much more food than you had been ingesting. Thus, he prescribed an appetite enhancer that had been developed for people sick with AIDS. His office scheduled a return visit in one week to chart your progress and to reconsider the question of chemotherapy. Both you and Rosie wanted to follow his recommendation.

"At least five more years," Rosie had demanded that night in your kitchen in Florida. You had delivered nearly two spectacular years. And now, as I watched you out of the corner of my eye getting your second wind, I knew you were willing to try for even more. You didn't *need* to be alive for one more second; you had been ready to let go from the outset, not wanting us to make a fuss. But, in the end, you came on board and masterfully engineered this gift of extra time for Rosie. The following day, after you had napped, you showered by yourself and then expressed a desire to walk again. You appeared definitely stronger and more vibrant, as if a portion of your physiology had experienced a rebirth. With Rosie on one side of you and I on the other, the three of us strolled arm in arm slowly down the road.

"So, Pop," I asked, "What do you think happens when you die?"

"Here we go again," you said, amused. You looked up at the nearby ridge of mountains off to the right, then glanced up at the clouds in the sky. "Actually, Bears, I'm not quite sure."

"Well, why are you requesting to be buried instead of cremated or potted like a plant in an urn?"

You laughed. "Old-fashioned, maybe. Actually, Rosie and I made a pact a long, long time ago, didn't we?" Rosie nodded. "I would be buried beside your Mom, and Rosie would be buried beside Norman." You smiled warmly and held Rosie just a touch tighter. "I guess, one day," you elaborated, "somewhere up there, when it's time, your mother and I and Rosie and Norman will get together and play bridge. We'll become a foursome. Right, Rosie?" She nodded again as she looked at you adoringly.

"What about you, Rosie?" I asked.

"I like what your father said. We both decided this together."

"We arranged for everything in advance," you continued. "When I go, you just call a number and this service takes care of all the details. We even picked out our boxes to be buried in."

"Wow. Anything fancy?" I asked.

"Wood. Simple. Not expensive." You looked at me as if searching for a reaction.

"Are you satisfied with your choice?" I inquired.

"Absolutely!"

"Rosie, what about you?"

"I'm with him." She smiled.

"You guys feel okay about this conversation?"

"Yes," you assured me. "And you?"

"I'm having the best time," I said. "I also have another question."

"You always have another question, but before you ask, let's turn around. I'm getting tired."

We switched direction and walked slowly back toward the main building.

Once you got your footing, I resumed our conversation. "So, Pop, do you ever think about what happens to you when you die?"

"Frankly, I don't give it that much thought. Right now, I'm living, so I think about living. I'll let God take care of the dying."

I chuckled in the face of your simple wisdom. "Well, since you mentioned that bridge game in the sky, Pop, what do you think might happen next, after the bridge game?"

"You want me to think so far ahead? Let me get to that bridge game first."

Smiling, I asked, "Any fears?"

"No, my boy. I'm ready. Actually, you've helped me become even more ready."

"How?"

"By making this a big adventure."

"It's been a big, big adventure for me, too, Pop." When we returned to the front of the main building, you sat in one of the chairs facing the valley and the distant mountains beyond. You drew in a deep breath and sighed.

"Abe, are you okay?" Rosie asked.

"Doing fine. Doing just fine." Within seconds, you fell asleep.

Rosie left me with you and went to prepare some food. I stared at your face. Your hair was gone. Bryn had cut the few straggly remaining strands just the day before. Your jacket draped loosely across your upper torso, now two sizes too big. Your shoes looked much larger than your feet. I noticed a slight tremor in your left hand. Yet, despite these obvious changes in your physiology, an uplifting quality of spirit emanated from you. I found you to be more attractive, more handsome — yes, handsome — than ever. Almost eighty-six years old, and getting ready to leave your body behind, you looked lean. Mean. Like a sleek greyhound. I know you asked Raun not to remember you as you have been these last weeks. But my memory, Pop, will be filled with your warmth, your love, and the simple reflections you shared on this day and on other days. These two years will be my memory of our lifetime together, and they will be more than enough to last a lifetime.

You opened your eyes again.

"Did I fall asleep?" you asked.

"For a short time. We took a big walk. You needed a little rest."

"Go now," you advised. "You've got so much to do."

"Everything has been covered," I said. "I don't teach until later. Right now, this is my time with you."

You surveyed the vista glittering in the sunshine. "Sure is beautiful. I feel like I'm a guest in heaven." A gentle wind caressed the leaves and bounced off the rocky ridges behind the Institute's campus, echoing against the hillside like the wood flutes played in mountain villages in Peru and Ecuador. "Do you want to talk some more?" I asked.

"You know, Bears, I'm from another generation. In my day, we didn't talk so much. We worked hard. We provided for our families. And then, at the end of our lives, if we were lucky, we got a few years to kick back and relax. In that department, I've been very fortunate. No complaints."

"Anything you would have done differently?"

"Well, sometimes I think I should have spoken up more."

"For example."

"With your sister. I guess I didn't want to make things more difficult if it wasn't necessary. I didn't follow the same practice with you."

"How come?" I asked.

You looked at me thoughtfully. "I guess I saw you as strong — too strong, too headstrong. As your father, I thought I needed to take you down a peg or two. Maybe I didn't have to do that, but that's what I did. It took a lot of strength for you and Samahria to do what you did with Raun, to create a place like this and to write all those books. I just wanted you to be reasonable."

"Do you experience me as reasonable?" I asked with genuine curiosity.

"Years ago, mostly no." You glanced in my direction and tapped my arm. "Now you're not only much more reasonable but I like you."

"I like you, too, Pop."

We burst out laughing simultaneously. Over a decade ago, in the course of that conversation in which I asked you if you would pick me from a roomful of people to be your friend, I told you I would not pick you from a roomful of people to be my friend and you admitted finally that you, too, would pass me by. Now, Pop, we were both picking each other decisively, and we had been doing it consistently for almost two years. "For the longest time," I said, "I thought you'd never get to know me. I believed you didn't really have any interest in knowing me. Do you remember, maybe about six years ago, that strange conversation we had about tombstones in a restaurant near your home in Florida?"

"My memory's getting rusty. Remind me."

"First I asked you what you would want written on yours, and you refused to answer. Samahria and Rosie didn't have much energy to participate, either. I kept trying to push the envelope. I wanted to know you. I wanted you to know me. But all I felt was the wall you put up against what you labeled as my obsession to have 'deep' conversations."

You lifted one eyebrow and smirked. "This is starting to sound familiar. Go on."

"At the time, I felt like an elephant trying to balance on a teacup. I said that on my hypothetical tombstone, hypothetical because I intended to be vaporized with my ashes cast to the wind, I would inscribe the notation, 'Bears. Trying to be happier, more loving. I did it my way.' Samahria responded by saying, 'That's for sure!' I liked echoing the words of that Frank Sinatra tune. Rosie smiled, but you looked at me blank-faced."

"Sounds like me," you noted, so relaxed and easy with our current conversation. At that moment, Pop, the warmth on your face and the twinkle in your eyes was anything but blank-faced. "Then, pushing up against your refusal to participate, I decided to go further and said to you, 'Pop, if I had to inscribe a tombstone for you that had a personal commentary from me, it would say: 'Here lies my father, the man who judged me all my life.'" I laughed aloud. "Remember that? Sorry, Pop, for the flamboyant commentary. Sometimes, when we teach, we heighten the stimulus purposely or make the comments bigger and more theatrical so the challenges are more vivid and the opportunities for solutions more compelling. I meant what I said during that breakfast, but you might have found what I said hard to digest because you looked stunned. I felt like a teenager again, wanting to shake you and, at the same time, feeling I had overstepped my bounds."

"I remember that remark," you said, shaking your head. "Actually, I didn't know how to respond. Rosie always told me I was hard on you during our phone conversations."

"Do you think you were?"

"I could have been easier on you, Bears. You have a different way of looking at the world than I do. You say people don't have to be unhappy, that they make themselves unhappy, and that they could learn to make new choices. People come from all around the world to learn that from you. Wonderful! But I didn't want to learn to make new choices. If I didn't like what you said, I was *happy* yelling at you." You laughed, enjoying your own commentary. "That wasn't ever good enough for you. You had to ask me 'why' I was angry. I didn't want to figure out *why*. I just wanted to say my piece and be done." You stopped speaking for a few moments, then whacked me on the shoulder with the back of your hand. You had the sweetest grin on your face. "Not only that. When you were younger, you had to have long hair and sport that beard of yours. You wore clothing hand-painted by your friends. Ridiculous! Frankly, you embarrassed me. And then you talked all these strange ideas. I'm for civil rights, too, but it doesn't mean I have to adopt children of other races. I'm for peace, too, but it doesn't mean I have to meditate or love everyone. Sometimes I would wonder, where did you come from? Not from your mother or me.

I guess everything you said or did seemed so extreme to me. Now your hair is short, thank God, and your beard is nicely trimmed, and you can carry on a reasonable conversation once in a while." You laughed, and I was so delighted by your outspoken comments. "Okay," you continued. "Now I understand more about where you're coming from. I don't mind your questions anymore. Sometimes, I even like them. It's not what I do, but it's what you do. This is not a concession speech. I'm just telling you what I think." You smiled.

"How do you feel?"

You puckered out your bottom lip thoughtfully. "Good. I

feel good. Bears, you think it's healthy to get things out, to discuss them. Sometimes, I think it could be better to let sleeping dogs lie."

"Well," I responded, "you and I have opposing viewpoints on that issue. And yet, Pop, we are talking more openly, more honestly now than ever — getting more 'things out,' as you say. Useful or not useful?"

"Between you and me, very useful," you admitted. "But I'm not sure about the rest of the world. Not everyone wants to have these probing discussions all the time."

"I treasure them. I get to know you and understand you more. Then there's more of you available for me to love. But I think there's a benefit for you, too, Pop. Do you remember that first week in Tulsa, when you not only had all the diagnostic tests but attended classes on meditation, nutrition, pastoral counseling — 'stuff' you normally disliked?"

"Yes. The people there are terrific. I was surprised; it was all very interesting."

"And do you remember what you said when I asked you what you had learned most after being there for that week?"

You looked up toward the mountains, searching for the answer. "I told you, my memory's not as good as it used to be." You paused for a minute, searching for the memory. "Yes, I do remember. I told you that I realized how closed I had been all my life."

"I was just delighted in how open you had to be with yourself and me to have made such a comment. Eighty-four years old at the time, and parachuting into new territory. What an inspiration, Pop!"

"So now I'm an inspiration."

"Definitely. I'm so enjoying you now."

"Good — enjoy me," you said.

Just as you concluded that comment, Rosie arrived with some food and hot tea. I helped her set the tray on your lap. "How about I leave you guys some time to spend alone?" I said, rising from the chair. "Pop can use a rest from all the 'deep talk,'" I joked. "If you need me, I'll be in my office."

You improved steadily over the next week, even insisting on driving yourself to the "infusion" center in Great Barrington, where you received your injections every other day. Rosie sat proudly in the passenger seat as you both took on your old driving roles. Later that week, Pop, I saw you zooming at a fast clip down the road, a cowboy at the wheel, defying your eighty-six years and acting like a teenager, passionately in love with the freedom of movement your vehicle allowed you. Family members came and went. David and Alan and their families visited, as did Kenny, Denise, and Jessica. Old friends of yours from Mohegan Lake visited. One time, I returned from class to find you and Rosie entertaining two couples on the front porch. You had dressed more formally than on previous days, wearing a green and blue plaid shirt, tan Bermuda shorts, and a baseball hat. Quite a dashing silhouette, Pop! With a proud smile, you announced that the six of you were about to drive to a local restaurant for lunch. You gave me that famous wink, acknowledging in a fleeting glance the irony that only a few weeks earlier none of us would have predicted that you would still be alive on this sunny afternoon.

I remembered the radiologist at the Cancer Treatment

Center of America in Tulsa asserting that every once in a while you meet a person, a patient, who defies all the statistics. With those rare souls, the doctor said, you must throw away all the textbooks. He identified you as just such a person. Given the virulence of your cancers and your advanced age, he might have realistically given you a life expectancy of three or four months. However, mirroring principles we hold dear in our work with people at the Institute, this thoughtful physician and his associates never stripped you and Rosie of hope. Instead, they supported you, encouraging you to live your life as fully as possible, never limiting what might be possible by giving you a grim edict about a limited future. They believed in the spiritual as well as medical component of your treatment, a perspective and sensitivity that medical professionals rarely demonstrate.

Now, as we faced another decision about your treatment, I decided to call the center and speak to Margie, who had been a key member of your care team there. She questioned, as did Kenny and I, the value of more chemotherapy and expressed concern about its potentially devastating impact on your already diminished vitality. Over and over again, she told me how much she loved both of you. Pop, she actually used the word "love." I never felt that I was speaking to a professional at a cancer hospital; this woman reached out like an old and dear friend. What a gift, and what a contrast to most of the people you encountered in your other medical and hospital experiences in Florida and New York! I had no doubt that Margie would have honestly delighted in watching both of you catch these precious last moments with your friends. Quality of life, Pop — that's what it's all about. We had conspired to provide you with a supportive environment in which you could retain your dignity and be surrounded by love.

After the excursion with your friends, you came into the living room, searching for a place to rest. The outing had drained your physical resources. Rosie gave you more medication for pain and you lay down on the couch and dropped off to sleep. An hour later, you awoke and asked me to take another walk with you.

I loved these special moments alone with you. You wrapped your hand around my arm to help support yourself and we exited the house, heading down the road carefully. Your eyes scanned the landscape, enlivened by the bustling of a family of Canadian geese that had made their home in one of our ponds. We stopped for a moment to allow the two parents to stroll across our path with their six little goslings, who followed them in an orderly line. Then they took flight in what appeared to be a training session for the younger geese. Flapping their wings furiously, most of the goslings managed to lift off the ground and stay aloft for almost two hundred feet before landing on a distant field. One straggler, who never managed to get off the ground, no matter how ambitiously he flapped his wings, ran on what almost appeared to be motorized legs in order to catch up with his family and rejoin them. "Always little ones," you said smiling. "And one day, like me, the little ones will grow old. What we can hope for is that we helped make it better for those who come next."

"Do you think you did, Pop?"

"I don't know if the sun's going to shine any brighter because of me, but I did my best."

"Maybe that's all any of us can ever do. We do our best. I like to believe that as we learn more, understand more, open our hearts more, then our best gets even better. I've seen you do that."

"Let's turn around," you said, shifting our direction back to the house. "Why do you pay me all these compliments?"

"I wasn't aware of complimenting you — just verbalizing what I think and see. Ready for another question?" You nodded. "How do you explain being so vibrant after being so sick no more than ten days ago? Beyond that, how do you explain how well you've done in general these past two years?"

You snapped out your answer, taking my breath away.

"Attitude, my boy," you said with conviction. "It's all attitude."

I laughed uproariously. "Want to join our teaching staff, Pop?"

"No. I'm happy just being a guest."

EIGHTEEN

We gathered in the kitchen to perform our nightly dinner ritual. Samahria concocted her special salad dressing. Rosie and Sage prepared lettuce, tomatoes, onions, and mushrooms. Raun offered to empty the dishwasher with Tayo while I set the table. Then Rosie and I selected an offering for you from among the stash of delicious provisions replenished almost daily for your consumption. When I reached for a slice of salmon, Rosie slapped my hand playfully.

"Away," she instructed. "That's for your father."

"Just a little piece?" I pleaded. "Tayo will get more tomorrow, right Tayo?"

"Yes, Popi," he asserted, amused by our interaction.

"What do you think, O Great Protector of the Salmon?" I inquired.

Rosie handed me a small sliver and said, "But that's it."

"You got it," I assured her, enjoying my minimal feast.

The energy among us had a very special spark. Although we might have shared meals for years and the specific activities we engaged in were familiar and seemingly routine, your presence in our home enlivened our moments in the kitchen with a heightened consciousness and a reverent spirit. Rosie had joined us so easily, fitting like a timeless member into our nuclear unit. Together, we did more than prepare the meal; we created a special ambiance among ourselves as a way of welcoming you into the kitchen and cherishing your arrival. We acknowledged your mobility as a gift. Although new blood tests still demonstrated a continued physical frailty, your energy level remained steady, and your pain, thankfully, under control.

Once the food had been set on the table, I left to fetch you from your room. "We're all ready for you," I announced.

You started to shift your weight in the bed, but I noticed you winced as you turned.

"Your back?" I asked.

"When did I take the painkillers last?"

"About three hours ago, during my last break from class. You want more now?"

"Yes," you said.

After you'd taken your medication, we walked together slowly down the hallway. Your gait appeared slightly more tentative than on previous days. Additionally, I caught you twice as you stumbled, your balance more precarious than ever. We took the stairs very, very carefully.

"You sure you want to do this? Don't forget: In this hotel, we have room service. We can bring the food up to you."

"No. I'm fine," you insisted.

"Are you lying, Pop?"

"Mind your own business," you snapped with a burst of your old feistiness.

"All right. Lean on me." You did not fight my suggestion and allowed me to support you every step of the way. At the bottom of the staircase, we walked arm in arm. I could feel you dragging your feet instead of lifting them off the floor. When we arrived at the kitchen door, you pushed off from me purposely and entered the room without assistance. I stayed very close but made sure I did not touch you unless absolutely necessary. I wanted you to be able to assert your independence for as long as you could, since being self-reliant was so important to you.

"Hey, Grandpa," Raun called. "You look great."

"No, I don't," you said, matter-of-factly. "I look lousy."

"Okay, Grandpa," Raun nodded, smiling, "you look lousy."

"Abe," Rosie protested, "you look damn good."

"For an old buck," you added.

Sage hugged you, and you patted her back. "Nice kid," you said quite genuinely. You always had a soft spot for Sage, and she always expressed great warmth with you.

"Gee, thanks, Gramps," she responded, not knowing whether to endorse or protest your comment.

Samahria hugged you and then moved ahead to pull out your chair. Tayo, although not tall, had developed broad shoulders, a huge chest, and a stance that often appeared as immovable as a brick wall. You eyed his form, Pop, pounded on his chest lightly with your fist, and declared, "Solid. Rock solid. How was football practice?"

"Good, Grandpa," Tayo noted, obviously pleased by your comments and recall of his beloved sport. When you sat down, you sighed and closed your eyes. Rosie eyed me with concern.

"Grandpa, do you hurt?" Sage asked.

You reopened your eyes. "A little. But your father gave me another pill, so I should be just fine soon. Come. Everyone sit."

We followed your directive obediently and took our seats around the table. At that moment, Bryn, William, and their daughter, Jade, arrived. "Don't worry, we're not going to eat," Bryn announced as she hugged you, "we're just visiting for a few minutes." William, who had been carrying Jade, deposited her into my lap. Then Bryn and William proceeded to hug and kiss everyone around the table. Jade peered up at you, Pop. You smiled and touched her nose. Although you demonstrated such sweetness toward her, you appeared awkward, as if you did not quite know what to do.

"Jade, honey, do you want to sit with your great-grandpa?" I asked as I lifted her in your direction. She pulled back but did not stop looking at you.

"Leave her," you suggested. William reclaimed his daughter, and he and Bryn took seats around the table. You then made the first move to initiate our gratitude circle, reaching out to hold my hand on one side and Raun's on the other.

"Nice move, Grandpa," Bryn said, smiling. You smiled back at her.

Once we had all clasped hands together, Samahria said, "How about we all look at Grandma and Grandpa." She gazed at Rosie and at you. "We want you to know that we feel your presence adds so much to this family."

We all fell silent for a few moments, and then Bryn spoke. "It's great having both of you here. Now Jade gets to know you." Bryn smiled at you, then leaned over and kissed Rosie, who sat next to her.

"How about we close our eyes," I began, "and then..."

"Before we close our eyes, I want to say something tonight," you interrupted. "We want all of you kids to know," you said, your hands still locked with mine and Raun's, "that your grandmother and I feel more than just welcomed here; we feel at home with all of you."

"You are at home, Dad," Samahria said.

I waited to see if you wanted to share more, but you cast your eyes toward your lap. "Okay," I began again, "how about we now close our eyes and take a few moments to be grateful that Grandma and Grandpa are with us, that we love them very much, and that we all have the gift of this meal to share. Also, tonight, maybe a special prayer for Grandpa's health."

In the quiet of my mind, I prayed to God not to follow my directive for your deliverance but to walk beside you in whatever way would be best. Long ago, I stopped instructing the universe how to unfold based on the limited vision of my pea brain and created prayers and visualizations that supported and trusted the flow of life's river. Oftentimes, as a result, my prayers began with a silent chorus of thank-yous. Even as I noted your discomfort tonight, I could see on your face and hear in your words the blessings you had obviously given yourself during this challenging time of transition.

After about a minute, everyone opened their eyes.

"Jade, darling," Bryn said in amazement. "You were such a good girl, so quiet." Jade had been fascinated by our communal ceremony and now glanced from face to face as we all laughed, enjoying her curiosity.

"I thought about going to Boston next week to go job hunting," Raun said, "but not if you need me here."

"We've got Ay-Tay," Rosie volunteered. "He's been great, helping us get all of Grandpa's favorite foods."

"Honey," Samahria said, "we appreciate that you stayed to help, but I think between all of us, we'll do just fine."

"Hey, Pop, you're not eating anything," I noticed. "Do you want something different?" You picked up your fork and put some potatoes into your mouth. No one spoke for a few seconds. We all watched you.

"Dad, we still have some ribs from last night," Samahria offered.

"Or we could start with dessert," I suggested.

You sighed and looked up at us.

"Not hungry, huh?" I said. "Then don't eat."

"He has to eat," Rosie insisted.

"Well," I countered, "maybe just not now." Pop, you appeared distracted. "Is it the pain?"

You glanced up at all of us. "I'm fine," you said unconvincingly. "I'll just nibble. You go on talking."

There was a long silence. Bryn spoke next. "Raun, I think it's a great idea for you to go to Boston. You had your year working in England and Ireland; now it's time to settle in here."

"Do you need me to do more research?" he asked me.

"No, Raun," I said. "We're in a holding pattern now. We have to see how Grandpa does."

"Go," you offered. "Between your dad and your mom, we have everything we could ever need. You continue living your life just like before."

"Grandpa, I could do some research," Tayo offered. "I helped Popi on the Internet. He could just tell me what you need, and I could find it."

You tipped your head, acknowledging his offer, and then announced, "I think I'm going to go upstairs."

Rosie and I both jumped to our feet to help you. You put

your hands on the table and pushed upward as I lifted you from behind. Perhaps the combination of the pain and the medication had sapped your energy. "Abe, do you want me to take the food upstairs with us?" Rosie asked.

"Whatever you want," you said with palpable lack of interest. She grabbed your main dish as I helped you move from the table.

"We hope you feel better, Grandpa," Sage said, visibly distressed.

"Here, I'll get the tea," Raun offered as he stood, lifting the cup.

We helped you up the stairs and into the bedroom. You indicated a desire to rest. Rosie stayed with you, although you instructed her to return to the meal. Within seconds, however, you drifted off to sleep.

When I returned to the kitchen, everyone wanted to be updated on your condition.

I described your journey back to the bedroom.

"Is he getting worse?" Bryn asked.

"I don't know," I said truthfully. "He's not always consistent, and the last blood tests were not great."

"Is he going to die soon?" Tayo asked, a question he would never have posed if Rosie had been at the table.

"He could. But we want to do everything we can to make it easy for him. To make him comfortable," I added.

"And that's where all of you can help," Samahria said. "Actually, you're doing it already. When he's not in pain, he enjoys being with you. So love him as you have been doing. And Grandma, too. This is a very, very difficult time for her. She needs just as much support as Grandpa."

"I feel sorry for Grandma," Sage said.

"Why?" Samahria asked.

"She won't have Grandpa much longer," she responded.

"Well," sighed Samahria, "she's dealing with it every day. When we take those walks every morning, I try to help her look at her feelings. But sometimes, she can be a tough cookie and avoid talking about what's on her mind. Imagine what it might be like for me if something like this happened to Popi."

"I definitely couldn't handle that," said Raun. "I love Grandpa, but I couldn't deal with it if something happened to you or Popi."

"Then let's work on that," I suggested to Raun. "I don't want you to be afraid."

"I think I'm like Raun," Bryn interceded. "I've watched you and Mom with Grandpa and Grandma. I feel I know how to be with them. I'm not at all scared. I can handle it. But if it were you guys, forget it. Dying is really heavy."

"Is it dying that's the problem or us dying, in particular?" Samahria asked.

Raun responded, "You dying in particular. Not that I don't have problems about me dying!"

"Tayo, how would you feel if we died?" Samahria asked. "Fine," he said matter-of-factly.

"Oh, c'mon," Raun objected. "You don't feel anything?"

"I feel fine," Tayo repeated. "I don't have any problems about death."

"Oh, the big football player," Sage quipped. "That's because you're only seventeen."

"I thought about death a lot when I was seventeen," Raun noted. "I used to think about it when I was ten and twelve."

"I think this is all really interesting, seriously," Bryn said, "but we have to leave and get Jade to bed. Let's save this discussion for brunch on Sunday."

"I'd like that," William said. "When my dad was sick, before he died, none of my family would really talk about it. It's very different here. Death doesn't seem scary in this house."

"That's beautiful, William," Samahria said.

"I wish my father had had this kind of dying experience," he added.

"I remember you saying that you crawled into bed with your father on that last night," I reminded him. "You knew what to do. You reached out to him, and that's what matters!"

"That's true," William said, smiling.

"I'll come visit Grandpa tomorrow," Bryn said, kissing Samahria and me. William gathered Jade's toys off the floor and lifted his daughter into his arms. After they left, we cleared the table together as we continued to discuss death in regard to ourselves and those we love. Although Sage and Tayo did not say a great deal, Raun had an insatiable appetite for the subject. Of all the children, he had had the most contact with you when you first arrived, Pop, and this experience had stirred up many thoughts and feelings.

You rallied the next morning, although you didn't quite regain the strength you had exhibited during the preceding week. That afternoon, Samahria asked me to join her in your bedroom. Apparently you wanted to have a meeting with us. You leaned up against the headboard, sitting almost upright in the bed. Rosie sat in the chair nearby.

"You both know how grateful we are to be here," you began, quite formally. Samahria and I smiled, acknowledging your words. "We really like it here, as well. How would you feel if we stayed on a permanent basis?"

"Wonderful," I said. "The house is big. Most of the kids are grown and gone, and there's lots of room for all of us. Besides, we love providing this — oh, what would I call it — this sanctuary for both of you."

"It would be great," Samahria mused. "I'd have a permanent partner for my walks every morning. Even when my sabbatical from the Institute is over and I resume, hopefully, a full teaching schedule, we could still walk before work." She touched your shoulder. "As long as this is our place, it's yours as well. Always."

I noticed Rosie staring down at the floor, obviously uncomfortable with the discussion. "What's going on with you?" I asked.

"I don't know why he's asking you this. We have our home in Florida."

"Oh, c'mon, Rosie," you protested. "With the shape I'm in, we're going to need help. I'm just asking in case we have to stay here for a long time. Okay?"

"Okay," she conceded.

"Look. We can do this one day at a time," I suggested. "But be assured that you can live here on a permanent basis if you want. We are not only open, but we would be honored. Seriously. Do you believe me?"

"Yes, I believe you." You smiled. "Thank you," you said softly.

"Thank you," I responded.

NINETEEN

After everyone else had gone to bed, I noticed the light in Raun's room still burning. I climbed the stairs to the third floor and found him lying in his bed, staring wide-eyed at the ceiling.

I glanced up at the smooth expanse of white painted plaster. "See any cracks?" I asked.

"No. But I'm not looking for cracks. I'm thinking."

"Well, that's exciting. Actually, my guess would have been that you had developed a keen meditative state with your eyes open ... or that you'd submersed yourself knee-deep in thought ... or that you'd had a stroke and possibly vacated your body."

"Popi, that's not funny."

"Why not? Do you believe you're going to leave your body one day?"

"Yes. And that's exactly what I have been thinking about."

"What a surprise!" I said, sitting on the edge of the bed.

"With all that concentration and mental calisthenics, have you come up with any earth-shattering insights?"

Raun sat up. "Listen, I don't want to have a dialogue with you asking all the questions and me answering. Don't get me wrong. I love dialogues. I loved them when I took the eight-week program at the Institute. I like it when you let me come to my own conclusions. But, in this case, right now, I want to know what you think. I like to hear your ideas; sometimes, that's very useful."

"Okay. You're on. What would you like to talk about?"

"Oh, c'mon, Popi. Death. Dying. What else?"

"Whose death? Grandpa's? Mine? Yours?"

"How about we start with mine?"

"Okay, what about your death?"

"I thought we weren't going to have a dialogue with you asking me questions?"

"We're not," I said. "But I have to ask you a few questions to understand the substance of what you want to talk about."

"Okay, that makes sense."

"So, what about your death are you concerned about?"

"Well," Raun continued, "I'm not afraid of being dead. I mean, I am afraid of dying, especially if it's painful. But I'm okay about being dead, sort of — well, not really. That's the problem."

"What's the problem?"

"I really like myself. Is that okay to say?"

"It's fine with me," I answered, suppressing my inclination to inquire if he thought it was morally defensible to sustain such a positive self-regard.

"So here's the problem," he continued. "You know I'm kind of an agnostic — well, maybe an atheist. I keep thinking that this might be it; you're here, and then you're gone, you're dead, and it's really over. But I can also conceive that something of your spirit goes on. I mean, you can make a case for that in physics, Popi. Matter can never be destroyed. It can be radically changed, like a volcano blowing off the top of a mountain. But it never quite disappears; it becomes lava or vapor. It just converts into another kind of energy — or, in terms of human energy, it becomes spirit. So, let's say my spirit goes on, only I have no memory of this life because I'm pure spirit and I, as my spirit, don't retain my personality. So then this vapor — not really a vapor, but you know what I mean — it continues in the universe but without my memory and my personality characteristics. As far as I'm concerned, then, this spirit, well, it's not really me anymore, not the me that I know and like. It's the abstract spirit of me, and who cares about that? That's still like dying into nothing."

"Wait, slow down," I said, enjoying his thoughtful rambling. "If you believe something of you continues, then there is no death, not in the 'nothing' sense of the word."

"For me, that's just about the same as 'nothing.'"

"Why?" I asked.

"Popi, I have so many great memories. Of course, there are some that I don't think are so great, and who cares about them? But I want to hold on to the great ones. And then, I still feel silly saying this, but I really like my personality. So, if I die and don't remember those great memories and do lose my personality, which I love, then I don't have anything that matters or, at least, anything that matters to me right now. Does all this sound a bit brain-dead?"

"No, Raun, this sounds very much 'brain alive.' You're raising important concerns and very, very profound questions. Do you believe in heaven and hell?"

"I don't think so. It's too literal for me, like trying to imagine a shelf somewhere in time or space, that's not really in time and space of course, where all the good people go, and then another shelf where all the evil people go. And then imagining a sort of limbo, a holding tank where you get processed for a portion of eternity. I can't quite grab on to that. It's easier to imagine just going to dust."

"Why, Raun?"

"I want to know what you think," he insisted. "Like, what do you think is going to happen to Grandpa?"

"I told you already what he said. He's going to meet up with my mom, and then Rosie will meet up with her first husband, Norman, and then, apparently, they will create a foursome and play bridge together."

Raun laughed. "C'mon, Popi. Be serious."

"You know, until this very moment, I never realized that maybe I am being serious."

"What's that supposed to mean?"

"Could you entertain the following scenario?" I asked, hypothesizing as I spoke. "The universe, or God's universe, depending upon your belief structure, seems to be in a constant state of expansion, with infinite elasticity. It has no discernible beginning or end, and therefore no walls or limits. Now, we live in this universe, on this dot that is Earth — well it's so small that, in terms of the universe as a whole, it's hardly even a dot. Anyway, on and in this dot, we are busy creating an avalanche of beliefs about good and bad, right and wrong, and so on. And these beliefs are powerful in molding our everyday life experiences. We are very serious about our belief-making, sometimes self-righteous. We even go to war with those who hold differing beliefs that we might see as threatening ours.

"When you were little and diagnosed as incurably autistic

and mentally retarded, the beliefs of the experts led them to advise us to put you in an institution. If we had done that, then you would probably be a nonverbal inmate of some mental facility right now, rocking back and forth in your own feces, and those experts would point to you and say how correct their beliefs had been. Instead, your mom and I decided to see you as providing us an opportunity to love and accept you and create a very special program and method to help you. After we had worked with you for years, you evolved into the amazing young man that you are. We had a different set of beliefs than the experts did; thus, we stimulated a completely different outcome. In this universe I'm describing, beliefs are often self-fulfilling.

"Now suppose, just suppose, this belief-making ability that we all have is a mirror of the ultimate creativity of the universe. And suppose, just suppose, that, as God has given permission in this universe for people to choose love or hate, to make peace or war — in the sense that space and free will are provided so people can make those choices — then maybe, in this possible universe, how it works in life is how it works in death. For example, in this infinitely expansive universe, those who believe they will turn to dust upon death in fact turn to dust. Those who believe in reincarnation and who think they will return as a cow or an insect will return as a cow or an insect. Those who believe in heaven and hell indeed find those shelves you talked about before. And those who see themselves as releasing a spirit or essence of their nature, without memory or personality, get to vaporize themselves in that way. . . . What do you think? It's something like a series of parallel spiritual universes created by our beliefs. Isn't that exciting?"

"Okay, Popi, let me see if I follow your logic. If I believe that when I die I'll retain my memory and personality, then I'll get to retain my personality and memory."

"Yes. Exactly."

"C'mon, you are just making this up."

"Of course. Exactly. It's all made up," I agreed. "Suppose that's the way it works in death, since it works that way in the lives of many of us dancing on our little dot. That would be God extending to us ultimate creation."

"Then the ball would be in our court," Raun concluded.

"Yes. And what if the ball has always been in our court? Only now we are going to acknowledge our involvement and take more conscious charge of our destinies."

"Sounds great, Popi, but that doesn't make it true."

"This is not about truth, Raun; this is about make-believe, the ultimate make-believe."

"Why would you believe this version of death?"

"Why not?" I asked. "Do you think going to dust is a more useful belief?"

"No," Raun said, "I like this one better."

"Good. Then it's yours to believe, if you want it."

Raun smiled at me. "You know I think it's crazy. I don't really buy it. But, Popi, I'm not dismissing it." Raun smiled. "I don't know why, but I'm feeling much better."

"Great. Now you can go to sleep," I suggested.

We hugged each other, exchanging kisses on the cheek.

As I returned to my room, I reviewed my conversation with Raun, realizing I had opened myself to an entirely new perspective from which to view your transition, as well as from which to embrace my own. Amusing myself, I conjured up a Hollywood version of your fanciful bridge game in heaven, smiling as I imagined you looking at me, off in the distance, and winking.

TWENTY

As the third week with you and Rosie in residence at our home unfolded, I spent time with you early each morning, then at lunch and dinner whenever possible, and for long hours afterward in the evenings. I made sure that I jogged back to the main building to visit with you during all my class recesses so that we could share every ounce of time available and explore whatever thoughts you wanted to consider. Although your willingness to have extended discussions had ebbed somewhat in the last few days, you always lavishly expressed your delight in seeing me.

One afternoon, as I rounded the front porch of the house, I found you sitting alone in a chair, facing the distant view. Though you had been napping, you awoke as I approached.

"I know your footsteps now," you smiled confidently without opening your eyes. "Bears, sit," you said, touching the chair next to yours. "Your class — what did you teach this morning?"

"Before I answer," I said, "can I refill your mug with some hot tea?"

"You don't have to," you responded, "Zoe just did it five minutes ago. She's gets me things before I even realize I want them." You shook your head with an appreciative smile. "Okay, now back to the seminar. Tell me about it."

"We did an exercise on how we make ourselves powerful and how we have made ourselves weak . . . or victims. There was a lot of laughter but also some super learnings about beliefs we hold that either strengthen our determination to be daring or erode our self-confidence."

"What do you mean?" you asked, still keeping your eyes closed.

I enjoyed your newfound curiosity about our work, but sometimes I questioned the sincerity of your increasingly frequent solicitations for more information about ideas and a philosophy of life you had criticized for decades. "Hey, Pop, do you really want to know more about the classes, or are you just being kind to me?" I asked playfully.

"I do want to know. And what's wrong with being kind to you?"

"Actually, Pop, you have been so damn sweet, I barely recognize you."

You opened your eyes abruptly. "I've always been sweet," you barked.

"Listen, cute guy, you are so full of shit."

"That's the prerogative of an old man," you asserted, amused by our exchange. "Besides, is that any way to talk to your father?"

"That's a perfect way, especially when my father has become my dear friend and my words are filled with love and straight talk — not judgments." I responded.

You took my hand into yours, smiled, and leaned your head back into the chair, allowing your eyelids to close again. "Tell me more about your class."

"After the group exercise," I said, "I listed on the easel three core or central disempowering beliefs and three alternative beliefs that could forever change our lives. Do you want to know what they were?" You nodded your head. "Okay. Here goes. Disempowering belief number one: 'I can't get what I want.' That belief kills off all sorts of wants or desires before they are even birthed fully in our minds, suggesting something's wrong with us, suggesting we're incapable rather than capable. Disempowering belief number two: 'The environment has limited possibilities.' With that belief, instead of seeing abundance and opportunities, we see limits and scarcity. Disempowering or inhibiting belief number three: 'The universe is inhospitable to us.' Believing this, we have to exert almost superhuman efforts to get what we want in the face of opposition from people and events that we identify as hostile to our efforts and goals." I smiled as I looked up at the sky. Certainly, I had labored under such assumptions for years, never questioning the burden that resulted from maintaining that kind of worldview. "It's a wonder that any of us who have ever held these beliefs could actually get out of bed in the morning and face the world. Now, what excited us in class was the idea of challenging these perspectives and entertaining the possibility of replacing them with more useful and helpful ones. Are you still with me?"

"Yes, my boy," you said. "Go on."

"Now here's the kicker, Pop: designing and adopting new, more effective perspectives to replace the old ones I just mentioned. So, empowering belief number one becomes: 'I can get what I want,' instead of 'I can't get what I want.' As soon as we come from that new place inside, our minds and hearts and spirits come alive with a wellspring of creative thoughts and dreams. Empowering belief number two: 'The environment has limitless possibilities.' From that vantage point, we start seeking and often discover options that weren't apparent before. And number three is my favorite because it flies in the face of most newspaper headlines and lead stories of television newscasts: 'The universe can be very user-friendly.' If we adopted that notion, we'd more likely envision and seek support rather than armor ourselves against anticipated hostility." I paused. "Still interested, Pop?"

"Yes, but don't keep asking me. My eyes are shut, but I'm listening." You raised your eyebrows as if accentuating your pronouncement. "Belief number two," you said with a flourish. "If we believe in limitless possibilities, we're more likely to find solutions to our problems. And belief number three: If we think the universe is friendly," you articulated carefully, with a smile, "then we might make a lot more friends. Yes? You see, I've heard everything you said."

"Actually, Pop, I love your rephrasing of what I said. Very folksy!"

"I'm a folksy kind of guy," you responded. "Go ahead. I'm ready for more."

"The big question is, When we dump the old limiting perspectives and form more hopeful or optimistic ones, does the world change? Maybe not directly. But our experience of the world does change, and that in itself changes the world. Because we've changed our beliefs, we've changed, and then we respond differently to life's twists and turns, the way you've chosen to see your illness as an amazing opportunity and adventure rather than a tragedy."

You nodded your head as you absorbed these ideas. "So," you asked pointedly, "do you now hold these...these empowering beliefs all the time?"

I laughed. "Twenty-five years ago, I never dreamed of questioning core beliefs or the so-called societal truths I'd learned growing up. I bought most of them hook, line, and sinker; I was a great student of the collective pessimism and, as a result, one miserable character. I'm doing better now, Pop. Perfect? No, no way. I trip and stumble, but maybe less frequently than in previous years. We're in charge of the beliefs we hold. Reforming or recasting my mind-set, even when I'm really challenged, helps me to be clearer in my intentions and to deliver more effectively the life experience I really want. But I feel I'm still very much a student of what I teach."

"That's good," you acknowledged.

"Pop," I said, "when Mom was sick, I never knew what to do, how to be with her. None of us did. Being scared can be very self-consuming. I've taught myself to see the world differently. I'm not scared now — not for me, not for you. How about you? Are you scared?"

"No, I'm not scared, either. Not about the cancer. And not about moving on."

"What about the pain?" I asked.

"It's been tolerable. Sometimes better. Sometimes worse." You opened your eyes, still clasping my hand. "How do you think Rosie is doing? Is she disturbed?"

"Why don't you ask her?" I suggested.

"I have. She says she's doing 'fine.'" You took in another deep breath and then released it with deliberate focus. "Quite a wonderful woman, that Rosie of mine." You paused again. "Bears, you didn't answer my question."

"She's dealing, Pop. During their walks every morning Samahria encourages her to talk, get stuff out, maybe change some ideas. Rosie and I bantered back and forth just yesterday about her taking more charge of your joint affairs — like learning how to balance the checkbook, understanding what's in those chaotic, crazy files you keep, and dealing with your income checks from Social Security and from your bonds. Samahria and I finally got her to open a bank account in Salisbury and go into town to do some shopping. We want to help her to be independent. Kenny and Denise have been super. You see them organizing all your papers and explaining to Rosie what bills have to be paid. But still, in regard to finances, when I look into her eyes, I see a wall."

"You're right," you said, acknowledging what you had observed yourself. "Okay, Bears, enough talk now. Let's just look at the view." Your eyes scanned the landscape and the clouds in the sky. "Heaven — I've come to heaven."

I knew that you were referring to more than just the scenery. Somehow, you had made heaven more and more your state of mind. Did you know, Pop, that I have no recollection of ever holding your hand as a child? But here we sat — you at almost eighty-six and I at fifty-four — father and son, friends at last, sitting together and holding hands. Heaven, Pop. This is heaven.

When I came at lunchtime to accompany you to the kitchen, I encountered a surprising scene. You sat in a chair by the window in your room. Rosie sat beside you, piles of paper spread out on the carpet in front of her. She had apparently opened the files you both kept and explored them well.

"Hey, hey," I said, "I'm awestruck. Not so much by you, Pop, but by you, Rosie."

"I hate this stuff," she quipped. "Really, I'm just doing this as a favor to your father."

You looked up at me with a mock-serious expression on your face, then smiled. Without missing a beat, you continued to instruct her. "After you pay the maintenance on the apartment, then you file it here," you directed, pointing to the alphabetized filing box. Rosie placed the receipt dutifully in the appropriate section. "Good," you said. "Now, let's do the tax form."

"Do we have to go through all of this?" Rosie whined.

"C'mon, Rosie. You've got to get used to this." Suddenly, tears gushed from your eyes, Pop. You started to cry. "Rosie, one day, you're going to be alone. I'm not going to be here. You're going to have to learn to take care of yourself." Rosie looked down at the floor, then grabbed her throat, holding back the emotion and the tears. Without responding, she walked out of the room. You pointed after her, clearly wanting me to follow Rosie into the hallway.

"Will you be all right?" I asked.

"Yes," you said, gaining control over your feelings and blowing out an extended column of air as you relaxed your chest. "Go with Rosie."

Rosie sat on the step of the staircase, looking aimlessly out the window.

"Do you want to talk?" I asked, sitting beside her.

"No," she said.

We sat together in silence for at least five minutes. "I know

I should learn how to take care of all those bills and the checks and the files," she said. "I know." Rosie looked at me and grabbed her throat again.

"What's happening?" I asked.

"I can't let go," she insisted as the tears finally welled up and flooded her eyes.

"Can't let go of what?" I asked.

"You know," she insisted. "I'm not ready to let him go. And he was doing so well."

"He's sliding a bit now," I said. "He's much more tired."

"I know. Bears, I lost one husband many years ago. It's hard to go through this again."

"What's the most difficult part for you?" I asked.

"I love him. It feels like we've been together forever. I'll just really miss him," she said as she cried. I put my arm around her and held her close. We didn't speak until I could feel her gaining her composure.

"Rosie, how can I help you with this?"

"By just doing what you're doing. I know it's good for me to talk about it, but sometimes I think if I talk more, it will hurt more," she said.

"Does it hurt more now?"

She shook her head, sighed, then started to laugh. "No. It doesn't hurt more. Actually, I feel like I can breathe again."

"Good. So does that mean you're going to survive?"

"Yes," she declared. "I can do this."

"You can do what?" I questioned.

"Learn the damn checkbook and whatever else. Okay, let's go back to your father."

"Do you feel okay? We can talk more if you want."

"No. I don't want to leave him alone. He'll worry."

We stood and walked back toward your room. You had your half glasses on the tip of your nose and looked up at us as we entered. "You ready now, Rosie?" you barked like a drill sergeant.

"I'm ready," she declared.

"Bears, give me the file over there." I picked up the box and brought it to you. I could see your level of fatigue increasing. "You don't have to do it all now. I can help you and Rosie later today or tomorrow." You dropped your shoulders, nodded, and gestured to us to help you back into the bed.

Once we had covered your legs with the blanket, you looked at Rosie, then back to me. "Rosie, when I'm gone, you can stay here, live here permanently with Bears and Samahria."

Rosie drew in a deep breath, about to allow herself to move into territory not previously traversed. "Abe, what are you talking about? We have our home in Florida. I'd go back to Florida."

"But it would be nice for you here," you said softly.

"May I interject?" I asked. "Both of you can decide whatever makes sense for you. Either of you is welcome to live here as long as you want. That's like a forever invitation. Rosie, do you hear me?"

"Yes. That's very nice, but we have our home in Florida."

"What about it, Rosie?" you asked. "You can stay here with them."

"No, Abe, I would go back to Florida."

You looked at me, Pop, seeming disoriented for a second. You, for your part, had to let go of trying to care for Rosie once you were gone. In these moments, Rosie had allowed herself to consider the unthinkable and envision her life without you.

"How about we leave you to nap; then it will be just about dinnertime. How does that sound?"

You sighed boisterously, shaking your head affirmatively. When I leaned over to kiss you, you grabbed my arm and held me close. We looked into each other's eyes. I could feel, in this moment, that you had begun to say good bye. I touched your face with my other hand. You smiled and kissed me.

"Abe, I'll sit with you until you fall asleep." Rosie said as she sat down on the bed and took your hand.

I left the room quietly.

The next day, as we prepared to take you for another examination by the doctor, you dressed more slowly than usual. Given the obvious erosion of your physical vitality, Samahria had brought breakfast to you in your room, but you declined to eat anything more than a single bite of the toast and a sip of tea.

Finally, you declared. "I can't go. I am just too tired."

"Listen," I said, "I can rig a chair, get some help, and make it easy for you to get to the car." You shook your head. "Okay, Pop. Do you want to lie down again?" Before I finished articulating my question, you sat down on the bed and tried to kick off your shoes. Rosie grabbed the sneakers, untied them, and gently slipped them off your feet. Together, we helped you resume a supine position in the bed. You bit down on your bottom lip. "Are you feeling pain?" I asked. You nodded.

"Abe, I just gave you your pills two hours ago. The doctor said every four hours. I can't give you more for at least another hour," Rosie said, clearly disconcerted by her own pronouncement.

"I have a thought," I interjected. "Even if we doubled the dosage, it's not going to be a catastrophe. Actually, the doctor said we can adjust the amount of medication we give him if the pain increases. Let's make him comfortable." As Rosie reached for the capsules, I continued. "Pop, how about we see the doctor without you — and see what steps he can advise to help you further?"

"Maybe we should schedule the appointment for another time," Rosie countered.

"Let's keep this appointment and then, if we want, make another for Dad at a later date," offered Samahria.

"In the meantime, Rosie, could you give him the painkiller?" I said. You opened your mouth to accept the medication, then sipped limply on the straw. "Pop, how does all this sound to you?"

"Whatever you want to do. You do what's best."

As we walked in silence down the staircase, I noticed Zoe at her desk.

"Zoe, would you do me a favor," I asked, "and sit with my dad while we go to the doctor?"

"Absolutely," said Zoe, jumping up from her chair.

"It's just about lunch hour anyway," I added. "We should be back before two."

"Does he want anything from the kitchen?" she inquired.

"I don't think he wants to eat anything right now," Samahria responded. "Just your company would be perfect."

Zoe scooted up the stairs as we left the house.

Driving up the winding country road, I said, "Rosie, maybe it's time to consider hospice. It will allow us greater control over his pain."

She looked at Samahria, as if pleading for an opposing comment. "I agree, we don't want him to suffer, right?" Samahria said, touching Rosie's arm.

"So this is it?" Rosie asked herself aloud. "So this is it?"

Samahria took her hand and stroked it. "Rosie, maybe it's time to take this next step — so we can help him."

"You're right. But, first, let's see what the doctor says."

"Sure," I concurred as we arrived at the chemotherapy facility where we were to meet with the oncologist.

The physician, surprised at the absence of the patient, listened as we described your condition. Rather than pushing for more injections or suggesting additional treatment, he concurred that hospice sounded like the next logical step and agreed to fill out the necessary forms. When I gave him the name of the person I had contacted at the local hospice association, he said he knew her well and that she would be the perfect person to speed the process along and initiate help with our home care.

When we got back into the car, Rosie eyed me suspiciously. "You have been talking to hospice all along?" she asked.

"Absolutely," I said.

"But you didn't mention talking to them," she countered.

"Actually, I did. But you weren't ready. I just wanted to make sure that if we needed their services, they would know about us and be able to accommodate Pop as a patient. This is not the big city, Rosie. I didn't know who would be available and how quickly we could get help. All I did was lay the foundation."

"Thank you," Rosie said softly as she gazed out the window and watched the passing countryside. "One last point. Before we contact hospice, I want to ask Pop. This should be his decision."

Samahria and I both concurred.

When we returned to your bedside, Zoe had dampened your mouth with a washcloth and now sat at the edge of the bed, rubbing your feet. "I'm giving him a foot massage," she declared, smiling. "He's loving it. Right, Abie?"

You grinned, totally captivated by Zoe's energy and love. She had adopted you like a father, Pop. "Zoe, you're the best," noted Samahria.

"I totally agree," Rosie said, glancing at Samahria, then looking back at me. "Your friends, the people on staff here, they're wonderful," she added as we all watched Zoe's fingers moving artfully over the bottoms of your feet.

"Wonderful people," you acknowledged, Pop, as you looked at Zoe, "and one angel."

"I'm really not that good at foot massage," Zoe blushed, flashing a soft, self-effacing smile as she received your compliment.

After Zoe left, we presented you with all the information we had gathered about hospice and about our meeting with the doctor.

"Do whatever you think," you said after hearing all the data.

"If we did hospice, we'd be able to control the pain better and make you more comfortable," Samahria elaborated. "They'll give us additional medications to use, be available to us twenty-four hours a day. This could be quite wonderful — they'll supply you with a health-care worker who'd come for a few hours every other day to sponge you, if you want, and give you a massage."

"I have talked with the local administrator and the nurse who would be supervising your case," I added. "You know me — I won't settle for just any kind of care for you. Pop, these folks seemed like they had real heart and wanted to help, really wanted to help."

"Sounds pretty good," you said. "Rosie, what do you think?"

"Whatever you want, Abie," she replied.

"Bears, what's your opinion?" you asked.

"This could only be good for you. And if for some reason it's not, we discontinue immediately. These folks are good people. They care about the patients and their families. They don't want to intrude, just to help. My vote would be a definite yes."

You turned to Samahria, who tipped her head affirmatively.

"Rosie?" you said, clearly placing a question mark at the end of her name.

She reiterated, "Whatever you want."

You turned to me, Pop, and nodded, inviting consciously the next installment of our unfolding adventure.

Leigh, the case supervisor from HospiceCare in the Berkshires arrived on Friday afternoon. First she visited with you, Pop, explaining the services that would be provided and respectfully asking you about any adjustments or changes you wanted made. Then she came to the kitchen, where Rosie, Samahria, and I were waiting. As we walked down the hallway toward the sitting room, she paused, looked around, and smiled.

"There is such great energy in this house. I felt it from the first moment I walked in." When we sat together, Leigh reached out and held Rosie's hand.

"This is difficult for you," she said, reassuringly. "This is hard for everyone. But you're his wife. This affects you and your life the most." Rosie's eyes filled with tears. Leigh continued, "We're going to try to do everything we can to help him. Do you have anyone you have talked to about what you're feeling?"

Rosie pointed to us. "We talk and talk." Regaining her composure, she added, "If you live with him," she continued, pointing at me, "you get to deal with everything you're thinking and everything you're feeling." Rosie then leaned forward and tapped my knee affectionately.

"That's excellent," Leigh noted. "Many people we serve have incredible difficulties handling this type of situation emotionally, and we can supply therapists to help. It doesn't seem like that's an issue here. It's wonderful you're keeping him at home. Looks like you've got everything in hand."

"Almost," I said. "We want more help with pain control."

"You told me that on the phone, so I brought some morphine patches, which I will show you how to use. Based on how he seems to me now, I think we might want to consider a morphine pump. Do you know what that is?"

"Yes," I said. "Could you explain it to Rosie?"

"Sure," Leigh responded, turning toward Rosie again. "It's a machine, run by a little computer, that puts medication directly into the bloodstream through an IV. When we install it, we can set the exact amount of morphine he gets. So if he needs more, we simply adjust the setting. In addition, the pump has an override button that allows you to give him extra dosages if need be just in case he experiences a breakthrough of pain. I will order one today. I'm sure we can get it here by Monday. Until then, we can use the morphine patches."

"And if that's not enough?" I asked.

Leigh looked at me knowingly. "I will have the doctor write a prescription for some synthetic morphine that you can put under his tongue. It's fast acting and can be used to supplement the patches. How does that sound?"

"Great," I said, squeezing her hand appreciatively.

"His mouth is very dry," Samahria added. "If we can get him to take water, we're in good shape. But, if not, any suggestions?"

"We can give you something to help with that. They look like large cotton swabs with sponges instead of cotton on the end. You leave them in water on the table beside him and you can use them to keep his mouth and lips moist. Does he like to be massaged?"

"Not usually. However, when Zoe did his feet yesterday, he seemed to really enjoy it," offered Rosie.

"Then he'll just love Maria. She has been trained and has lots of experience with hospice patients. She'll be very sensitive and caring with him. Trust me on that."

During the next ten minutes, Rosie provided information for medical and Medicare questionnaires and signed the appropriate forms. Then, as Leigh stood at the door to leave, she reminded us that her staff would be on call around the clock, and that if necessary, we could get a nurse to come in the middle of the night.

"Can we give you a hug?" Samahria asked.

"Funny," Leigh said, "when Bears greeted me at the door, he hugged me like an old friend. I feel I know all of you." She embraced each one of us and departed.

Armed with the morphine patches, I went back upstairs into your room with Rosie.

"Nice person," you said.

"Definitely a very sweet lady," I agreed. "How's the pain factor?"

"Bearable," you acknowledged.

"Then why don't we try the patch that Leigh explained to you?" As I placed the patch near your shoulder, Rosie raised the bottle of water off the table beside your bed. You resisted her offering. "Cute man, if you take some of that water," I said, "you will be more comfortable." You eyed me curiously, then angled your head to accept the straw. "Later," I added, "we can decide whether you want to eat dinner in the kitchen or have room service."

"In the kitchen," you said. However, you remained in bed and ate very sparsely from the tray served to you later that evening.

The following morning, Kenny and Denise visited again. This time, they came without Jessica, who had seen you one evening earlier in the week. As had become our tradition, Samahria and I left to give them special time alone with you and Rosie. Denise, who had been trained in massage, worked on pressure points around your shoulders and head as you sat in bed. Although they remained somewhat aloof in my presence, Kenny displayed a touch more warmth than he had initially, and both of them addressed us more easily now as "Bears" and "Samahria."

In the evening, I returned to your room to assist you in case you wanted to eat in the kitchen. You had faltered when walking to the bathroom earlier in the morning, requiring support.

"What do you think, sweet man, downstairs or upstairs?" I asked.

You pointed downward.

"You got it. I'm going to kneel by your bed. You put your hands on my shoulders, and I will put my hands around your waist. When I get up, you get up with me. Okay?" You nodded. "We'll do it slowly, easily. Ready? Here we go." As I pushed up with my legs, you hung onto my neck and pulled yourself to a standing position. While you seemed proud of your accomplishment, Kenny and Denise's faces registered deep dismay as they watched. "Okay, Pop, we're halfway there — well," I laughed, "sort of. Now we do a power assist. Here, I'll get on one side and tuck my arm under yours. Kenny will take the other side." Without a moment's hesitation, Kenny moved quickly to your side and put his arm under yours. Together, we moved slowly down the corridor. Samahria and Denise followed. Denise put her hand in front of her mouth, obviously trying to digest how much your condition had eroded since their visit the previous week. At the staircase, I positioned myself below you. Kenny came from behind. Together, we moved methodically down the steps. "You're doing great, Pop," I cheered. "Still showing a bit of feistiness. But any time you want to stop to rest, let us know." You indicated your desire to continue down the stairs. Suddenly, you began to lose your balance. I righted your body without commenting. "How about we stop for a moment? Yes?" You paused, took in a few breaths as if to garner more strength, then indicated your desire to continue. "We're off, Pop. Kenny's got you. I've got you. We're having a dance, Pop. Three guys, dancing right on the stairs." You started to laugh, bracing yourself against the banister on the last step. "Okay. Time out for Pop to laugh." Kenny, Rosie, Denise, and Samahria began to laugh.

"You know, you're crazy," you said to me. You gave me one of those soft glances, Pop, touched my cheek, and then commanded, "Let's get going!" As we walked through the center hall into the living room, Samahria moved quickly in front of us and opened the door to the kitchen. Tayo awaited our arrival.

"Ay," Tayo grunted. "Hot and sour soup, Grandpa. I got you ribs, too. I got a lot of ribs so Popi can have some."

"Very kindhearted of you, Tayo," I said. "Did you get the dishes Kenny and Denise wanted?"

"Everything," Tayo said. "What's that?" I asked, pointing to the pizza box on the counter.

"Oh. I stopped at Brothers. I know Grandpa loves Chinese food, but we've been eating it so much since Grandpa and Grandma came. I got a pizza for Sage and me. Bryn and William are coming over later, and I know William likes pizza."

"No problem; you don't have to justify it," I said smiling. "But you sure know how to take care of yourself." Tayo smirked as he pulled out the chair for you, Pop.

"Big shoulders," you observed as you passed my son. "You're a good kid, Tayo."

"Thanks, Grandpa," he responded.

"That's our Ay-Tay," Rosie added.

Samahria explained to Kenny and Denise the meaning of Rosie's nickname for Tayo. We all took our places around the table. None of us knew that this would be your last meal in the kitchen.

Later that evening, while Kenny stayed with you and Rosie in your room, Samahria spent a few hours alone with Denise. Denise had graciously offered to see if she could help Samahria with the persistent pain in her joints and back. As they spent time together, they began to build a bridge across the abyss of years of separation and silence. The next morning, Sunday morning, Kenny and Denise sat with you and Rosie while Samahria and I spent time with our children and granddaughter. Before he and Denise left to return to their home in Pennsylvania, Kenny pulled me aside.

"I know you have another doctor's appointment on Tuesday. Do you think he'll make it?" Kenny asked.

"Frankly, I don't know. Given we've started with hospice, I'm not sure it's relevant anymore. But whatever happens, I'll call you."

"Thanks," he said. "Thanks for all that you're doing."

Several hours later, I received an unexpected and moving e-mail from Kenny and Denise.

Hi, Bears:

Denise and I have become aware of how much we appreciate all that you and Samahria have done and continue to do. Your love and support for Pop and Rosie has given them unending comfort and guidance. We wanted you both to know that all that you've been doing, and the way you're doing it, has also given us tremendous peace of mind. We welcome this, and thank you for it.

We again would like to offer ourselves in any way at all that we can continue to help in this joint journey that we are sharing together.

Love, Denise and Kenneth

TWENTY-ONE

The next day was difficult for you, and you remained in your room instead of venturing downstairs. We launched the day together before the sun came up. Several times, I helped you extricate yourself from the bed in order to use the bathroom. In each instance, I positioned myself behind you, wrapped my arms around your chest, and mobilized you by pushing my legs up against yours from behind and sliding them forward, inching us across the floor until we reached the bathroom. I talked to you to encourage you and keep you motivated as we moved.

"You keep defying all previous records. Still mobile, Pop. You're doing great. We're a team. You and me. Getting from one room to another. Pop. How you doing?"

"I'm doing," you said.

"Just doing, huh? You could decide you're having a good time. I'm having a good time." I suggested. You smiled. "Caught you!" I exclaimed. "One genuine smile as we shuttle to the bathroom. I know, I know; you don't have to say it — I'm crazy."

"If you keep talking so much, how am I going to pee?"

"I'm done. No talking while you're urinating. We can make this a religious experience. Or we can do this as a meditation."

"How about I do it just as a simple pee?"

"Perfect, Pop," I said. "One simple pee."

Recognizing the amount of effort required for you to sit and then stand again, I stood steadily by your side, holding you up so that you could relieve yourself without altering your position. You stood tall, Pop. You were withered. Tired. Aged. Yet you had incredible grace as you stood on the tile floor in the winter of your days. As the vitality in your body diminished, your spirit shone brighter as if the force of your nature made a more soulful than material presentation. I felt like I had become your knight, standing guard in the twilight, assuring your safety as you prepared one day soon to walk through death's door.

After we returned to the bedroom, I stayed with you and Rosie for the next three hours until I had to prepare for class. Bryn arrived before I left, spending an hour with you before she departed to work with a family from Sweden who had come to the Institute with their autistic daughter. Samahria and Rosie prepared your meals, although you refused the food and just sipped some water. Samahria took an extra long walk with Rosie later in the morning, then sat with you and Rosie for several hours in the early afternoon. During my class recesses, I read to you, first from Richard Bach's *Illusions,* especially the opening passage about the many creatures clinging to the bottom of the river and the one among them who dared to let go and trust the current to take him home. Then I read from pages of poems and prayers that I use in the courses I teach. Later in the day, I canceled my meetings and afternoon dialogue sessions, replacing myself with other staff mentors in order to be with you.

When I returned to your bedside, you appeared extraordinarily fatigued. The level of pain had increased, especially in the areas of your lower spine and kidneys. We gave you additional medication. I called Leigh, who assured me we would have the morphine pump by morning.

Something within me shifted as I walked back and forth between my room and yours throughout the night. I experienced a new sensibility, a heightened sense of alertness. Shapes and colors appeared laser-sharp to my eye. The slightest whoosh of air coming through the open window suddenly seemed more audible than ever before. The call of birds and distant geese danced in my ears like sections of an orchestra birthing a natural symphony. My fingers exploded with a full spectrum of sensations, no matter what I touched. The imprint your body had left on mine after I lifted you and walked you to the bathroom tingled at the edges of nerve endings on my chest and arms long after the event. Phrases that I had repeated to you replayed in my mind like old sweet tunes that I wanted to hum: "You're the best guy." "You're doing great." "Thank you, Pop." "This is my honor." "We're having an adventure." I also recalled the phrases that you repeated to me: "Heaven, I've come to heaven." "You know, you're crazy." "Here we go again." "I'll leave the dying to God."

After you arrived here you had moved away from the beckoning abyss you cried out to embrace so eagerly in the hospital and created your own second coming, Pop. You opened your heart to me in ways I would never forget. I know you wanted to give Rosie more time and more opportunities to ready herself for your passing. Indeed, you had utilized this time so wisely. The image of the two of you balancing your checkbook together was a most meaningful portrait, a testament illustrating how you guided her shrewdly toward the next stage of her life. I knew we had now begun the last dance, Pop.

That trusty little alarm clock in my head continued to awaken me every half hour, permitting me to check in on you, assist you to the bathroom or help you with water or medications. The promenades down the hallway became the glue that cemented all the activities into a journey without end. Sleeping, awakening, walking through the darkness, looking out the windows at the stars, helping you, holding your hand, refilling the water container beside you, putting the straw in your mouth, talking to Rosie, hugging Rosie, saying a prayer, crawling back in bed, snuggling with Samahria, whispering my gratitude to God. Then up again, moonlight on the balcony, cool wood against my feet, back into your room, a capsule under your tongue, replacing the morphine patch, stars visible from the windows, tears of love and joy on my pillow. Thank you, Pop.

TWENTY-TWO

At seven o'clock on a Saturday morning, I drove through the gates into the parking area at Crossroads Stables. Almost thirty years had passed, and yet every detail of the buildings, the fencing, the jumps, and the fields remained curiously the same. Jerry — you remember Jerry, Pop — he, too, appeared exactly as I had remembered him, not a single day older in spite of all these intervening years. Unkempt and caked with mud as usual, he swaggered toward my car.

"Hey, your father phoned right after you," Jerry yelled. "He wants you to wait for him. He should be here any second."

"My father called?" I asked, flabbergasted.

"Yes, yes," he insisted, ignoring my evident surprise. "Kahlil's in his stall." Jerry shook his head in mock disgust. "You ought to consider getting rid of him. He's too crazy. I know you like Appaloosas, and Teddy at Long Meadow said he's got a real beauty coming in. Well mannered. Big, like Kahlil — almost seventeen hands. Why don't you take a look?" Before I had a chance to answer, he ducked into the main barn and disappeared from my view.

"What's going on?" I protested aloud. No one answered. I slipped out of my car slowly and stood motionless in the parking lot for a few minutes, too disoriented to take even a single step in any direction. Ellen, Jerry's wife, appeared suddenly. She walked quickly from the main barn to the office, smiling and waving at me. God, Pop, she didn't look any older either.

"Coming through!" someone shouted from behind. Instinctively, I moved away from the voice. A man, leading two horses by a rope, brushed by my side. Although the landscape was familiar, I felt awkward and displaced. I knew I could not remain in the parking lot indefinitely; so I headed cautiously toward the second, smaller barn where Kahlil used to be housed. To my surprise, I found him in his stall, characteristically spirited and skittish as I approached.

"Good luck with him today," said Lauren, the stable hand who cared for him for years. "When I brought in his bucket of grain, he acted so spooked that I thought, 'Damn, this morning that App's gonna trample me.' I got the heck out of his stall real fast." Shaking her head, she bent down, picked up a sack of feed, tossed it into the wheelbarrow, and exited the barn. Kahlil had backed toward the rear of his stall, snorting and banging his front legs on the dirt floor. He peered at me through the wood slats encasing him. How bizarre it felt to see him again. When I entered the stall, I said, "Hey, big guy," words I had repeated to him a thousand times previously. Kahlil marched right up to me and pushed his head affectionately into my chest. As I stroked his long, muscular neck, I felt extraordinarily excited and confused at the same time. Thirty years! It had to be thirty years! How could I be here, after all these years, with this amazing creature that I had loved once so dearly? How could he still be alive?

Kahlil and I had learned to ride together. During our first months (our chaotic honeymoon), I, totally inept and a novice at horsemanship, attempted to school this absolutely "green" Appaloosa gelding. You called me nuts, Pop. Even by traditional training standards, Kahlil had been an unusually skittish and high-strung animal. He bolted at the slightest noise and often reared in response to other horses, bicycles, and cars. One of his eyes was large and dark brown, but the other was a beautiful, bizarre, humanoid blue eye, called a "watch eye" — deemed by horse folklore to signify a dark force in an animal. Certainly, Kahlil lived up to this reputation by resisting any attempts at grooming by the stable staff and by catapulting me off his back over and over again.

However, after a period of several months, I gained more skill and confidence in my riding and Kahlil became more responsive, though he was never docile. Even as we developed a solid, respectful partnership, Kahlil declined to give me absolute rule. Often, he'd pull on the reins to signal his desire to run, or cast his eyes toward a fallen tree and pound the ground with his front legs until I allowed him to race forward and make the jump. At other times, as if to acknowledge the give-and-take of our relationship, he would follow my lead, turning or stopping or galloping ahead based on how I shifted my body in the saddle. Now, as I continued to stroke Kahlil, I realized how much I prized this mysterious, somewhat unpredictable, friend.

Jerry entered the barn, talking as he walked past: "I suggest you saddle him up real soon. Your father doesn't like to be kept waiting. He'll have Poco ready to go within minutes after he arrives." Jerry knew you, Pop — no nonsense. We had been boarding horses and riding together for six years. When you brought Rosie out here, you put yourself into a lower gear, becoming patient, easy about time and the trail ahead. Sometimes, prior to our jaunts, the three of us would share a morning coffee with Jerry and Ellen. However, when you came to ride with me alone, you didn't want to dally. You wanted to saddle up and get moving.

As I grabbed the saddle from the rack at the back of the stall, Kahlil shook his head up and down and banged his left front leg several times against the closed door.

"You got it, kid," I said. "I'm taking you out." I couldn't quite believe what I was doing. Kahlil must have died years before. How could I be draping this blanket and saddle on his back, placing the reins over his head and sliding the bit into his mouth? Just then, I heard you call my name.

"Barry. Let's get going!"

"A minute more, Pop," I said dutifully, wondering why you hadn't addressed me as Bears.

I tightened the strap around Kahlil's belly, rechecked the bridle, inspected his hooves, and then led him from the barn. Perched atop your beloved palomino and sitting tall in your handsomely carved Western saddle, you looked down at me impatiently. "Come on, we don't have all day," you huffed as you directed Poco toward the meadow and the trail beyond. Although frugal in most areas of your life and of moderate financial means, you had allowed yourself one indulgence, horseback riding. And although our relationship had tended to be quite muddled, with you often annoyed or angry with me, you and I had managed to forge this single area of interaction where we could find common ground.

As I placed my foot in the stirrup and pulled myself up into the saddle, I couldn't keep my eyes off you. The hair on the sides of your head was thick, dark, and slicked back handsomely. Your shirt, tucked tightly into your jeans, outlined your trim upper torso and muscular arms. You were totally in command, like a mythic general atop his favorite mount. You could not have been more than fifty-five years old. My age, Pop. But how could that be possible? And yet, here you were, still in top form and riding Poco once again. Apparently you did not notice how old I'd grown or how young you'd become. I kept thinking that if I dared to suggest that this had to be a dream, you would disappear. I nudged Kahlil with my right foot, and he moved forward smartly. Just as we passed the tractor, Ellen started it. Kahlil bucked, slamming his body into an open barn door and snapping off the upper latch. The noise his rump made slapping the wooden barrier spooked him even more; he pranced nervously in a sideways direction.

"Easy, easy, easy," I said reassuringly. "I got you, my friend. Easy does it." Kahlil seemed to calm once he allowed himself to hear my voice.

"I'm sorry!" yelled Ellen.

"Listen, when I get back, I'll take care of that latch. Okay?"

"It was my fault," she responded. "We'll fix it. No big deal. Did Jerry tell you about the Appaloosa for sale at Long Meadow?"

"Yes, thank you," I said as we lurched forward, knowing I had no intention of trading this spirited, passionate creature for an inhibited, well-mannered animal. Besides, I loved Kahlil. I trotted past the barn complex until I had brought Kahlil alongside Poco. "Let's head out through the woods toward Old Westbury Farms," you suggested, leading the way at a comfortable gallop until we entered the trail at the edge of the forest. Then you slowed Poco to a walk as we negotiated the first steep incline down a rocky ledge. When the path leveled, we moved ahead once again at an easy canter until we reached the next incline.

"Pop, isn't this strange?" I asked, wanting you to acknowledge how utterly peculiar it was that we should still be riding together.

"What are you talking about?" you responded. "The weather's great this morning. Warm but cool. If you can just keep that horse of yours under control, we'll have a fine ride." You appeared oblivious to the impossibility of the situation.

As we left the confinement of the trail and crossed the first in a series of huge meadows, I pulled alongside you again. I did not know quite what to say.

"Kahlil almost took down the barn before," you quipped.

"I know, Pop, but he and I had a quick talk. He's got his act together now."

"Can't fool me," you said. "Some creatures can never be tamed." You looked at my horse as we rode and then, to my utter surprise, said, "Actually, that's what I like about that damn horse."

"Really?" I exclaimed. "I thought you hated Kahlil."

"He's a pain, all right. Wouldn't take much to dislike him." You paused, smiling, and said, "But he's got real spirit." At that moment, you snapped your reins lightly and pulled ahead in a controlled gallop. I nudged Kahlil to lunge ahead. Once abreast of you, I asked, "How come you never told me that you liked Kahlil before, that he had spirit? I thought you agreed with Jerry — that Kahlil was crazy."

"I didn't say he wasn't crazy. I said he's got spirit. Like you. And you have to negotiate with spirit; you never tame it." You smiled again, not a smile consistent with your disposition during your earlier years but a smile filled with the warmth and wisdom now more familiar to me. You tightened your legs around Poco, increasing the speed of your gallop.

I encouraged Kahlil to move faster and within seconds found myself right back beside you. "You seem different, Pop."

"I am," you said.

"How come? Why are you different this morning?"

"This is a very special ride, my boy. Nothing like the others."

"How's it different, Pop?" I asked.

"You'll see," you said as you directed Poco into a full gallop.

Standing up in my stirrups, I flicked my reins, riding in a style I adored. Kahlil sprinted ahead into a full gallop, flying across the landscape like the wind. As you turned to see me gaining on your position, you laughed and nudged Poco with your boot, increasing your speed. "Go, Kahlil! You're free," I shouted as I leaned forward. "You are free!" Usually Kahlil could easily overtake Poco, but somehow your horse managed to move faster than ever. You and that animal, now lathered in sweat, glided forward into a time warp. Suddenly, I could see your every movement as well as Poco's in elegant slow motion. Your body, athletic and agile, mimicked the graceful mechanics of your horse. You moved together like two seasoned dancers at the apex of your art. Although you raced your horse through the tall grass and across the open field, you maintained a curiously relaxed and disengaged expression. "I'm doing it," you said.

"Doing what, Pop?" I shouted, trying to gain enough speed to close the gap between us.

"You know," you said confidently. You spoke in a normal voice. In spite of the wind and the pounding of the hooves on the ground, I heard you perfectly, as if you had spoken from inside of me.

Nevertheless, I yelled to you. "What do I know? What am I supposed to know?"

You smiled at me, and to my amazement, Poco's form became even more energized. His legs lunged forward, extending his gait as well as increasing his velocity. I kept nudging Kahlil to catch up. As you crested a grassy ridge and sped along a high plateau, I followed. The dirt, kicked up from the ground beneath Poco's hooves, formed a cloud of dust behind you. You pressed your horse to move faster, guiding him to hug the split-rail fence as he ran. Finally, in an effort to catch up to you and simultaneously give Kahlil total control, I released my reins and put my hands into the air while continuing to stand in my stirrups. In the past, whenever you observed me riding that way, you'd scream at me to stop. This time, however, you looked back and watched me with what appeared to be an approving grin. Then, you, too, stood in your stirrups and put your hands in the air. I could not believe my eyes. Suddenly, I found myself instructing you to sit back down into the saddle. You shook your head, saying, "Just one more field."

"What does that mean?" I shouted, knowing that at least five more interlaced fields lay ahead.

"One more field," you repeated. Instead of turning predictably to the right, you eased back into the saddle and veered left into what should have been a thick forest. A huge meadow we had never traversed spread out before us.

"Let me catch up!" I yelled, concerned about depressions or unexpected holes in the ground. "We can do this together." I reached out to grab your hand, and you extended your arm toward me as you said, "Who will be left to remember what we did?"

"I will, Pop," I assured you. "I will remember."

"And when you're gone, then who? Who then will remember?"

"I don't know, Pop. Maybe, in the end, no one will be left to remember. Please, give me your hand." I angled my body, extending my reach farther until our fingers moved within inches of each other. As I lunged to grab your hand, I felt myself falling off the horse.

At that instant, my eyes opened wide into the darkness. I could hear the clock clicking on the counter. My heart raced. The galloping motion lingered in my body as I jumped from the bed onto my feet in one swift movement. Almost an hour had passed since I checked you last. A full hour! What happened to the trusty clock in my head? Within seconds, I had made my way rapidly down the hallway to your room. As I approached your door, I slowed my pace purposely. Before entering, I stopped and listened. I could hear you breathing. I stood alone, in the corridor, calming my racing heart and just listening. Finally, I walked quietly into your room.

"He's been sleeping more soundly," Rosie whispered.

"Great," I said, realizing that the morphine pump we received that morning had allowed us to make you more comfortable and minimize your pain. You had the most relaxed expression on your face, Pop, similar to your expression when you rode Poco into that last field. Only you had aged about thirty years in the thirty seconds since the end of my dream.

I reached down and clasped your hand firmly.

Although you remained asleep, I could hear your voice in my head.

"Who will be left to remember?" To my surprise, I heard you repeat the question, this time adding words that were not in my dream. "Who will be left to remember — what we did, who we loved, and how we cared?"

TWENTY-THREE

In the morning, you again requested my assistance to get to the bathroom. I did not know this excursion would be the last time you would leave that bed alive. Rosie and I eased you into a sitting position, and then I wrapped my arms gently around your torso and lifted you to a standing position. Rosie grabbed the morphine pump as she untangled the intravenous tubing taped to your wrist. Noting her efforts, you tried to assist.

"Abe, it's okay," Rosie said. "I've got it."

Almost too exhausted to talk, you whispered, "Gimme," indicating that you wanted to carry the pump. Rosie handed it to you immediately.

"Pop, give me a second to get behind you and we'll be off," I said as I circled to your back and slid my arms around your chest in an action we had performed many times over the past few days. For me, this special ritual with you had become like lighting candles in a cathedral, where we bring alive a flame of faith and hope. Your bedroom and the bathroom ahead had become part of my cathedral. "Ready, Pop?"

"Ready," you responded.

"Here we go," I said, moving my legs against the back of your legs, propelling you forward once again. "We're up and running. Yes, sir! It's you and me again, sir, making tracks. You can almost see the dust flying behind us." I thought about my dream and our race across that last unfamiliar field. No longer astride your mount, you shuffled slowly across the floor, holding the pump limply at your side. Although others might have despaired in the face of such a contrast, I experienced every step you took as triumphant. Even as I felt you sagging into my arms more heavily than usual, I had only the greatest reverence for your determination. "You're one fantastic dude, Pop. People who have climbed Mount Everest say they do it one step at a time. We're doing our Mount Everest right across this floor."

"One step at a time," you echoed as you looked down at your feet.

"And you are doing it so elegantly. It's all perception, Pop. I only have eyes for the wonder of what we're doing." I meant every word I said. You stopped at the entrance to the bathroom, resting for a moment. You glanced back at me out of the corner of your eye. "Not far to go, Pop," I said. "A few more feet. Is this manageable for you?" You nudged me, indicating your desire to continue. "Come on," you muttered. "We got some more elegance to do." I laughed. You smiled. Once inside the bathroom, I stood at your side, supporting you as you stood by the toilet. Hardly any fluid at all passed from your body. Nevertheless, you waited as if anticipating a larger physical event that did not occur.

"What do you say we return to your room?" I suggested finally.

You shook your head. We waited. And waited. And waited. At last, a small stream of urine cascaded into the bowl. You grinned.

"A class-A accomplishment, Pop," I said, celebrating your achievement. "And I was here as the witness. Rosie," I shouted, "we got some action going here."

"I hope it makes you both very happy," she bantered.

"What do you say, Pop? Did it make you happy?"

You looked into the toilet, then glanced back me. Although your arm remained at your side, you gave a thumbs-up sign with your hand and tipped your head regally to celebrate your stunning success.

"I'm happy," you volunteered, flashing me a spirited though somewhat sleepy smile.

"Me, too," I whispered as I looked directly into your eyes. "I love you, Pop."

You nodded, responding in a raspy voice, "I love you, too."

This was as unlikely as it gets. Two grown men, poised over a toilet bowl, talking about happiness and expressing love.

When you sat back down on the bed, you winced.

"Your back?" Rosie asked.

You squinted and nodded.

"Let's give him an extra dose," I said to Rosie. "Okay? I'm going to hit the button on the pump."

"He just got into bed. Maybe we should give him a few minutes," cautioned Rosie.

"Why?" I asked. "Administered this way, the morphine works almost instantly. But it's your call, Rosie."

"Abe," she said, "do you want something for the pain — or should we wait, since you just got back in bed?"

"I'd like something for the pain," you said softly. Rosie

looked up at me as I leaned over and pressed the button. The very audible whine of the machine filled the room with its mechanical music as it sent an extra dosage of medication directly into your bloodstream. Your body relaxed noticeably within twenty to thirty seconds and you promptly fell asleep.

Signaling to Rosie to follow me, I ambled down the hallway away from your room and invited her to sit beside me at the top of the staircase.

"Why the hesitancy about extra medication from the pump?" I asked.

"You don't let me get away with anything," she responded.

"We're a team. Part of being a member of this team is that we help each other, support each other, and love each other. Right?" Rosie nodded. "So I'm not trying to catch you at anything. But you really don't look at home with that machine. How come?"

"I can't talk about it," Rosie said.

"You can if you want to. But you have to decide. I can't get inside of you to help make this easier. If I could, Rosie, I would. But if you talk about it, allow yourself to feel whatever you're feeling, then you'll give yourself a chance to find a way to be with Pop that won't hurt."

"Who said anything about being hurt?"

"No one," I admitted. "I'm just guessing."

"Well," Rosie responded, "it's a good guess."

"What's the hurt about?"

"The machine. People use that pump, Bears, when there's no hope."

"No hope for what?"

Rosie glared at me, then softened her expression. "No hope that he's going to come around again."

"What does that mean?" I asked.

"He did it when he first came here. He got out of that bed and walked. He smiled, laughed, and ate in the kitchen with all of us. We even went to the restaurant with..." She stopped talking midsentence. "I know, Bears. I've been letting go — more and more. I'm really grateful for this time. He's been very happy here. I guess I still want more. Is it okay to want more?"

"Sure. But Rosie, I don't want more for Pop if he doesn't want more. You guys have had the best life together. He really worked hard at hanging out a bit longer with all of us. He's tired now. We've just got to let him go."

Rosie nodded her head. "You see, Bears, as long as he's breathing, even if he's sleeping, we're still together. There's a little piece of me that keeps holding on." Her tears started to flow finally. This time she did not grab her throat in order to subdue her emotions. Instead, she allowed herself to sob, her chest heaving as she released months of anguish. I put my arms around her, loving her, Pop, and loving you.

That afternoon after class, I returned to your room. Rosie and Samahria sat at your bedside. You had steadfastly refused all offers of food or even water. To make you more comfortable, they moistened your mouth and lips with wet sponges.

"Why don't you go out and stretch for a couple of minutes?" I suggested. "I'll stay with him."

As they left the room, I climbed up onto the bed beside you and took your hand. You opened your eyes and looked at me.

"Can I get you anything? Anything at all?"

"No," you whispered.

"How's your throat?" I asked. You opened your mouth to signal the dryness in your throat. I grabbed a sponge and brought it to your lips. You sucked on the wet edges, then pulled it into your mouth with your tongue. "Does that feel good, Pop?" You nodded almost imperceptibly. After a few more moments, you signaled to me to remove the sponge.

You exhaled noisily and then with the sweetest smile said, "I'm ready, my boy."

"I know, Pop. You just let me know whatever I can do to make this easy and comfortable for you. Okay?"

"Okay," you said.

"Do you know how much everyone has been loving you?" You dipped your head affirmatively. "Whenever you're ready, Pop, you can just take off."

"Like a bird," you joked.

"Sure, why not? Just like a bird," I laughed.

You took my hand and held it tightly. "You know I can't thank you enough," you whispered.

"We had the best time, Pop. I'm so grateful for these weeks and for the last two years. It filled a lifetime for me — in terms of me and you."

"For me, too." Tears filled your eyes as you smiled again. I could feel the wetness on my own face as I looked at you. You attempted to wipe the tears, but your hand fell short of its mark. Immediately, I used my fingers to push the tears from the corners of your eyes. "Make sure Rosie's okay," you said.

"You know I will," I answered. You tapped my hand, nodding your confirmation. "So Pop," I said, "you can relax into this process now and let go whenever you want. You're safe here. And if you need more than the normal cycle of medication for the pain, we can help you with the button on the pump." You closed your eyes and drifted off to sleep. I remained beside you, content to sit motionless, never once needing to adjust my position. And you, Pop, you never let go of my hand.

About an hour later, you awoke, somewhat uncomfortable. "How are you doing?" I asked.

"I'm doing," you said. We both grinned. I offered you some water. To my surprise, you responded affirmatively. I put the straw into your mouth, allowing you to take a few meager sips before you pushed the bottle away. Then, as you requested, I gave you another container in which to relieve yourself.

"Would you like to talk? Or would you like me to read to you?"

"Read," you instructed.

I read from Bach's *Illusions* once again, then read some more poems. You seemed to drift in and out of consciousness as I went from one reading to the next. Rosie and Samahria came back, stayed for a while, then left to prepare dinner. Twenty minutes later, you opened your eyes again.

"Hi, Pop," I said. "I'm still here."

"Me, too," you commented playfully.

"Ready to have your visit with God?" I said, alluding to a comment you had made in a previous conversation.

"Is God ready for me?" you joked.

"What do you think?"

"I'll let you know when I get there."

I laughed aloud. "Fair enough, sweet man."

You closed your eyes again. I could see by the way you moved your head against the pillow that you were experiencing discomfort. "Any pain?"

"Yes," you sighed.

"Want a little extra help with it?"

"Yes."

"Okay, here it comes." I pressed the button on the morphine pump. Within a few minutes, you fell back to sleep again.

We ate a quick dinner in the kitchen; then we all returned to your bedside. Tayo stopped in several times, wanting to know how you felt. On one occasion, he sauntered in very quietly, went over to Rosie, hugged her, then hugged Samahria and me as he exited. Zoe came by, bringing glasses of water and tea for everyone. Bryn visited later in the evening, alternately holding Rosie's hand, then Samahria's. Before she left, she climbed up on the bed next to me and put her hand on your shoulder.

"I love you, Grandpa," she said, looking down at you with a big smile. Although you did not acknowledge her presence or comment, I had no doubt that her energy reached you. Bryn leaned her head on my shoulder and added, "I love you, too, Popi."

"Thanks for loving me," I whispered, "and for loving your grandfather." During the next few hours, we talked to you as much as we could but in ever decreasing fragments of time. More and more, you receded into a deep landscape within.

My left hand cradled your head against the pillow. The fingers of my other hand created a soft cocoon around your arm, which lay limply on the blanket. I had now been sitting cross-legged on the bed next to you for hours. I could not discern whether you could hear me, but I kept speaking anyway. In every manner possible, I wanted you to feel our love and experience our presence at your side.

"You're doing great, Pop. It's Bears. Rosie is here. She's doing fine. She loves you. Dad, you have the best wife. And, in her eyes and our eyes, you're the best.

Samahria's here too. She adores you. We all do. We're here with you as you take this journey. We're cheering you on. It's okay to let go whenever you want and have your visit with God. Pop, we love you."

The room had become a sacred sanctuary where the lines between life and death blurred.

The next morning, the hospice health-care worker visited, offering to give you a sponge bath and a light massage. You accepted the kindness, although your focus felt more inward now. After she left, you fell asleep again. I took my position beside you on the bed and placed my left hand under your head again. When I put my right hand into yours, you squeezed it. I exerted a gentle pressure against your fingers to acknowledge your greeting.

"You don't have to open your eyes, Pop. I wanted to share with you a portion of a sunrise meditation I lead in our Inward Bound program. You might like it."

I took a deep breath and let myself slide into a most quiet and peaceful place inside.

"The sky above. The fields below. The sun. The moon. The light. The darkness. The comings and the goings. Always, always the comings and the goings. A circle without end, Pop."

You opened your eyes and looked up at me. I smiled, then bent over and kissed you on your cheek. Within seconds, you closed your eyes and drifted back into yourself. The soft light of the table lamp put a golden glow on your face. Your arm twitched several times as if releasing energy. The rhythm of your breathing appeared somewhat strained but mostly steady, except for those infrequent occasions every few minutes when you stopped in mid-breath, frozen in silence and stillness, only to begin again, usually with a deep inhalation. As I watched you, I realized I had been following your breaths with my own, entraining my respiration to yours. We can walk together up to death's door, Pop, but we each enter alone. I kept visualizing a little baby floating in the liquid of its mother's womb and feeling the undulations of birthing contractions. Dying out of that womb meant being born into the daylight. Were you getting ready to be born?

I remained at your side, always holding your hand. Minutes melted into hours. Sometimes I stayed silent, leaving you alone to continue your internal process of disengagement. At other times, my words to you echoed in the quiet of the room. Rosie sat nearby, watching and listening. Samahria floated in and out of the bedroom like a mystic phantom, coming to your side to touch you or kiss you or tell you how much she loved you and then disappearing silently through the doorway. We had each carved out a special place for you in our hearts.

"I'm here, Pop. Right beside you."

As I listened to the sound of my voice, I could feel my love for you pouring from every cell in my body.

"I will not leave you, Pop. You can still count on me, on all of us. We are all loving you. Rosie's still doing fine. Bryn visited early this morning. You were sleeping, Pop, but she talked to you anyway — like I'm talking to you now. She told you how deeply she cares about you. You're her special grandpa; she so enjoys your gruff, understated affection toward her and treasures you as the elder of the tribe. But Pop, I know you know that. If you're in any pain, just give me a sign — squeeze my hand, nod your head. We want to make you as comfortable as possible."

Although I watched carefully for a signal, any gesture, even a fluttering from your closed eyelids, I did not detect any meaningful movement or response. Nevertheless, I remained vigilant.

Zoe tiptoed into the room and taped onto the footboard of your bed a handwritten piece of paper with the words "God is good." We smiled at each other as she withdrew silently from the room.

Bryn returned again during her lunch break. She kissed you, Pop, read the message pasted to the footboard, then crossed the room to hug Rosie.

"Grandma," she said, "when you and Grandpa first came to live here, you brought all your jewelry in a bag, but you never showed me what's inside. I'd love to see your jewelry." "Bring me the bag from the top shelf in the closet," Rosie ordered in a grandmotherly manner. Bryn retrieved it forthwith and gave it to her. Rosie smiled as she pulled out the first item. "This bracelet was my mother's," she said while modeling it on her wrist and admiring its craftsmanship. "But I never wear it," she admitted. Soon afterward, Rosie extracted a pair of earrings that had been her mother's as well and held them at the side of her face. "They don't look very good on me." She put her hand back into the bag and this time retrieved a necklace given to her by you, Pop. Many of the other articles in the bag had also been gifts from you. Her expression softened. She placed it around her neck for both her and Bryn to admire.

Suddenly Bryn pointed to the only piece of jewelry Rosie wore — a very thin, silvery ring that, when compared to the bounty in the bag, looked like an inexpensive trinket. "Grandma, what about this ring?" Rosie's eyes melted into the sweetest expression as she stroked the ring and looked at you in the bed.

"Years ago," she said, "when I first met Grandpa, we went to Hawaii. Now, we weren't married yet," she continued with a sly smile, "and I didn't want anyone to know I was traveling with a man I wasn't married to." Rosie giggled. I had never seen her giggle quite like that before. "In those days," she continued with a mischievous smirk, "people didn't do that. Your grandfather, being the gentleman he is, walked me into a Woolworth's right down the street from our hotel and bought me this ring so I wouldn't feel uncomfortable. It cost $1.25. I wore it all the time, so that if anyone looked, they'd think we were married. And I've been wearing it ever since, for over twenty-five years." She stared at the ring, cherishing the memory.

I could see Bryn struggling to hold back her tears. Rosie's prized possession had not been any of the shiny jewels in that bag. Instead, she wore a dime store ring that looked as if it came from a bubble gum machine as a symbol of your love relationship.

After Bryn went back to work, Kenny, Denise, and Jessica entered the room. Although we had been in continual contact by phone, they had not seen you in almost five days. I had warned them that you would look different — that you had lost more weight and, in some fashion, appeared less imbedded within your physical form. Kenny bent over and kissed you. Jessica took your hand as tears came to her eyes.

"He's still having his adventure," I said softly. "I'm glad that you're here. I'm sure he will be, too." I gave them some time to adjust to the current situation and your presence in the bed, then, raising my voice, I said, "Pop, Kenny, Jessica, and Denise are here."

You opened your eyes and looked at them.

"Hi," Kenny said softly.

"Hi, Daddy," Jessica whispered.

"Here," I said, sliding off the bed, "sit with him. There's plenty of room."

Kenny and Jessica took positions on either side of you as Denise seated herself near the foot of the bed.

"How do you feel?" Kenny asked.

In a barely audible, raspy voice, you said, "Okay."

"Pop, I'm going to go downstairs," I interjected, "so you guys can have some time together. But first, I'll explain to them about the pump and the sponges and water." I reviewed how we were helping to make you comfortable. They listened very attentively as I pointed to the pump and showed them how it worked. I also informed them of Rosie's discomfort concerning extra dosages of morphine that you might receive.

As I turned to leave, Jessica picked up the sponge and wet your lips. You acknowledged her gesture by nodding.

"I won't be far away if you need me," I said.

We spent the evening by your side. From time to time, you awoke, looked around long enough to catch us smiling at you, then closed your eyes again. I took up my position cross-legged on the bed next to you. Again, I cupped my left hand behind your head while using my right hand to clasp your hand gently. I wanted you to feel our continued presence, wanted our love to soothe you like a cradle, wanted you to know that all of us — Rosie, Samahria, my siblings who were here, my children, and I — continued to embrace you. You were not alone. You remained part of a circle, our circle, that had no end. My brother and sister watched me with you, keeping their energy consistent to the ambiance that character-ized our vigil. Their ability, in these moments, to be totally present and loving with you added an incredible depth to the warmth and solidarity that I believe we all experienced. As you slipped in and out of consciousness, I kept talking to you.

"We're all here, Pop. Kenny, Jessica, Denise, Samahria, me. Rosie's on the chair, looking at you, loving you. We're all loving you. You are the best guy. We've had the best time with you. You can let go any time you want. We're all rooting for you."

I looked over at Rosie. Her eyes met mine; then she turned away. Earlier we had two discussions about how she might tell you that she'd be okay if you let go. The expression on her face told me she hadn't said that to you.

"The sky above. The fields below. The sun. The moon. The light. The darkness. The comings. And the goings. Always, always, the comings and the goings. A circle without end, Pop. A circle without end."

Kenny watched me and listened to my words. He appeared relaxed with my verbalizations. Later that evening, he spoke. "Pop, we love you. We really love you. We're all together." His eyes moistened.

"Hey, Pop," I added. "You can let go and leave when it feels right. We're ready. Any time, Pop, you can go have your visit with God."

"Bears, do you think he'd want to hear what you just said?" Denise interceded, "The part about having a visit with God?"

I smiled at her, Pop. "Oh yes, we've talked about having a visit with God. Even discussed bridge games in the sky. Thanks for asking."

Several hours later, in the center hall, I talked with Jessica.

"Is there anything more I can do for you while you're here?" I began.

"No. I'm fine," she said. "Can I use your phone?"

"Of course; you don't have to ask. Jessica, how are you doing with this?"

"How would anybody feel? It's not easy," she answered. "Although I was watching you upstairs with him and you seemed so...so relaxed — but I'm not sure that's the right word."

"Grateful would be my word," I said. "I used to think that if I could wish Pop an ending for his life, I would have wished for him to just drop over while sitting in a chair or to die peacefully in his sleep. Maybe many people would have that dream for those they love. Never would I have wanted him to have an extended illness like cancer. And yet I am so grateful for his cancer. I am so grateful for the challenges and transformation it brought him — and for this expanded time to express so much love."

Jessica shook her head. "Grateful for his cancer! You know, I'll never understand you." Shaking her head, she walked away from me.

Suddenly I realized how strange I must have sounded. For me and from my chosen perspective, these past two years had been glorious, filled with unexpected opportunities to love you, Pop, and to see you open your heart. For her, Pop, this period of time had been difficult, filled with pain and a nagging sense of loss. Although I had suggested on numerous occasions that she speak with you about her issues and concerns regarding herself, her family, you and Rosie, she wasn't able to do that. Jessica represented our past, Pop, where the truth of what we thought or felt remained submerged beneath a friendly and often false smile or burst forth in angry and frequently inarticulate statements.

After Kenny, Jessica, and Denise left to go to their motel for the night, Rosie, Samahria, and I stayed with you. Once again, I hopped onto the bed and took up my post beside you. Every time I placed my hand within yours, you squeezed it, oftentimes now without ever opening your eyes.

"Hey, Pop, you're doing just great. Do you want me to read to you or say some prayers?"

You shook your head.

"Okay, then, do you want me to keep talking to you?"

You nodded.

"Great. Let me tell you who's in the room with you right now. Rosie is sitting in the chair by the window. She has the greatest expression on her face. That's one strong lady you've got. Samahria's sitting in another chair right next to you. She's eyeing you right now with that exuberant smile of hers. Kenny, Denise, and Jessica went to the motel. They'll be back in the morning. Oh, Pop, Zoe sends her love. She doesn't want to intrude; she only wants you to know you're in her prayers. And then there's me, Pop. Thank you so much for letting me help you. Getting to know you and you getting to know me has been an unexpected treasure in my life. Thank you, sweet man."

My tears kept coming as I gazed at your face. You pressed my hand, letting me know that you heard my words. It took an enormous effort for you to communicate. Just seconds after expending that energy, you faded back into that unfathomable recess inside.

"Take our love with you, Pop," I whispered in your ear.

The next day, I so appreciated how Kenny helped each time I gave you the extra morphine, especially in the face of Rosie's resistance. We never discussed a plan of action, but soon, communicating with eye gestures, we began to act in tandem. I would slide the pump under a pillow and just as I pressed the button, Kenny would cough loudly to camouflage the whining sound of the pump. Several times, Rosie glanced at us momentarily, then looked away. I think she knew exactly what we were doing, Pop, but found some comfort in not having to listen to the noise.

While I sat alone with you, still cradling your head and holding your hand, I admired the soft expression on your face. Although you had not been conscious for hours, I decided to whisper to you anyway. "Pop, whenever you want, just let yourself go. Whenever you're ready, you can have that visit..."

In the midst of my sentence, you opened your eyes suddenly and looked directly at me. Then, as if we had been in the midst of a conversation, you asked with total lucidity, "Visit. What visit? Where am I going?"

"Remember, Pop? Whenever you're ready, you can have that special visit with God."

Your face broke into a big smile, then you began to laugh with gusto. I didn't know where you found the strength. I laughed as well, enjoying your humor and joyfulness. You took a deep breath, closed your eyes, and drifted back into that place within. Your grin lingered and lingered. How beautiful you looked, Pop. What an inspiration! I could feel every fiber in my body cheering you on. You were going home to God.

That evening, your breathing patterns ebbed into a rhythm of apnea as your body loosened its grip on life. You would draw in a breath, then pause for as many as twenty seconds before exhaling and pulling in the next huge breath; then you would stop breathing again prior to taking the following breath. We watched you for hours, Pop. Nothing about what unfolded felt distressing. The room appeared frozen in a time warp filled with love.

I again asked Rosie to tell you that you could let go. She said she had done so the night before but admitted her pronouncement had lacked conviction. Rosie and I talked further about her releasing you from a deep, deep place inside.

"Pop will know, Rosie. It's got to come from your heart."

"I'm trying to get my heart ready," she murmured.

"I know. You're doing just fine," I said as I hugged her.

Later, as she stood at your bedside and watched you take those big gasps for each breath, tears streamed down her checks.

"It's time, isn't it?" she whispered. I nodded.

As the buildup of fluids in your throat further inhibited your breathing, I asked Kenny and Jessica, who had just returned, to help me roll you on your side in order to clear your passageway. Afterward, when we eased you onto your back, you opened your eyes once again and appeared to be in considerable distress and pain. The movement had brought you to the surface of your body and amplified your physical sensations. Rosie watched somberly from the hallway. I hit the button of the morphine pump and gave you medication orally as Kenny wet your lips and tongue with the sponge. Slowly, you drifted back into that oddly soothing rhythm of breathing apnea. I vowed not to turn you again.

Kenny, Jessica, and Denise went back to their motel for the night. I sat up on the bed beside you again. My legs began to numb from sitting cross-legged for all these hours, but my hand under your head and the other hand clasped within yours felt so vibrantly alive with your energy. Even so, I felt you moving further and further away into some secluded cavity within. I had been talking to you for days, and I wondered whether my words and comments kept drawing you back into the room and into this world. So I decided to use only touch and to be silent for longer periods of time — to give you space. At times, I engineered a mass exit from your room, including Rosie and me, announcing the fact to you so that if you felt more comfortable letting go without an audience, you would have the opportunity. Pop, this dying process felt very gentle and very peaceful. I hoped that was your experience, too.

I stayed with you for a few more hours, then took catnaps, awakening every thirty minutes to check on Rosie and you. Sometimes, when I reached your room, I found Samahria already there, sharing the watch.

At two in the morning, you started making a loud gurgling sound with each breath. Some folks call this the death rattle. It wasn't scary, just very loud and different — like no other sound I had ever heard. I had embraced your impending death so fully that no sounds or gasps could mar my sense of peace and completion. Rosie had difficulty listening to the noises in your throat. "It's music, Rosie," I said. "This is Pop's music."

"I wish I could hear what you hear," she responded.

"For some of us, this is the last song we get to sing," I added.

"You just want to make everything wonderful, don't you?"

"That's my job," I said, smiling.

As your breathing became more labored, I stayed closer to you and Rosie through most of the night, walking the hallway, visiting with you and talking to you. A number of times, I remained outside the door to allow Rosie her private time with you.

By six o'clock on Sunday morning, the increased accumulation of mucus in your throat had significantly compromised your breathing. You seemed to be drowning.

Rosie lay in bed beside you, her hand on your arm, her head on your shoulder. "Rosie," I said, "I'm so sorry, but we have to turn him over again to clear the fluid from his throat."

"No," she said as she started to cry, "Please don't touch him." She reminded me of my vow not to turn you again.

I withdrew into the hallway, closed my eyes, and took a few deep breaths. I did not want to go against Rosie, Pop. You had asked me to let her decide, and I intended to keep my commitment to you. Nevertheless, I still wanted to turn you over. I didn't want you to suffer. Returning to the room, I said, "Rosie, he can barely breathe. We have to help him. We have to turn him again — we have to do it right now. Please," I pleaded, "let me turn him over."

She watched you, still crying. "Okay," she whispered finally as she backed away from your form.

I put my hands under your shoulders and back and rotated you very gently onto your side. A thick fluid poured from your mouth. As soon as your windpipe cleared, your breathing, no longer blocked by the pooled mucus, returned to those firm though infrequent gasps for air. I rolled you slowly onto your back again. Your eyelids opened wide. I leaned over you, trying to search those eyes that no longer appeared to see. You seemed agitated, as if we had once again disturbed your process. I got down on my knees beside you and started rubbing your chest.

"Pop, you're doing great. It's Bears. I love you. Rosie is here. She's doing fine."

At that moment, Rosie put her hand on my shoulders. "I did it, Bears," she whispered. "From deep down. Just a little while ago, I told him that I would really be okay, that I wanted him to let go." Tears flooded my eyes. She had released you, and I knew this would make the journey easier for you now. I felt so excited for you both. You could let yourself go home now. I kept rubbing your chest.

"Pop, you don't have to keep this up any more. You don't have to take another breath. Rosie told you, Pop.

She loves you, and she'll be okay now. So will I, Pop. We'll take care of Rosie. We'll all take care of each other. You did that last breath beautifully, but you don't have to take another one. You can let your spirit free."

I felt you draw in another breath and hold it again.

"This could be it, Pop. You could just let this out and not take another breath in. We just want this to be easy for you."

Your breathing relaxed momentarily and your eyes closed. I continued rubbing your chest and talking to you. I decided I would help you do this, Pop, and I would not ever leave your side again until you were free.

"You can do this, Pop. You don't have to take another breath. It'll be easy."

I noticed the next breath appeared to be much shallower.

"You're doing it. That's it, sweet guy, you're letting go."

Rosie crawled into bed next to you, pressing her body against your arm. I could hear her crying. You started to draw in another breath as I continued to rub your chest very lightly.

"You don't have to complete this one, Pop. You could just let it go." Your chest expanded only partially, then you relaxed into yourself.

"That's it, Pop. Go to God."

About thirty seconds passed. Still stroking your now immobile chest, I watched the pulsation in your neck continue. Then another twenty seconds, then another. The visible pulse in your neck disappeared.

"Pop, you're really doing it. You're letting go. I'm so excited for you."

Another thirty seconds passed.

"My God, Pop, you did it! You are the best. Hurrah for you! Take our love with you, Pop."

I could hear my voice getting louder as if part of me stood as a witness outside of my body.

"Keep going, Pop. We're cheering you on. You're free now. You did it! You did it!"

The struggle to breathe had ended. Your body became extraordinarily quiet. Motionless. Warmth still radiated from your chest into my hand. Though your spirit had been set free, your energy still embraced me. Rosie stopped crying and sat up next to you, admiring your form. A few seconds later, you opened your eyes and a single tear rolled slowly down your cheek. I gazed into the vacant, dark, bottomless pools of your pupils. You were gone. I turned to Rosie, who watched that single tear glide down your face and smiled at you adoringly.

"What do you think the tear means?" I asked her.

"It's your father telling us he's okay," she said. "He's saying thank you and good bye."

A tear of joy. A tear on leaving this life and going to God. A tear of love.

I sat back down on the bed, crossing my feet beneath me as I cradled your head once again with one hand and held onto your fingers with my other hand. Somehow, Pop, I felt your spirit, still within your body and outside of it at the same time. Your skin remained supple and warm. Your face looked at ease and elegant in repose. I thanked God for this privilege, for the honor of being with Rosie and you in this way. With very gentle fingers, I closed your opened eyelids. I had never felt so filled with love and God in all my life.

TWENTY-FOUR

Rosie asked that your body remain in the room all day. She wanted to go to your cottage in New York, promising to return in the afternoon to say one more final good-bye to you. I brought Samahria into the room. We sat on either side of you, holding your hands. Then Bryn came and Raun and Sage and Tayo. Kenny, Denise, and Jessica returned. The air in the room felt holy, as if our energy still mingled with yours, Pop. I continued talking to you, sometimes aiming my voice at your relaxed figure, sometimes smiling as I looked up and around the room. Tears gushed from my eyes as a cry exploded from my throat, releasing a feeling of awe and wonder bigger than my physical form could contain. I had not wanted you to suffer, and I believed we had achieved that goal. Kenny walked over and put his arms around me. As the hours passed, your body cooled. But your face, Pop — your face became even more radiant and stately. How utterly handsome you appeared in death!

Jessica knelt beside you and touched your shoulder. After a few minutes, she looked up at me and said, "Pop's death was as beautiful as Mom's was horrible." She recalled, decades ago, watching Mom racked with pain as she occupied a sterile, anonymous hospital bed bordered on each side with metal railings. Her arm and hand, resting on the sheet, twitched by her side, and Jessica remembered how she had stared at Mom's hand, not knowing what to do, not able to touch her and soothe her. "I couldn't even take her hand," she whispered, shaking her head incredulously. We returned to your side. Several hours later, Rosie rejoined us. When I phoned your brother, Max, to tell him that you had finally set yourself free, he listened in silence, then said, "What is often difficult in the eyes of men and women is easy in the eyes of God."

EPILOGUE

After the burial ceremony, we all met at David's house. Kenny and Denise invited Samahria and me to accompany them into a separate, private room. They held our hands, Pop, as they expressed their gratitude to both of us, our staff, and the place that had allowed you to have such a "good death," referring to the love and care they had witnessed as a source of great comfort to them personally. Then they handed us a check for one thousand dollars made out to the Option Institute. What a distance we had come since those phone conversations in which Kenny said he would not address us by our names or do anything whatsoever that would endorse us and our work. Both Samahria and I were deeply touched by their warmth and sincerity. Over the past several years, Kenny and I have continued to communicate, especially regarding Rosie — working together to ensure her care and welfare. Kenny and Denise spent a weekend at our home the first summer after your death. We talked, laughed, and shared warmly, something I believe would be meaningful to you, Pop.

To honor their desire for privacy, I have changed their names and disguised their identities and those of their family members in this narrative. I have done the same for Jessica and her family. Samahria and I reiterated our offer to have Rosie stay with us, but she like you, Pop, covets her independence. She returned home to Florida soon after your funeral and from there wrote us the following letter.

My dearest Bears and my dearest Samahria:

You'll have to read this mush letter because it's easier for me to get the words out on paper than to wait for that little door in my throat to open.

I need Dad to help me put my feelings (our feelings) into words. Just to express a "thank-you" is not enough. How could we ever repay you for the love, the caring, the support? It was overwhelming for me to watch you totally take charge of everything, get all the help we needed, and not let me do a thing or worry about a thing. Bears, your strength enveloped me and gave me the strength to go on. Samahria, I'll always treasure our walks together, your sweetness and concern, and the closeness and secrets we shared. My grandchildren, Bryn, Raun, "Ay-Tay," and Sage are so warm and comforting to me. I love them dearly.

Bears, I'll always treasure that last Sunday morning, when you and I were alone with Dad — how you were struggling all night, trying to figure out how to get him to "let go" and not suffer any more. You did it, rolling him over with your strength and gently loving him and talking him into leaving us physically. We'll always have those wonderful memories of our great times together. You and I were so exhausted that last morning but relieved and happy for him. We knew that he was, at last, at peace.

I love you both for being there for your father and me and feel so grateful and fortunate to be a part of your family. I hope we'll always remain as close as we were during Dad's illness.

Love you both,
Rosie

I love and treasure Rosie so deeply. She remains an active and key part of our lives, as I know Samahria and I are in hers. When she is away from us, we burn up those long distance telephone wires with frequent hour-long conversations. We have the same kind of probing, playful, and loving conversations you began to allow in the last years of your life. Although you structured a wonderful trust mechanism to care for Rosie, we help her and assist her in every way we can. Our special friendship has grown even more dear.

Rosie is in my heart, Pop. I will always stand by her.

As I was completing this book, Pop, Rosie phoned from Florida with the most wondrous story. She had been sitting in the bedroom when suddenly she heard a loud thump in the apartment. She investigated immediately, walking through the house to check the front door and windows and also searching the walls to see if the recently hung framed photographs of you that I had sent to her had fallen. Everything appeared to be in order. Searching further, she opened the large storage closet in the hall. There she noticed that a carton had, indeed, fallen from a shelf — a carton that had occupied the same spot for years and years. When she bent down, she saw on the floor, just behind the place where the carton had fallen, a box wrapped in tissue paper. She withdrew the package and brought it into the living room. When she removed the tissue paper, she began to cry, Pop — not tears of sadness, but tears of surprise and joy.

At the beginning of your last summer together, both of you had been strolling in a shopping mall when Rosie spotted a beautiful carved Chinese jewelry box in a store window. You had suggested she buy the box for herself, but when she noted the price of several hundred dollars, she refused, insisting that the two of you continue your walk. Apparently, you had returned secretly to the store, you sly fox, and purchased the box for your beloved. You put it in that closet, Pop, and you never had the opportunity to give it to her. But death could not prevent you from expressing your love. That thump in the night — was it your thump? Rosie believes she received, besides your gift, a sweet message of reassurance from you. Yes, Pop, she has the box, but you can know that the thin silvery ring on her finger will never be housed in one of its drawers.

You did not build a skyscraper with your name on it. You didn't write a best-selling novel, become a movie star, or sing a famous tune. Your name will not appear in the history books. And yet what you did, Pop, will be as enduring and memorable as any work of art. You lived simply, with dignity and integrity, passing this way and leaving some of us richer for having known you and having experienced your love. Were you perfect? Hardly. Did you make mistakes? Sure. But did you learn to fly? Absolutely. Like a bird. You were never the father of my dreams, but in the end, you became the father of my heart. Who will be left to remember what we did, who we loved, and how we cared? Who will be left to remember? I will, Pop. I will remember.

FINAL REFLECTIONS AND GUIDING PRINCIPLES

The following principles created a frame of reference that not only guided me during my journey with my father but also enabled me to take action by expressing a kind of love that was, concurrently, tangible, tender, and awesomely empowering. I am forever grateful to have had the opportunity to walk this road.

AUTHENTICITY. Authenticity holds the promise of building bridges between people where none existed previously. Authenticity allows us to remove masks, break down walls, and create communion with others. Authenticity can be part of a cradle of love in which I allow you to be you and you invite me to be me. No masks. No charades. Straight talk. Real talk. Opening our hearts and minds to ask questions and share our own concerns, fears, confusion, insights, and joy.

False smiles and surface commentaries leave a sick person isolated and very much alone. People who are aging, ill, or dying know they are aging, ill, or dying. The conspiratorial game of silence or misinformation (saying "You look great" when you know the person looks gaunt or tired or wasted) closes the door to communion with our loved ones, for as we attempt to protect them, they, in turn, stay silent to protect us. But by asking sincere questions and expressing sincere thoughts and feelings, we open a gateway to others, allowing them to talk about what matters most to them.

LISTENING/BEING PRESENT. Active listening means making another person the total focus of our attention so that we can be supportive, caring, and responsive. Providing our afflicted ones with opportunities to cry, to laugh, to share stories and anxieties gives them a safe place in which to be themselves and be heard, validating any suffering and pain they may experience. In the midst of large families, many people grow old and die alone because no one has dared to listen. Instead of thinking about other things in our lives when we're in the presence of someone about whom we care, we can simply stay present.

ACCEPTANCE/RECONCILIATION. Many people realize at the end of their lives that they have much unfinished business. Letting go of our judgments and accepting a person who is grappling with death provides a meaningful conduit for healing. Oh yes, we might have our own unfinished business, our own regrets and expectations not met — we may even hold grudges. To open our hearts in the face of these barriers, we have to either process these concerns and confusions with a friend, mentor, or therapist or put them aside. Every time we discard the viewpoint, even if only momentarily, that another person is "bad" or "wrong," we give ourselves a greater opportunity to see and understand that person's humanity (clarity, prejudices, love, fears, comforts, discomforts) and let go of our judgments. Acceptance lives on the other side of a discarded judgment and oftentimes provides a fertile field for reconciliation.

GIVING THEM CONTROL. Allowing our aging parents or ailing loved ones control over their lives and their deaths means honoring them and helping them to retain a sense of dignity. The hospital death (dominated by high-tech life-prolonging measures and monitored by well-intended professionals) often robs people of the simplest dignities — privacy, the right to eat and sleep and see loved ones when they want, the warmth of familiar surroundings and people. If our parents or loved ones want to deal with their illness at home and die at home, let's be open, supportive, and active in fulfilling those wishes. We're not alone or without support in this; today, there are over 2,000 hospice organizations in the United States dedicated to helping people to live and die in the arms of their loved ones.

EXPRESSING LOVE. Don't hold back when expressing your love. Even if it means breaking with more conservative traditions, we *can* open our arms and hug each other. We *can* hold hands. We *can* put our heads on the shoulders of others and invite them to lean on us. We *can* share tears.

Remember, love is: (1) Accepting others: assuming that our parents and loved ones have done and are doing the best they can, letting go of our expectations of them as we might wish them to let go of their expectations of us; (2) Wanting the best for others and making that desire the pervasive underlying attitude in all our interactions with them, bringing to life that sentiment in every one of our 51 trillion cells whenever we think of or encounter them; (3) Being useful to them by taking action to help them get the best (their best, not ours). In order to love someone, we have to first fill ourselves with love. Not only do the ones we love benefit from such an action, but we, ourselves, benefit from the love we generate that now fills our own cup. Love them now.

PERSONALIZING PAIN RELIEF. Physicians and attending health professionals often regulate pain medication according to the dictates of some statistical norm, based on prescribed milligrams and time factors rather than the particular patient's experience of pain. Make sure you find compassionate and "user-friendly" doctors and nurses who can and will accommodate the needs of your loved one. Many hospice professionals have been expertly trained to provide responsive and responsible pain relief and comfort for their patients — even educating the patient and family so they can regulate this area of treatment themselves.

LETTING GO. Letting go is not just a state of mind; it can also be an action. People hang on to life and suffer beyond measure in order to accommodate and support the perceived needs of those they love. We can help the people we love to free themselves by telling them, even encouraging them, to let go when they feel ready. Often, those who are close to death hold on for the sake of loved ones who are not ready to let them go. To help those dying to free themselves, we can acknowledge aloud that we will survive and thrive while always keeping them close in our minds, our hearts, and our prayers. What a reassuring message to give to those we love!

BECOMING A FORCE OF NATURE. If we choose to help our loved ones during critical times of transition, it's best to become self-empowered so that as caregivers and gatekeepers, we can stand tall even in the face of opposition (have no doubt that there will be opposition). Here are the keys to becoming such a force:

- **Clarity of Purpose.** We can begin every experience, every relationship, by setting clear intentions, asking ourselves what we want to be or do or get from an experience. This is clarity of purpose. When my father first called me about his illness, I asked myself exactly how I wanted to be with him. Deciding to make loving him and serving him my focused mandate, above all else, helped guide all my subsequent decisions.

- **Conviction.** Once we set a course, once we clearly identify our purpose, we can develop a set of beliefs to support the process of fulfilling that purpose. Oftentimes, people make decisions to take new jobs or create new relationships while filled with doubts, regrets, and pessimism. Muddled beliefs or lack of conviction can lead us to miss our mark.

When we worked with our son Raun, we decided to make the attitude of love and acceptance the foundation of our approach and program with him. We sensed a baseline rightness about our perspective — not a self-righteous rightness, but a deep personal and pervasive understanding that our approach would not only "do no harm" but would in fact be the most respectful and, we hoped, the most effective strategy for piercing the veil of autism and helping him bond with us. If we could successfully build a bridge into his world, then we had a chance to help him learn and grow. Believing in our son and having faith in the course of action we took to reach him made all the difference. And that has been the key. Conviction about our clarity of purpose helped us mold ourselves to become forces of nature in our son's life. I did the same with my father.

My father's call for help when he became ill gave me a very special opportunity. For the first time, I created a clear purpose for my relationship with my father. I had made up purposes as a husband, as father to my children, as a teacher, and as a writer. What was my purpose or intention in my role as a son? To love my father and serve him, I decided. The decision to adopt that intent did not feel like a burden. In fact, my role as a son, which had been like a ship without a rudder (me, in relation to him), finally had a steering mechanism. Creating direction in my life with my father liberated me to give him the best of what I had learned through the years.

Once I decided to devote myself to respect, love, and serve him as a son, I formulated beliefs to support that purpose. If I wanted a loving experience with him, I would have to model it. Even if he never knew or understood me, I could at least come to know him if I opened my heart, *really* opened my heart. Samahria's insightful saying, "The one who loves the most wins!" always echoed in my brain. I could never lose; I would only win by showering him with my love because in order to love my father I had to first fill myself with love. We can't give what we don't have! During those two years, I watched my ability to love expand exponentially, thanks to my experience of loving him.

- **Daring Action.** Having a purpose that is supported by conviction, that internal feeling of rightness about who we are and what we are about to do, provides the platform, even the diving board, for our dive into experience. But daring to live our purpose and conviction inspires daring action, including a willingness to stand alone, if necessary! When professionals tried to discourage us from creating our program with Raun (counseling us to put him in an institution), when family and friends distanced themselves from us rather than join our effort to save our son, we stayed the course even though it meant acting alone initially. The healing that came for our son and subsequently for other children in successful programs set up by the courageous families we have trained, all came from that willingness on our part and on the part of other parents around the world to stand alone and go for their dreams with their children, despite the prognoses and lack of support. Daring Action.

With my father, daring action meant serving him even when others disagreed with my role, fought with and criticized me, venting their anger in my direction. It meant juggling my professional responsibilities, when necessary, in order to explore additional new developments and treatment protocols that could impact the disease process in his body. It meant energizing myself so I could be keenly alert, sensitive, and helpful during those two- and three-hour long-distance phone conversations we would have several times a week after the initial diagnosis. It meant carving a space in my heart and in my mind that would be totally available to him, at all times, day or night. Ironically, none of those actions felt daring. I did exactly what I wanted to do based on my clarity of purpose and the deep conviction supporting it.

- **Passion.** I've found in our seminars and workshops that different program attendees demonstrate profoundly different degrees of commitment. Some arrive without any spark or vitality to enliven the very experience they have just used their hard-earned money to purchase and will spend precious time attending. Invariably, this lack of energy limits the benefits they might attain. But then, other folks lean forward as soon as one of our facilitators begins a workshop. Wow, those participants are up and ready! They demonstrate, usually from the very beginning, a commitment and involvement that is filled with energy, excitement, and enthusiasm. These participants invariably report profound learning.

Statistical studies support my observations, demonstrating that our learning curve soars when we study or participate with enthusiasm. Are we half asleep or wide awake? Do we have passion? It does not require shouting from the rooftops or running around the room with hands flying. Passion defines the vitality of our participation as spouses, lovers, parents, friends, workers, teachers, and students.

- **Persistence.** Most people give up their dreams after knocking on the door of opportunity only once or twice. Some of us never knock on that door.

At our learning center, when we help people to move through their depression, conduct sessions with folks experiencing relationship meltdowns, train parents to stimulate and educate their children, we always, always, always encourage persistence. Stay the course. Keep coming back. Keep the ball you want in play. The individuals who leave their depression and psychotropic medications behind or who revitalize their marriages or who negotiate happy divorces all stay with the learning process until they reach their personal goals.

These fundamental codes of conduct and underlying attitudes are neither complex nor beyond our reach if we identify clear intentions from the outset. When I first learned of my father's metastasized cancer, I made a commitment deep inside to love him and serve him as he began this final adventure of his life. Dying is no more unnatural than living. It is not a sign of moral or physical ineptitude. It can be the opportunity of a lifetime for reconciliation and the expression of love. But we don't have to wait for someone we love to be challenged by aging, illness, or impending death to invoke these principles. We can love them now.

During the Middle Ages, Christian monks greeted one another with the salutation "Memento mori," which means "Remember, you must die." Thus with every encounter they reminded themselves and each other of the impermanence of life and the preciousness of each moment. From the time my father shared his diagnosis with me until he took his last breath, we practiced dying each day — letting go into the present moment and beholding with gratitude the wonder of our shared experiences.

SUGGESTED READING

Other Books by Barry Neil Kaufman

During our travels throughout the world, people continually ask Samahria and me for support materials regarding our work with individuals, couples, families, groups, and businesses. They are looking for a way to deal successfully with a relationship or a career challenge, to cope with their own illness or the illness of someone they love, to help a child facing difficult challenges, or simply to put new vigor into their everyday lives. Our answer to them is similar to what we share with those individuals who attend any of the programs offered at our international learning and training center, the Option Institute. The core of what we teach begins with attitude: making self-acceptance, personal empowerment, happiness, and love tangible and useful. In addition, we provide tools and systems to enable profound and lasting personal change.

The path is not long, difficult, or painful. Although we, ourselves, are still very much students of what we teach, we now offer books, audiotapes, and videos to help people on this journey:

Happiness Is a Choice

This book not only presents a simple blueprint that empowers the decision to be happy (to create inner ease, comfort, and peace of mind) but it also shares six shortcuts to happiness, each of which opens a doorway into an openhearted state of mind. This book contains the best of twenty-five years of experience working with tens of thousands of people, condensed into an easily digestible, step-by-step journey to self-acceptance and empowerment.

Note: This book and the other books listed here were written by Barry Neil Kaufman. There is another book entitled *Happiness Is a Choice* that is unrelated to Barry Neil Kaufman's work. Mr. Kaufman's book is published by Fawcett Columbine (Ballantine Books/Random House).

Son-Rise: The Miracle Continues

The best-selling book *Son-Rise* was made into an award-winning NBC television special, which has been viewed by 300 million people in over ninety countries. This new book, which replaces the original, presents the expanded and updated journey of Barry and Samahria Kaufman's successful efforts to reach and heal their "unreachable," autistic son, and it also includes the inspiring stories of five other families, from among the thousands of families helped by the Kaufmans, who used the same loving approach and educational principles to heal their own special children. Give this book to anyone you know who has a special child or who wants to find an entirely new, loving, and effective way to parent or live their own life. Original version published by Harper & Row and Warner Books; currently published by H J Kramer.

PowerDialogues (Limited edition)

This book shares one of the core teachings of the Option Process system of personal development, called the Option Process Dialogue, or PowerDialogues. This most comprehensive guide-book and working manual is now being used as the primary text in certification programs at the Option Institute. Step-by-step, the reader learns to master a powerful and life-changing Socratic form of inquiry using a logical system of nonjudgmental questions. This book is a valuable tool for those interested in personal exploration and development and for those helping professionals wanting to integrate this process as a fundamental method of transformation and healing for all those they assist. Published by Epic Century Publishers.

To Love Is to Be Happy With

This book presents the practical and powerful Option Process system for self-empowerment, self-reliance, and self-trust, enabling readers to redesign their attitudes and their lives. Readers learn a simplified version of the Option Process Dialogue (see above) in order to replace inhibiting beliefs with beliefs that will liberate them to become happier, more loving, and more empowered.

Our emotions and behaviors are fueled by our beliefs. Given this basic premise, *To Love Is to Be Happy With* helps us learn how to identify specific beliefs, jettison those that do not serve us, and create new ones that allow each of us to become the person we have always wanted to be. Although the Option Process Dialogue has been honed and further refined in the years since this book was published, it remains as relevant and helpful as the day it was written. Originally published by

Coward, McCann and Geoghegan, Inc. Current edition published by Fawcett Crest (Ballantine Books/Random House).

Giant Steps
This book presents ten intimate and uplifting portraits of the Kaufmans' transformative mentoring process in action. In this book, the reader holds hands with young people on special journeys who learn to break through pain and triumph even in the face of challenge and crisis. Published by Fawcett Crest (Ballantine Books/Random House).

A Miracle to Believe In
This most revealing portrait of Barry and Samahria Kaufman's working and healing lifestyle focuses on the years before they established their world-renowned learning and training center. *A Miracle to Believe In* gives an in-depth picture of their family and the group of daring volunteers who came together to help a family from Mexico find doorways into their special child's world and create bridges of communication, sharing, and love. It also provides a blueprint for work with children, adolescents, or adults with special needs. Originally published by Doubleday and Company, Inc. Currently published by Fawcett Crest (Ballantine Books/Random House).

Additional books by Barry Neil Kaufman: *A Sacred Dying, FutureSight,* and *Out-Smarting Your Karma and Other Pre-Ordained Conditions.*
These books are available at local bookstores and libraries and can be ordered by mail through Option Indigo Press. Special sales: All books are available at special discounts for organizations, individuals, and groups purchasing them for fundraising and educational purposes.

Videos and audiotapes, including the twelve-tape Option Process Series, The Keys to Option Mentoring (The Dialogue Process), No Risk/No Fault Parenting, Body Vital/Stress Free Living, The Empowered Leader, Making Love Last, and many others, are also available by mail order from Option Indigo Press.

For ordering information and a free catalog, contact us at:
Option Indigo Press
2080 South Undermountain Road, Sheffield, MA 01257-9643
1-800-562-7171
www.optionindigo.com

The Option Institute Learning and Training Center, founded by the Kaufmans in 1983, offers weekend, weeklong, and eight-week training programs to individuals, families, businesses, and groups throughout the year. These programs include general focus seminars such as Empowering Yourself, Shortcuts to Happiness, Inward Bound, Road to Greatness, CouplesCourse, ParentingCourse, Revitalize Your Spirit, and Living the Dream. Special focus workshops include courses such as PowerDialogues, Radical Authenticity, Optimal Self-Trust, Fearless, Exceptional Woman, and Group Leadership Training, as well as certification programs in mentoring/counseling and teacher certification programs to help children challenged with autism spectrum and related dysfunctions.

For information regarding workshops, seminars, counseling sessions, and motivational talks by Barry Neil Kaufman and Samahria Lyte Kaufman, and for information about the Option Institute as well as services for individuals, families, businesses, and groups, please call or write for free literature or free consultations with program counselors.

BARRY NEIL KAUFMAN

THE OPTION INSTITUTE
International Learning & Training Center
2080 South Undermountain Road
Sheffield, MA 01257-9643
Phone: 1-800-71-HAPPY
Fax: 413-229-8931
www.option.org

ABOUT THE AUTHOR

Barry Neil Kaufman is the author of twelve books on the Option Process® and The Son-Rise Program®, including the best-selling *Happiness Is a Choice,* a blueprint of simple, concrete methods to empower the decision to be happy, *Son-Rise: The Miracle Continues, To Love Is to Be Happy With, Giant Steps, PowerDialogues, A Miracle to Believe In, A Sacred Dying, Future-Sight,* and *Out-Smarting Your Karma.* Mr. Kaufman's books are available in twenty-two languages in more than sixty countries. He has twice won the Christopher Award for writing, and he and his wife, Samahria Lyte Kaufman, have won the Humanitas Award for their screenplay of the NBC Movie, *Son-Rise: A Miracle of Love.*

Mr. Kaufman is cofounder and codirector, with his wife, of the Option Institute International Learning and Training Center in Sheffield, Massachusetts, a nonprofit educational organization and worldwide teaching center for the Option Process. The Institute, a year-round facility offering empowering personal growth programs and seminars for individuals, couples, families, and groups, uses life-changing experiential learning techniques designed to greatly improve health, career, relationships, and quality of life. Professional certification training programs and individual counseling services are also available.

Additionally, the Kaufmans and their staff give motivational talks at conferences, lead workshops and seminars, lecture at universities, and appear in mass media throughout the world.

The Option Institute is also the home of the Autism Treatment Center of America™. This division of the Institute grew out of the Kaufmans' innovative and successful work with their once-autistic son, Raun, now a thriving young man who contributes greatly as an international lecturer, seminar leader, and counselor at the Option Institute. Work at the Autism Treatment Center is centered on The Son-Rise Program, a groundbreaking treatment method for autism spectrum and related developmental challenges. The Kaufmans and their staff also counsel and instruct families wanting to create home-based, child-centered teaching programs for their own special-needs children. Additionally, they train professionals in their methods.

The Kaufmans have six children and three grandchildren and live in western Massachusetts.

For more information about seminars and courses taught by the Kaufmans and their staff, call The Option Institute at 800-71-HAPPY (800-714-2779), visit www.option.org, or write The Option Institute, 2080 South Undermountain Road, Sheffield, MA 01257-9643, USA.